BEDFORD BY THE RIVER

Max Lock Group

An impression of the proposed cultural and recreational centre east of the TOWN BRIDGE, *showing the covered* SWIMMING POOL, THEATRE, BOATHOUSE, RESTAURANT *and* CINEMA, *with the tower of* ST. MARY'S CHURCH *in the background.*

BEDFORD

BY THE RIVER

A Town Planning Report by Max Lock FRIBA, MTPI, *David Grove* BA (OXON), *and Gerald King* ARIBA

LONDON · JOHN MURRAY · 1952

Members of the Group

MAX LOCK, FRIBA, MTPI

Author of: Middlesbrough Survey and Plan, 1946; The Hartlepools Survey and Plan, 1948; Civic Diagnosis;
Reconstruction in the Netherlands; Outline Plan for the Portsmouth District, 1949

D. A. TOOKEY, BA(OXON)   D. J. GROVE, BA(OXON)

G. W. KING, ARIBA   I. F. RUTHERFORD, ARIBA   ANN LUBIN, MA   MARY BOLTON (SECRETARY)

G. J. EASTON, ARIBA   JOAN CLARK (LONDON OFFICE)

Assistants

A. J. S. FROST   R. EFEMEY, BA(OXON)   W. A. BISHOP   MRS SINFIELD   MISS KEY

AUDREY ROBINSON   JOY MAXWELL AND JANICE FREEZER (BEDFORD TRAINING COLLEGE)

Members of the Town Planning Committee, 1950–51

THE MAYOR, ALDERMAN RICHARD TURNER, JP

ALDERMEN: JOHN A. CANVIN, JP, S. B. MORLING, JP, A. L. NICHOLLS, MC, JP, F. A. RICKARD, COLONEL G. H. WELLS, TD, DL

COUNCILLORS: P. GARNET HALL,* C. N. BARROTT, C. A. E. C. HOWARD, A. A. JONES, MRS D. GEE, J. M. BERRIDGE

* Councillor P. Garnet Hall died 24th September 1950

This book has been published for the Bedford Corporation by

JOHN MURRAY (PUBLISHERS) LTD
1952

It has been designed and produced by

NEWMAN NEAME LTD

and printed in Great Britain by

W. S. COWELL LTD

Contents

Maps

NOTE *Not all the names mentioned in the text will be found on the relevant maps. The two large folding maps in the back pocket show street names throughout the town, and those in the central area also appear on the front end-papers. The back end-paper provides a key to the outline base of Maps* 1, 2, 3, 5, 6, 8, 10, 11, 12 *and* 14. *The one-inch Ordnance Survey map of Bedford and district is reproduced on Map* 7.

Diagrams

Tables

Illustrations

The tailpieces were drawn by Gerald King

" Bedford by the River "

Preface

THE WORDS of our title are taken from the refrain of the Bedford School Song. They are not simply a compliment to the famous school, but also a recognition of the fact that Bedford is essentially a riverside town. The river brought it into being, has affected its growth in many ways and is a continually recurring factor in the planning of future development.

Many Bedfordians have long been aware of the need for planning to enhance the merits and remedy the defects of the town; this was shown in particular by the survey carried out in 1944 by the Bedford Council of Social Service and published last year. We have found inspiration from this voluntary effort and have sought to carry further the lines of investigation which it opened up.

In a work of this nature we could not have obtained results without the fullest co-operation of all concerned, and we have been fortunate in the kindness and consideration that has been shown to us in the carrying out of the task. I am grateful to the Town Planning Committee for the time they have given to detailed consideration of every stage in the proposals. These have also been discussed with the full Council on three occasions, and informal meetings with the Alderman and Councillors of each Ward proved extremely valuable.

During the past year I have enjoyed the close co-operation of the Borough Engineer and Surveyor, Mr C. H. Blakeway, M Inst Mun E, F R San I, and his staff, and have been helpfully advised by the Town Clerk, Mr G. F. Simmonds, MA, LL.B (Cantab), on all major issues involved. I should also like to acknowledge with thanks the advice of the Medical Officer of Health, Dr G. K. Bowes, MA, MD, MRCP, DPH, and the indispensable help in the housing survey of the Chief Sanitary Inspector, Mr F. C. Haynes, MSIA, Cert RSI, and his staff.

My special thanks are due to the Mayor, Alderman Richard Turner, JP, for his vision and grasp of both the ideals and practical objects of town planning. It is rarely that a technician has such enlightened and positive guidance from a layman.

The County Planning Officer, Mr E. Sterne, BSc, AMICE, MTPI, has given many helpful suggestions, and was good enough to let us use the survey information and statistical data already collected by his Department.

In considering our recommendations in relation to the regional programme, we have had the assistance of the Regional Officers of the Ministry of Local Government and Planning, the Board of Trade, the Ministry of Labour and the Ministry of Transport.

The preparation of a town planning report can no longer be considered a one-man-job, and I have been unusually fortunate in the intelligent and hardworking team who have shared the work with me. Their names appear elsewhere, but I would like to give special mention to Mr Douglas Tookey and Mr David Grove. Mr Tookey worked with me at Portsmouth and carried through the valuable pioneering stages of our work in Bedford. He was unfortunately unable to stay for the completion of the job, and was succeeded as Assistant Consultant by Mr Grove, who directed most of the survey work and has undertaken a major share in the compilation of this report.

We have been deeply impressed by the way in which the citizens of Bedford responded to our appeals for co-operation and assistance. In particular the assistance of a number of schoolboys and schoolgirls in the routine work of sorting statistical information was invaluable, and we are grateful to the Headmaster of Bedford School (Mr Humphrey Grose-Hodge, MA, FSA) and the Headmaster of the Harpur Central School (Mr A. B. Wignall) for allowing them to help. A full list of organizations and individuals consulted by us appears on page 136.

Because the two local authorities of Bedford and Kempston embrace a simple community, it is out of the question that one part of the area should be considered without the other. Both have therefore been included in these outline proposals.

Finally, I do not think that this report should be issued without particular reference to the interest and helpfulness of the local Press. The thoughtful and stimulating articles and illustrations in the *Bedfordshire Times* have maintained the public interest in the future of the town.

Although the circumstances of our time have placed many obstacles in the way of much needed improvement of the physical environment, we are convinced that there is a keen awareness on the part of the Corporation and the Public of the importance of seizing every opportunity of making Bedford an even better place to live in.

Max Lock.

Foreword

by the MAYOR OF BEDFORD, *Alderman Richard Turner*, JP

IT IS FORTUNATE for me that the publication of *Bedford by the River* should come within my term of office as Mayor, for it is a privilege to write the Foreword.

I am reminded of my early days here, when the Town Crier was still active—this was before the days of the motor car—when the bicycle had hardly come into existence and when the only traffic in the High Street was the butchers' and bakers' horse-drawn carts or the doctor's brougham, and when a man with a red flag walked in front of the steam roller on its way through the streets.

Saturday was busy, as on that day the carriers' carts brought visitors from the villages to shop—only a few years earlier the fairs were held in High Street twice a year.

The change and the growth of the town have been rapid and the coming of the motor car has presented us with many problems. Large new housing estates have been developed and the town has suffered from the lack of comprehensive planning in the past. The two road bridges across the river, sufficient for the traffic seventy years ago, have not been added to since that time and this is the main reason for congestion in our principal streets.

New roads and river crossings must be our first consideration if we are to solve the traffic problems. New housing estates must be planned to meet the needs of our ever-growing population and to replace houses which are growing old. These new estates must provide houses of various types, including homes suitable for old people, together with shops and all that goes to make life pleasant.

Although Bedford was fortunate in escaping large bomb damage during the last war, a plan for its orderly development is essential.

The main factor with which the Town Council has always had to contend is the heavy expenditure which would be involved in bringing about the necessary improvements. This, coupled with six years of war and the years of austerity which followed, has not made the problem easier.

The passing of the Town and Country Planning Act has meant that this problem has had to be faced with courage. In consequence the Council appointed Mr Max Lock, FRIBA, MTPI, as their Consultant, to advise upon the proposals which the Town Council should ask the County Council to include in the Development Plan, and this report is the result of a year's energetic survey and study by him and has been agreed by the Council step by step.

I recommend it to all who read it as a comprehensive report on the planning problems in Bedford and the remedies suggested to relieve them.

A plan is often thought of as something which 'came into force on an appointed day'. Nothing is further from the truth; development is going on all the time and the purpose of a plan is to steer that development in the right direction. Thus, while many of the remedies will not operate for many years, every development in the future will be designed to fit into its place in the scheme for gradually overcoming our planning problems.

Engraved by Hillard from an Original Drawing by J. Walker. Published Sept. 1, 1791 by Harrison & Co. No. 18 Paternoster Row London.

Preamble

'By this time the pilgrims had a desire to go forward, and the shepherds a desire that they should; so they walked together towards the end of the mountains. Then said the shepherds one to another, "Let us here show to the pilgrims the gate of the Celestial City, if they have skill to look through our perspective glass". The pilgrims then lovingly accepted the motion; so they had them to the top of a high hill called Clear, and gave them the glass to look.'—THE PILGRIM'S PROGRESS

Bedford's very name indicates that there was a town on this site even before the building of the **medieval bridge.** Here was one of the most important crossings in all the 150 miles of the Great Ouse—at the head of navigation and midway between the Fenlands to the east and the Midlands to the west. This position determined that Bedford would become the most important market in the district, and in time the county town. Indeed, Bedfordshire is not a geographical entity, but simply the area that could be most conveniently administered from Bedford. The old bridge with the gatehouse in which **John Bunyan** was confined for a short time made way for the present Town Bridge soon after 1800, and towards the end of the century, when Bedford was growing rapidly, this was supplemented by the Prebend Street Bridge. Today, after seventy years of further growth and the development of new functions, there is an urgent need for more river crossings. Three new bridges are proposed—one in the town centre, another at Queen's Park and a third at Newnham.

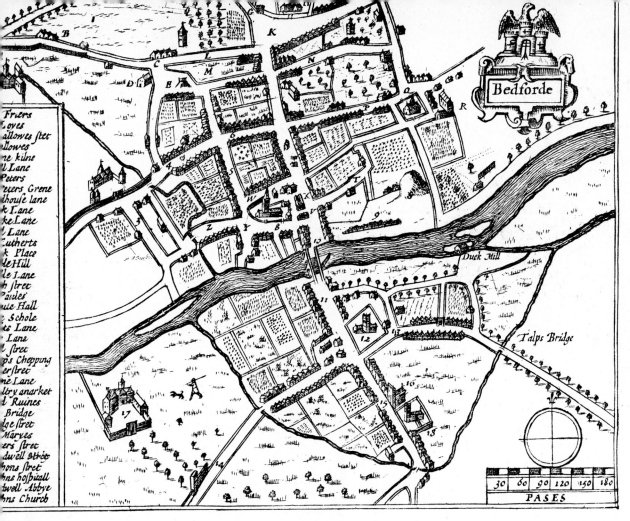

Speed's Map shows the small market town north of the river in 1610. Map 5 (page 45) pictures the growth of Bedford during the following three-and-a-half centuries and the further expansion that would occur in the next twenty years if our proposals were carried out. Matthiason's drawing of **Wing's Bridge and the Swan Hotel** (*opposite*) expresses all that is finest in the Bedford scene. But a bridge built in 1813 could not cope with the traffic of the twentieth century (*top right*) and in 1940 its width was doubled (*bottom right*). At the time there was a lot of criticism; now even the critics admit that little was lost and much gained. But the problem of congestion is not yet solved and we propose further necessary measures. Like the widening of the Town Bridge, these should be boldly conceived and executed in such a way that the business of the town can be carried on and that the essential character of Bedford is preserved and enhanced.

Most centres of administration and distribution are also educational and cultural centres, but Bedford has a special role in this respect because of its four famous schools endowed by the Harpur Trust, and the two training colleges. **Bedford School** is an ancient foundation, but its present buildings date from the period of rapid expansion at the end of the nineteenth century. The former regulation that only residents of the town could send their children to the schools had a profound effect on Bedford's physical development and social character. The schools have enriched the sporting life of the town as well as its cultural life. Bedford has one of the most noteworthy **Rugby Football Clubs** in the country and the **Annual Regatta** is the highlight of the year on the Ouse.

Bedford's educational functions can be attributed largely to the accident of the Harpur bequest, but its rapid development as a manufacturing centre in the last seventy years is due to manifest advantages of site and communications. **The Queen's Engineering Works,** now the town's biggest factory, was established in 1894. It has been followed by several other important works,

most of which are still expanding. Despite the growth of industry, Bedford's links with the countryside remain as strong as ever. The weekly cattle market and many other urban services attract farmers from a wide area. The most important event in the agricultural calendar is the **County Show,** in recent years held in Cardington Meadows.

There is comparatively little blighted housing in Bedford, but there is the sharp contrast found in most English towns between palatial middle-class quarters and dreary areas where many people still live. We cannot duplicate **de Pary's Avenue** but we can ensure that a similar dignity and grace is embodied in the new developments that will replace streets like **Dane Street** that are demolished during the next twenty years.

Though much of Bedford's housing is below modern standards, some of its open spaces are fine examples of urban landscape; Bedford Park is noted for its interesting layout and large variety of trees. **The Embankment** overleaf is the town's most characteristic feature.

1

" This design for Bedford seeks to make more of the merits and to mitigate the drawbacks, to solve the problems that have arisen from the unbalanced expansion of the last seventy years, and to provide for balanced expansion during the next twenty "

A review of the proposals

Bedford is a town of many functions. First and foremost today comes manufacturing industry; several important engineering works and many other kinds of factories give a wide range of employment to both men and women. Secondly, Bedford is a prosperous shopping, business and professional centre, serving a wide district. Each week 90,000 people come in by bus, and it is estimated that more than 100,000 people living outside the town (i.e. twice the population of Bedford itself) look to its central area for major urban services. Thirdly, Bedford has been for many centuries and still is the chief market town in the county, and as such preserves a wholesome balance between the interests of town and country. Fourthly, it is the administrative centre of Bedfordshire, housing the County Council offices and the Law Courts, as well as a number of branches of the central government and the offices of the Bedford Rural District Council. Fifthly, Bedford is a minor tourist centre. It has no ancient cathedral, castle or colleges to attract visitors, and much of the surrounding countryside is flat and somewhat uninteresting, but in the River Ouse—both within and without the town— it has a unique tourist attraction. The full potentialities of the river and its setting have not yet been exploited and they could draw many more visitors to Bedford. Finally, it is well known the world over for its schools, built up on the sixteenth-century foundations of the famous Harpur Bequest. The schools have coloured and consolidated the cultural life of Bedford in much the same way as the influence of John Bunyan has stamped and strengthened its religious life.

Bedford remained a small market town until after the middle of the nineteenth century, and so it escaped some of the worst evils found in towns which expanded suddenly during the Industrial Revolution. It has reached its present medium size through two periods of rapid growth —from 1880 to 1910 and from 1930 to the present day. This growth was stimulated in the first place by its increasing importance as a market centre, which in turn encouraged the development of the other functions mentioned above, though these were partly due to special factors described in Chapter 2.

During these years there have been considerable changes in the physical fabric, but the pattern of land use does not yet conform completely to the new role of the town. The area of the town centre and the layout of the road system remain much as they were in the middle of the last century, but owing to the slow development of neighbourhood amenities and cross-town roads they have had to bear the full weight of the subsequent expansion. The result is the present confusion of land uses and serious traffic congestion which have become a direct threat to the prosperity of the town. The removal of this threat is one of the main objects of the proposals. This problem of unbalanced development is common to most old towns which have grown rapidly during the last hundred years, but in this case its solution is complicated by difficulties peculiar to Bedford. The meandering river bordered by flood land, and the railway lines converging from five directions over an almost flat site, have hampered the extension of the road system and placed rigid barriers between neighbouring residential areas.

One of the outer neighbourhoods which has grown very rapidly in the present century is Kempston, a separate Urban District, even though physically, economically and socially it is part of Bedford. However the local government problem may be solved, it is clear that any land use plan for the development of Bedford and Kempston must treat them as one urban unit. The reader will observe that our proposals have been made with this unity in mind.

The Registrar-General's estimate for the population of Bedford in December, 1949, was 53,180 which allowed for the floating population. We estimate that in April, 1950, the population was 51,500, excluding boarders at the schools, students at the colleges and other temporary residents. Our estimate of the population of Kempston is 9,000. It is assumed that in twenty years the two towns will have grown from 60,500 to at least 75,000, and possibly 80,000, as a result of the natural increase of the present population, and of immigration to meet the needs of existing industries and of the National Aeronautical Establishment at present being built three miles north of the town. We think that three-quarters of the people associated with this project would wish to live in Bedford, and only a quarter in the villages. The prospect of this large influx together with the need to house the large number of families on the present waiting list and those who will be displaced from blighted dwellings, means that some 8,000 new homes ought to be provided during the next twenty years. Bedford and Kempston need to build about 400 houses per year, as well as making essential improvements in neighbourhood services and cross-town communications and extending the main shopping centre.

THE BALANCE SHEET Before outlining the main proposals the principal advantages and disadvantages of Bedford may be summarized. The merits are as follows:

1. A compact town centre with a busy, friendly atmosphere, and a convenient grouping of shops, administrative offices and markets.
2. The River Ouse, providing unique recreational facilities, and bringing broad wedges of open space right into the heart of the town.
3. A good variety of jobs in manufacturing and service industries.

4. Excellent educational facilities and a strong cultural life.
5. Comparative absence of sprawling residential development, preserving easy access both to the centre and to the surrounding countryside from most parts of the town.
6. Mutual interdependence of the urban and rural populations.
7. A central position in the country as a whole and particularly good communications with London and the Midlands.

The following are Bedford's chief drawbacks:

1. It has grown big enough to demand a full range of urban services, but not yet quite big enough to support them.
2. The main shopping streets and the markets are seriously congested.
3. There are two railway stations situated too far from the town centre and from each other, and both with inconvenient means of access.
4. About 1,500 acres of land, or nearly one quarter of the total area of Bedford and Kempston is liable to flood, and about another 500 acres, mainly in the north of the town, are boulder clay, giving somewhat unstable foundations.
5. The river and railway barriers obstruct cross-town communications and cause daily journeys to work to be longer than they need be in a town of this size.
6. Inter-war extensions to the town, particularly on the south, have been developed simply as housing estates, without adequate neighbourhood amenities. As in most towns, considerations of architectural appearance and tree planting were severely restricted in accordance with the practice of the period.

SUMMARY OF PROPOSALS This design for Bedford seeks to make more of the merits and to mitigate the drawbacks, to solve the problems that have arisen from the unbalanced expansion of the last seventy years, and to provide for balanced expansion during the next twenty; to the ends that the town may perform its main functions more efficiently, and those who live by them may have a more satisfactory environment. It is therefore desired to incorporate the following improvements in the town:

1. To build a Western Relief Road and bridge to free the town centre of north-south through traffic and to link the outer neighbourhoods on the west and south (*pp.* 20 *and* 57).
2. To bring all traffic from the south into the town by Ampthill Road (*pp.* 20 *and* 58).
3. To make three new inner road links, including a new bridge east of the town centre, completing a continuous ring road, and to re-design the junction of Midland Road and Prebend Street at the foot of Allens' Bridge (*pp.* 20 *and* 59).
4. To build a Central Relief Road and new bridge duplicating the 'spine' of the town centre, and to re-design the junction at Willmer's Corner (*pp.* 20, 61 *and* 68).
5. To construct a new road east of High Street to give access from St Paul's Square to the back of the shops, to new car parks, to Castle Road and to the Embankment (*pp.* 22, 64 *and* 70).
6. To construct four cycle tracks and bridges to complete the new system of cross-town communications on the west and south (*pp.* 22 *and* 58).
7. To build a westward extension of the main shopping centre north of Midland Road in the Allhallows Lane clearance area (*p.* 68).
8. To establish a new bus station in Horne Lane close to the shopping and administrative centres and their proposed extensions (*pp.* 64 *and* 68).
9. To provide sites for a new Shire Hall and County Offices on the old Cattle Market in Commercial Road (*p.* 74).
10. To build a new Assembly Hall and Community Centre south of Horne Lane (*p.* 74).
11. To build a recreational and cultural centre on the south bank of the river east of the Town Bridge, to include a new cinema, theatre, covered swimming pool and restaurant (*pp.* 75 *and* 121).
12. To re-site the agricultural markets south of Cauldwell Street and west of the Central Relief Road, together with an abattoir, a cold store and a car park for 250 vehicles (*p.* 77).
13. To make good the present deficiency of car parking space in the town centre (*p.* 70).
14. To use 119 acres of land for future industrial development and to build flatted factories and warehouses to accommodate some of the businesses displaced from the central clearance areas (*pp.* 22, 76 *and* 91).
15. To demolish 1,300 of the oldest and most decayed dwellings in the town (*pp.* 23 *and* 95).
16. To overcome the present housing shortage, re-house the people displaced from blighted areas and provide for the probable increase of population by developing a number of housing sites on the outskirts and by building at a high density in clearance areas on the edge of the town centre (*pp.* 23, 77 *and Chapter* 6).
17. To make good the lack of parks and public gardens in certain neighbourhoods, and of adults' sports fields throughout the town, and to make much better use of Bedford's major amenity—the river (*p.* 28 *and Chapters* 6 *and* 7).
18. To maintain the present large acreage of allotments by providing new plots on the outskirts to replace those nearer the centre which are required for houses, schools and factories (*pp.* 26 *and* 95).
19. To accommodate the thirteen new schools required to implement the 1944 Education Act in Bedford (*p.* 31).
20. To provide an adequate number of local shops, public houses, community and welfare centres in existing and new neighbourhoods (*p.* 31 *and Chapter* 6).

COMMUNICATIONS By far the worst of Bedford's problems is the congestion in the town centre resulting from the continued growth of retail trade on traditional sites which are too small to support any further extension. The traffic which serves these shops has greatly increased, and in the absence of any by-pass the flow of through traffic grows yearly. The fact that Bedford has only two bridges makes matters worse, and there are no cross-town roads to relieve the central streets, due principally to the difficulties of bridging the rivers and the railways.

From this it might seem that expensive by-passes would be necessary to solve the problem. This was thought to be the case by the Ministry of Transport and the County Council, as well as by the Bedford Corporation, until the Origin and Destination Census carried out in September 1950 showed that a much simpler solution would meet the need. It is not necessary to by-pass the town on the north or the east; a western relief road is all that is wanted to cope with the problem of through traffic.

The Western Relief Road. The Origin and Destination Census made it clear that any by-pass must carry both the streams of London traffic from A.6 and A.600 to the west of the town. The line proposed by the Ministry of Transport and shown on Map 7 (*p.* 62) does not pick up traffic from A.600. The proposed alternative shown on Map 8 (*p.* 63) would leave A.600 at Cotton End, cross Elstow Road at its junction with Mile Road, bridge the Bletchley Line to Ampthill Road, continue across Kempston Road through Austin Canons to a new river bridge, and thence proceed northwards through Queen's Park to Bromham Road and Clapham Road. This proposal has the further advantage of keeping clear of land that is required for new housing. It would relieve the town centre of north-south through traffic, and at the same time act as a connecting link between the southern and western neighbourhoods, thus meeting two of Bedford's most vital needs.

The approach to Bedford from the South. Elstow Road and London Road meet in a dangerous junction between two railway bridges. To overcome this difficulty a proposal had previously been made to take all traffic from the Luton-London Road (A.6), into Ampthill Road by a new link from just south of Elstow Village to Cow Bridge. This proposal is recommended because Ampthill Road is a more suitable main approach than Elstow Road, and because the new link will by-pass the historic and charming village of Elstow. If the proposed Western Relief Road were carried out, Ampthill Road would also be able to take traffic from the Hitchin-London Road (A.600).

The Inner Ring Road. Though large scale and costly outer ring roads are unwarranted, an inner ring road is needed to give Bedford's spider-like road plan a useful web. Parts of the inner ring, including Prebend Street Bridge, already exist, and it could be completed by three new links: from the re-designed Prebend Street/Midland Road junction, via Rutland Road to Bromham Road opposite Union Street; from Park Avenue /Kimbolton Road to Newnham Avenue/Goldington Road along the edge of Laxton's Nursery; from the bottom of Newnham Avenue, across the river by a new bridge, and through Cardington Meadows to the re-designed junction at Willmer's Corner (Map 9, no. 34, *p.* 74).

Central Relief Road and Bridge. The Western Relief Road and the Inner Cross-Town Roads would take perhaps as much as a third of the traffic at present using the Town Bridge. Since the flow of vehicles may well increase by more than a third during the next twenty years, further measures would be needed to reduce congestion in High Street and St Mary's, and to improve circulation throughout the town centre. A Central Relief Road is required. The proposed line of this road has been chosen so that it would also solve two other pressing problems—the extension of the shopping centre and the siting of a new bus station. With relatively little demolition the new thoroughfare can be built from Willmer's Corner northwards across Cauldwell Street and down Holme Street to the proposed new bridge at Batts' Ford; from there it would continue over Commercial Road, along River Street, across Midland Road and through a new square into Gwyn Street and Hassett Street, whose carriageways lie only ninety feet apart and can be combined into an open boulevard terminating opposite the High School in Bromham Road. This last section of the Central Relief Road would be the western limit of the proposed extension of the shopping centre in the clearance area bounded by Midland Road, Harpur Street and St Loyes. The new bus station would also lie on the Central Relief Road north of its junction with Horne Lane on the site of the two existing market yards. Here it would be centrally situated between the present shopping and administrative centre, the new extension of the shopping centre, and the new administrative buildings in Commercial Road; it would also be conveniently near the main railway station.

Access East of High Street. The last of the road proposals is for a

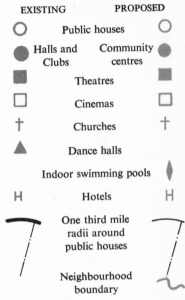

Half Bedford's hundred pubs are in and around the central area. So are most of the town's meeting places; the few in the outer neighbourhoods are quite inadequate, particularly south of the river. Fifteen new public houses and seven community centres would help to redress the balance. Kempston and Goldington will eventually be able to support neighbourhood cinemas. Sites for new churches have been suggested in the principal development areas.

new road from High Street, opposite the south side of St Paul's Square, across Ram Yard and Mill Street, and up Duke Street to Lurke Street, with a branch to the Embankment west of the Castle Mound. These new links would serve a number of purposes. The road from the Embankment would replace the awkward and dangerous turning at the head of the bridge; the new road would relieve Mill Street of much of the traffic from Castle Road to the west, and it would give access to the back of the High Street shops and to the proposed new car parks serving this part of the shopping centre.

Cycle and Pedestrian Ways. Four of these are proposed to supplement the Western Relief Road and complete the new system of cross-town communications on the west and south. Two would bridge the river from Queen's Park to Kempston, the first from Honey Hill to the Grange, and the second from Ford End Road to Austin Canons; the other two would cross the railways to connect Ampthill Road with Elstow Road by way of Sandhurst Road, and Elstow Road with London Road, by way of Newton Road and Dents Road.

All these new roads are necessary to solve Bedford's traffic problems and to provide an adequate road system for the larger town of the future. But they cannot all be carried out at once. The Western Relief Road would make the biggest single contribution to the relief of congestion, because it would carry both through traffic and cross-town traffic. But the Central Relief Road would increase rateable value by opening the way for an extension of the commercial centre, and this would help to meet the cost of reconstruction throughout the town. For this reason it is suggested that while both roads are urgently needed, the inner one should be begun first. The cycle tracks on the west and south could be completed long before the new roads and would facilitate cross-town communication and shorten daily journeys to work.

The road proposals and the traffic surveys on which they are based are more fully described in Chapter 3 (*p.* 52) which is fully illustrated with maps and diagrams.

INDUSTRIAL STRUCTURE AND PROPOSALS Diagram 5 (*p.* 82)

shows that Bedford's wide range of functions is mirrored by a great diversity of occupations. The 'profile' is based on statistics relating to the whole area covered by the local Employment Exchange, which is why agriculture and brick-making figure prominently. Engineering is the biggest single source of employment, but Bedford is not dominated by one establishment as are Oxford and Crewe. It will be seen from Map 11 (*p.* 84), that there are a large number of factories varying greatly in size, processes and products. There has been a steady expansion of manufacturing during the last seventy years, and several firms in the town contemplate building further extensions, and in some cases entirely new premises. Thirty-seven and a half acres have already been proposed for industrial development, and there are an additional eighty-one acres within the boundaries of Bedford and Kempston particularly suitable for new factories. The total of $118\frac{1}{2}$ acres comprises the following:

	Acreage	Number on Map 11 (*page 84*)
A. ALREADY PROPOSED		
Mile Road	18	4
Willmer's Field	5	6
Fenlake Road	$2\frac{1}{2}$	8
Goldington	12	9
	$37\frac{1}{2}$	
B. NOW PROPOSED		
Newton Road	$1\frac{1}{2}$	5
Western Relief Road	14	3
Chantry Avenue	47	1
Spring Road	9	2
Ampthill Road	$3\frac{1}{2}$	7
St John's	3	10
Pilcroft Street	3	11
	81	
GRAND TOTAL	$118\frac{1}{2}$ acres	

Most of these sites are fairly small parcels of land adjoining the railway in the main industrial zone. Their use would maintain the concentration of industry in the south-west quadrant, and the road proposals would improve accessibility from other parts of the town. In this way Bedford's people would be able to make the most of the wide range of occupations available in the main industrial zone.

The biggest individual site is at Chantry Avenue, and it extends the main industrial zone into Kempton, where large housing sites are also available. Both the Chantry Avenue site and the small site adjoining the Goldington neighbourhood would be ideal for female employing industries.

Bedford at present falls under the Board of Trade's ban on the building of new factories and major extensions in the south of England. At the same time, national planning policy has declared in favour of the dispersal of industries from central London, and Bedford, which has received many factories from London during the last fifty years, could well receive more. Other towns at a similar distance from London, such as Oxford, Cambridge and Luton are approaching the point of industrial saturation. The land which it is suggested should be reserved for industry would more than satisfy the needs of existing firms, and housing sites are available for a population of up to 80,000. Bedford's industrial expansion cannot therefore be considered to have come to an end.

A more detailed analysis of the existing industrial structure of the district and a review of present prospects are given in Chapter 5 (*p.* 80).

HOUSING Neither the expansion of existing firms nor the introduction of new ones will be possible to any extent until the housing problem has been eased. As well as providing homes for a large number of immigrants during the next twenty years, Bedford must build houses for people on its present waiting list and for those who will have to move when blighted housing is cleared. It is estimated that about 5,000 people in Bedford and Kempston, or nearly one-tenth of the present population, are seeking homes. Blight clearance will affect another 4,100 people who will be displaced from the main clearance areas between Midland Road and Bromham Road; north of Tavistock Street;

and in the Duckmill Lane and Pilcroft Street areas; as well as from isolated pockets of blight in outlying parts such as Old Kempston, Goldington Village and Mile Road. Of the 2,125 houses found to be blighted, it is proposed that 1,300 in the worst condition should be demolished during the next twenty years, averaging only sixty-five houses per year. The reasons which have governed this decision are described in Chapter 6 (*p.* 93).

Housing sites are available in the area to accommodate just over 30,000 people; 9,000 of these are already living in the town, and the remainder could be immigrants, bringing the total population to about 80,000. All these sites are shown on Map 12 (*p.* 101), together with the proposed residential density at which they should be developed. We believe that, as in most towns, the extensions to Bedford during the last thirty years have been spread over an unnecessary amount of land. The narrow house with the long deep garden cannot be justified in a town where the acreage of allotments is more than twice the recommended national standard. It is proposed that future developments should be at a density of thirty/fifty persons per acre, rather than at the prevailing density of twenty/thirty persons per acre. The proposed density on each housing site has been considered in the light of the existing provision of open space and neighbourhood amenities in the vicinity. Some of the sites will be entirely residential and here the density can be as high as fifty. Others will need open spaces, shops and community buildings, and here the overall density can be thirty persons per acre. The new estates should be laid out with wider house frontages, shallower gardens and more communal open space; flats should be provided among the houses, especially in the central area where they can rise to several storeys. If a plan is to be reasonably economic, dwellings must be grouped in such a way that the extension of streets and piped services is kept to a minimum. Above all, the growth of the town must take as little agricultural land as possible.

The bulk of the new housing would lie in the north of the Borough and in Kempston. Nearly 15,000 people could live in the two new neighbourhoods at Goldington and on either side of Kimbolton Road. Thus

Map 2

STAGING
OF THE PROPOSALS

	Acquisition	Development
First stage		
Second stage		
Third stage		
Fourth stage		

This map shows tentative suggestions
for a programme of development in
Bedford alone. The work is divided
into four stages. Under present
circumstances it is not possible to tell
how long each stage would last, but it
is expected that the total programme
outlined in this report would take a
minimum of 20 years. A forecast of
the time taken to implement any
one of the stages requires an exact
knowledge of the building labour
force available in each year, which
in its turn depends upon national
circumstances which do not at the
moment allow a reliable estimate to
be made. The first stage would include
the new bus station, the flatted factory,
all the cycle tracks and part of the
central road proposals; the first houses
would be built in Goldington. In the
second stage the Goldington neighbourhood would be completed, the land for
the Putnoe and Kimbolton Road
neighbourhoods acquired, and
the main central redevelopment carried
out. The principal scheme in the third
stage would be the construction of a
considerable length of the Western
Relief Road, which would be
completed in the final stage.

the second half of this century would witness a turn of the tide in Bedford, for major developments would once more be north of the river. They would be as great as those which peopled de Pary's and Queen's Park in the closing years of the last century. Houses on this side of the town would be convenient for people working at the National Aeronautical Establishment at Thurleigh; but the increased distance of these sites from the main industrial zone in the south-west makes more urgent the proposed improvements in the road system, particularly the Eastern Cross-Town Road from Newnham Avenue to Willmer's Corner.

In Kempston the population may eventually be almost doubled by building on a large number of sites scattered throughout the built-up area, the largest being on either side of Elstow Road and in Woburn Road and Cemetery Road. These would fill some of the gaps in the present straggling development in the Urban District and lay the basis for the establishment of a proper neighbourhood centre.

NEIGHBOURHOODS Communications are the framework of the town and industry its means of livelihood, but the immediate environment of people's homes is the neighbourhood in which they live and in which they spend most of their leisure. In considering the provision of local amenities such as schools, shops, churches, public houses, parks and playing fields, it is necessary to divide the town into smaller areas and provide within each an adequate standard of services. In a medium-sized town no residential neighbourhood is as self-contained as the suburbs of a large city, and the citizen's principal loyalty is, and should be, to the town as a whole, as its centre is not far distant from any part of the outer districts. But in Bedford the time has long passed when the whole population could look to the town centre for all their amenities, and, in fact, the physical and social nature of the town extensions during the last fifty years has given rise to fairly well-defined neighbourhood units. We have distinguished eight of these. Because the physical barriers of the river and the railways split the town into areas too small to support a full range of services, and because different amenities have to be considered in relation to different sizes of population, we have

further divided six of these neighbourhoods into sixteen subdivisions. The boundaries are marked on Maps 1 (*p.* 21), 3 (*p.* 29), 12 (*p.* 101), and 14 (*p.* 110), which show the existing and proposed provision of the principal neighbourhood services. The following is a list of the neighbourhoods and the subdivisions showing the present and proposed populations:

NEIGHBOURHOOD	PRESENT POPULATION		PROPOSED POPULATION	
1 QUEEN'S PARK		5,200		6,250
2 BROMHAM ROAD				
(a) Poets' Corner	3,925		4,675	
(b) Alexandra Road	2,175		2,050	
		6,100		6,725
3 BLACK TOM/DE PARY'S				
(a) Black Tom	4,800		4,700	
(b) de Pary's	3,900		12,400	
		8,700		17,100
4 GOLDINGTON		1,750		8,600
5 NEWNHAM				
(a) Rothsay Road	2,120		1,945	
(b) Castle Road	4,420		4,060	
(c) Wendover Drive	1,310		1,195	
		7,850		7,200
6 CAULDWELL/KINGSBROOK				
(a) Southend	3,930		3,605	
(b) Elstow Road	4,530		4,655	
(c) London Road	7,040		6,465	
(d) Harrowden Road	1,500		2,775	
		17,000		17,500
7 KEMPSTON				
(a) Old Kempston	3,400		7,110	
(b) New Town	3,970		6,645	
(c) Austin Canons	630		580	
		8,000		14,335
8 TOWN CENTRE				
(a) North of River	3,920		2,745	
(b) South of River	1,980		1,105	
		5,900		3,850
GRAND TOTAL		60,500		81,560

The future populations are based on calculations shown in Table 9 (*p.* 134).

The character and problems of each neighbourhood and its subdivisions, and the proposed improvements during the next twenty years, are described in Chapter 6; the main principles governing the provision of local amenities are discussed in the remaining sections of this chapter.

ALLOTMENTS (Map 3, *p.* 29 and Table 1, *p.* 27). Most houses in Bedford have their 'barn' and this local name for an outhouse is among many evidences of the town's close link with the countryside. One of the most important from a planning point of view is the strength of the allotments movement. There are at present 571 acres of land in Bedford and Kempston cultivated as allotments, or 9·4 acres per 1,000 population, that is, more than twice the standard of 4 acres per 1,000 recently recommended by the Allotments Advisory Committee, a standard which has not yet been achieved in many other towns.

Many of the existing allotments are temporary, and insecurity of tenure has lowered standards of cultivation. One of the objects of our proposals is to earmark a sufficient area of permanent allotments which will not be taken for any other use for at least twenty years. It would be possible to do this simply by deciding to preserve all existing allotments intact, but this would be to ignore the relationship between allotments and all the other uses of land which have to be integrated.

Some of the allotments are in built-up areas on land which would make excellent sites for houses, schools and factories. The allotment movement in Bedford deserves every consideration, but even 4,000 allotment holders and their families are hardly more than one-fifth of the total population, whereas everybody is affected by the need to be close to shops, schools and workplaces. Wherever we have faced a choice between planning short journeys to work and the town centre or short journeys to allotments, the first has been preferred, and in consequence it is suggested that a total of 225 acres should be zoned for other uses. This represents thirty-nine per cent of the total allotment acreage in the area. Sixty-one per cent of these allotments would be taken for housing, seven per cent for industry and roads, and thirty-two per cent for schools and open spaces.

The principal allotments to be disturbed are numbered on Map 3:
Cave's Lane (13) for private housing
Eastcotts Road (24) for Corporation housing
Winifred Road, Queen's Park (1) for a Secondary Modern School
North of Elstow Village (28) for adults' sports fields
Part of Brickhill (10/11) for cemetery extension
Evans Field, Bromham Road (3) for private housing.
The remaining eleven patches of allotments suggested for other uses are all less than six acres.

Two hundred and sixteen acres of new allotments are suggested on the outskirts of the built-up area—some of them just outside the Borough boundary. These will not be much further from the residential areas than are the existing allotments, but have been sited so as not to interfere with the compact development of the town.

The proposed sites are:
West of Queen's Park at Honey Hill Farm (59)
South of Mile Road (62/63)
North of Putnoe Street beyond the Goldington neighbourhood (60)
Around Kempston Sewage Works in Woburn Road (65/67)
South of the Kempston Boundary on either side of the main railway line between Ampthill Road and the new link from south of Elstow to Cow Bridge (64).

The total area of allotments would thus be reduced by only nine acres, but since the population is likely to increase by about one-third, there would be a reduction in the standard to 6·9 acres per 1,000 people. This does not necessarily mean that any existing allotment holders would have to give up their plots altogether, though many would eventually have to move to new plots. For one thing the immigrant population are not so likely to be affected by the special factors which have given rise to the strong allotment movement in Bedford, and will probably not even want four acres per thousand. For another thing, a number of the present plots are very large—almost smallholdings in fact—and should be shared out so as to accommodate the greatest number of tenants. Finally, in some cases the more economical layout

Table 1: ALLOTMENTS (*the numbers refer to Map 3, page* 29).

NEIGHBOURHOOD	EXISTING ALLOTMENTS				PROPOSED NEW ALLOTMENTS		TOTALS[2]	
	DISPLACED		RETAINED					
	Location	Acreage	Location	Acreage	Location	Acreage	Present	Future
	1	2	3	4	5	6	7	8
1—QUEEN'S PARK	1 Winifred Road 56 Cox's Pits 24·9	18·9 6·0	0 Allen Park 2 Quenby's Field 54 Eastern Gas Board 55 British Railways 37·2	5·0 17·2 14·0 1·0	59 Honey Hill[1]	31·7 31·7	62·1	68·9
2, 3 and 4— BROMHAM ROAD BLACK TOM DE PARY'S GOLDINGTON	3 Evans Field 5 Fairhill (part) 10, 11 Brickhill 13 Cave's Lane 83·7	8·7 1·5 15·0 58·5	4 Bromham Road 5 Fairhill (most) 6 Franklin's Brickfield 7, 8 Hoo Farm 9 West of Cemetery 12 Old cycle track 14 Barker's Lane 15 Haynes Field 126·2	2·0 20·0 2·1 51·9 35·0 4·2 6·4 4·6	60 North of Putnoe Street[1] 61 North of new Power Station 64·7	53·7 11·0	209·9	190·9
5—NEWNHAM	17 Newnham Avenue 18 Newnham Avenue (part) 22 Longholme 4·5	1·25 1·25 2·00	16 Bunyan Field 18 Newnham Avenue (most) 19 Brown's Close 20 Brown's Close 21 Barker's Lane 62·6	5·1 48·2 1·0 5·8 2·5		—	67·1	62·6
6—CAULDWELL/ KINGSBROOK	23 Alamein Avenue 24 Eastcotts 28 Elstow Village[1] 60·8	2·1 33·8 24·9	25 Duchess Road 26 Nicholls Road 27 Mile Road 29 Meltis Works 30 Edward Road 31 Cauldwell Walk 57 Rope Walk 58 Ampthill Street 44·7	0·3 0·8 30·9 3·1 4·6 3·3 0·5 1·2	62 South-East of Mile Road[1] 63 South of Mile Road 27·2	19·2 8·0	105·5	71·9
7—KEMPSTON	34 Orchard Street 37 Elstow Road 40 Hill Grounds (part) 50, 51 Beatrice Street 52 Kempston Road 50·9	30·7 3·7 3·0 9·5 4·0	32, 33 Ampthill Road[1] 35 Cryselco Works 36 Bedford Road 38 Margetts Road 39 Duncombe Street 41 Hill Grounds (most) 42 St. John's Street 43 Wyatt Road 44 Mill Lane 45 Water Lane 46 Ridge Road 47 Durler Avenue 48 Hill Rise 49 Grange Field 53 Cauldwell House 75·8	17·7 1·0 1·1 3·9 4·0 19·5 2·3 1·0 0·8 1·7 2·5 0·5 0·2 15·6 4·0	64 Ampthill Road[1] 65 North-East of Sewage Works 66 South-West of Sewage Works 67 North-West of Woburn Road 92·1	50·0 14·0 3·6 24·5	126·7	167·9
BEDFORD AND KEMPSTON		224·8		346·5		215·7	571·3	562·2

[1] Outside the Borough Boundary.
[2] Column 7 is the sum of Columns 2 and 4—Column 8 is the sum of Columns 4 and 6.

Source: Borough Allotments Manager and Field Survey.

Table 2: LIST OF EXISTING AND PROPOSED EDUCATIONAL ESTABLISHMENTS (*Key to Map 3, opposite*)

a	Ampthill Road Infant and Junior	p	Putnoe Junior (PROPOSED)*	ee	Bedford Modern School
b	Clapham Road Infant and Junior	q	Goldington Junior (PROPOSED)*	ff	Dame Alice Harpur School
c	Goldington Road Infant and Junior	r	Goldington Secondary Grammar (PROPOSED)*	gg	Convent of the Holy Ghost
d	Priory Street Infant	s	Cave's Lane Secondary Modern (PROPOSED)	hh	North Bedfordshire College of Further Education
e	Priory Street R.C.—to be discontinued, building to become part of d.	t	Bedford Secondary Technical (PROPOSED)	jj	Elstow Primary and Secondary Modern
f	Queen's Park Infant and Junior	u	Bedford Roman Catholic Secondary modern (PROPOSED)	kk	Bedford Physical Training College
g	Silver Jubilee Secondary Modern	v	Harpur Secondary Modern (to be discontinued)	ll	Rushmoor Preparatory School
h	London Road Junior—to be removed	w	Bedford Road Primary and Secondary Modern	mm	St. Andrew's School for Girls
j	Goldington Green Infant and Junior	x	Up End Primary (to be discontinued)	nn	Queen's Park Junior and Secondary Modern (PROPOSED)
k	Pearcey Road Infant and Junior	y	Church End Primary (to be discontinued)	oo	Roman Catholic Primary (PROPOSED)
l	Kingsbrook Junior Infant (PROPOSED)	z	Kempston Junior Infant (PROPOSED)	pp	Bedford Training College
m	Harrowden Infant and Secondary Modern (PROPOSED)	aa	Kempston Infant (PROPOSED)		*For proposed sites see folding map 'Future Land Use'.*
n	Putnoe Infant (PROPOSED)*	bb	Kempston Secondary Modern (PROPOSED)		
o	Goldington Infant (PROPOSED)*	cc	Bedford School		
		dd	Bedford High School		

of plots on the site could increase the cultivated proportion of the present total acreage.

Some interference with allotment holders is inevitable in the implementation of proposals covering every aspect of land use in a large area, but it should be regarded by them as the price that has to be paid for gaining security of tenure and a recognized status in the County Development Plan.

OPEN SPACES (Map 3, opposite, and Table 10, *p.* 135). Bedford and Kempston already have 5·6 acres of parks, gardens and other public open spaces for every 1,000 of their population. This is nearly twice the recognized standard of three acres per thousand.

They also have in Bedford Park, Russell Park, the Embankment Gardens and Kempston Grange, first-class examples of the landscaping of urban parks.

But, as in the case of other amenities, the distribution of open spaces among the various neighbourhoods is now seriously unbalanced. When Bedford and Russell Parks were acquired by the town towards the end of the last century, almost the whole population of the Borough lived

north of the river and though these open spaces were on the very edge of the built-up area, they were easily accessible from most parts of the town.

Today, when half the population live south of the river and in Queen's Park, the Cauldwell/Kingsbrook neighbourhood has only 1·6 acres of parks and public gardens per thousand people and Queen's Park has only two acres. It is proposed to correct these deficiencies by a sixteen acres extension of the London Road Recreation Ground, between the London Road and Harrowden sub-divisions of Neighbourhood 6; and by the provision of public gardens at Cox's Pits and west of the new Secondary Modern School in the green belt between Honey Hill and Biddenham. The new roads and cycle tracks south of the river would bring the Recreation Ground within fairly easy reach of the whole of the Cauldwell/Kingsbrook neighbourhood, and it should be laid out and planted as imaginatively and ambitiously as were the existing parks seventy years ago.

Certain existing and proposed open spaces, especially the river walks and Cardington Meadows, have been excluded from the calculation of neighbourhood standards, because they serve the whole town. The proposed extension to these, together with the new neighbourhood

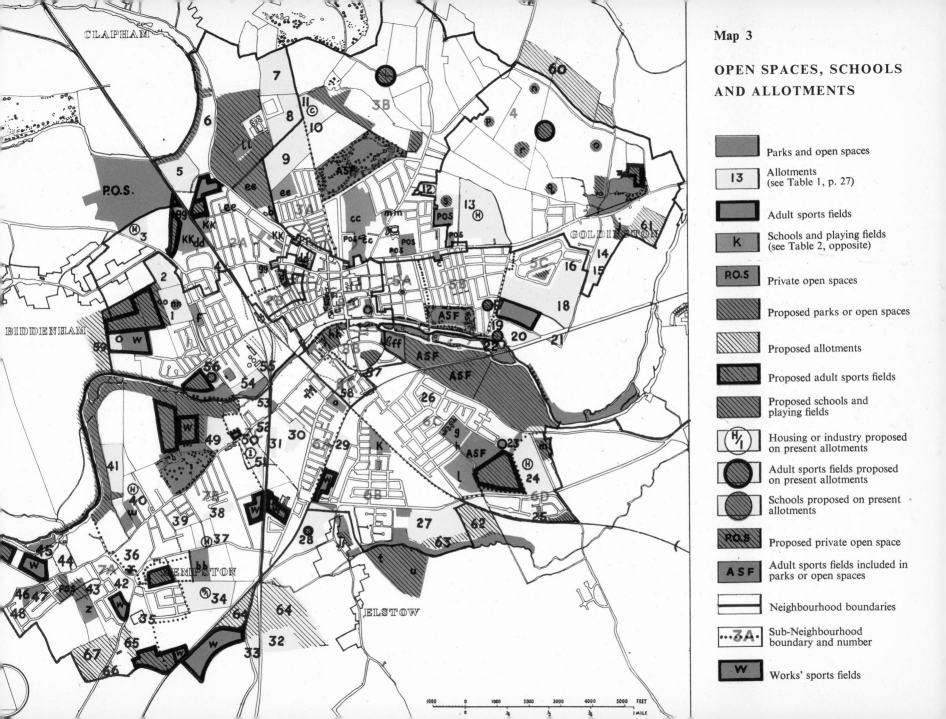

Map 3

OPEN SPACES, SCHOOLS
AND ALLOTMENTS

	Parks and open spaces
13	Allotments (see Table 1, p. 27)
	Adult sports fields
K	Schools and playing fields (see Table 2, opposite)
P.O.S	Private open spaces
	Proposed parks or open spaces
	Proposed allotments
	Proposed adult sports fields
	Proposed schools and playing fields
H/I	Housing or industry proposed on present allotments
	Adult sports fields proposed on present allotments
	Schools proposed on present allotments
P.O.S	Proposed private open space
ASF	Adult sports fields included in parks or open spaces
	Neighbourhood boundaries
3A	Sub-Neighbourhood boundary and number
W	Works' sports fields

CLAPHAM

BIDDENHAM

GOLDINGTON

KEMPSTON

ELSTOW

1000   0   1000   2000   3000   4000   5000 FEET

0   ¼   ½   ¾   1 MILE

open spaces, would raise the overall standard to 8·7 acres per 1,000 for a future population of 80,000. The total amount of land would be slightly more than doubled from 341 to 712 acres. Although well above the recognized minimum, this standard is not achieved at the expense of competing uses, since some of the large additions of public open space are on land liable to flood which could not be developed in any other way.

Small neighbourhood open spaces and children's playgrounds should be incorporated in the design of the new neighbourhoods and housing estates. At Goldington, where the biggest population increase is to take place, it is hoped that the grounds of the Hall and the Bury adjoining the existing village green will eventually become available for public enjoyment.

The river and its banks will remain Bedford's premier open space, and some suggestions for their improvement are given in Chapter 7. We have been privileged to read a personal unofficial letter addressed by the late Sir Herbert Trustram Eve to the Mayor of Bedford in March, 1933. In this he made certain suggestions about the future of the Wingfield Estate at Biddenham, including the possibility that parts of the river banks and adjoining land might become the property of the Corporation, so that they might be open to the public in perpetuity. This letter will no doubt form the basis of negotiations regarding the further development of the river walk.

ADULTS' SPORTS FIELDS (Map 3, *p.* 29, and Table 10, *p.* 135). As in most towns, there appears to be a deficiency of sports facilities for the general public and this stands in sharp contrast to the excellent private sports fields used by the Harpur Trust Schools, the Training Colleges, and the Rugby and Tennis Clubs. At present there are only 2·3 acres of sports fields per 1,000 of the population, and this standard includes the recreation grounds owned by a number of large firms in the town. The National Playing Fields Association recommend a standard of six acres per 1,000, but it is thought that a standard of four acres for the future population will meet the demands expressed during the survey of clubs and other organizations.

To achieve this standard means adding 208 acres to the existing 133, or more than doubling the total amount of land devoted to physical recreation.

An attempt has been made to distribute the new fields evenly between the neighbourhoods, and in all except the Newnham neighbourhood, where no increase is possible, the standard of four acres per thousand would be reached.

The main proposals are for sixty acres of sports fields in the Kimbolton Road Estate, which will also serve the existing populations of Black Tom and de Pary's; twenty-five acres in the Goldington neighbourhood, together with pitches and tennis courts in the grounds of Goldington Bury; increased facilities in London Road Recreation Ground; pitches in Cardington Meadows; pitches and tennis courts on the land between Elstow Village and the Bletchley railway line to serve the Southend and Elstow Road subdivisions (at present the worst off in the town); at Cox's Pits and in the Biddenham green belt to serve Queen's Park; and in Kempston, pitches north of the Grange, south-east of the sewage works and in Cemetery Road.

The playing fields in Newnham Avenue should be developed as a Stadium serving the whole town and the surrounding district, with facilities for all the major sports and adequate accommodation for the biggest local events.

A number of the larger firms in Bedford have extensive sporting facilities, notable examples being Allen Park at Honey Hill, the Igranic Sports Ground at Kempston, and Robertsons' field on the Ampthill Road. The Britannia Sports Club is seeking a new ground, and this could be provided north of Kempston Grange. In the course of the industrial survey several of the smaller firms expressed a strong wish to to have sporting facilities of their own, rather than relying on the use of public pitches, and many favoured the suggestion that some sort of association of small firms' sports clubs should be set up to acquire pitches which they would share. It is suggested that if the Cosmic Works were to join such an association, their field, which has been ploughed up since the beginning of the war, could be shared.

SCHOOLS (Map 3, *p.* 29, and Table 2, *p.* 28). Education is a primary function of Bedford by virtue of the large area served by its well-known public schools and training colleges, and of the number of families who have settled in the town to take advantage of these facilities. Educational buildings and playing fields take up a large area of land, including some of the best sites in the town. The four Harpur Trust schools alone have seventy-two acres, more than all the existing local authority schools in Bedford and Kempston, which occupy fifty-four acres.

The County's Educational Development Plan is not yet complete but a number of proposed sites have been selected in co-operation with the officials of the County Council. These proposals allow for the expected increase in population, though minor adjustments may have to be made. Existing schools with a total area of thirteen acres would eventually be discontinued and new schools on sites totalling 206 acres would be built. The area devoted to primary and secondary education, excluding the Harpur Trust Schools and the College of Further Education, would thus be increased by more than five times. This is one measure of the improvement in educational standards to be attained when the 1944 Act is implemented.

The main proposals are:

(i) Secondary Modern Schools at:
   Queen's Park (on the allotments west of the proposed Relief Road) (nn)
   Harrowden (on the far side of Eastcotts Road) (m)
   Cave's Lane (to serve de Pary's and Newnham neighbourhoods) (s)
   Goldington neighbourhood (r)
   Kempston (Elstow Road) (bb)
   Kempston (Cemetery Road) (aa)

(ii) Secondary Technical and Roman Catholic Secondary Modern Schools just south of the Borough Boundary between Elstow Brook and the proposed Western Relief Road from Cotton End (tu).

(iii) Infant and Junior Schools at:
   Queen's Park (Secondary Modern site)
   Harrowden (Secondary Modern site)
   Putnoe neighbourhood (n, p)
   Goldington neighbourhood (o, q)
   Kempston (Elstow Road)

Sites have been suggested for nursery schools in the proposed layout of the Goldington neighbourhood, and nursery schools should also be built in other new housing estates and in existing neighbourhoods. They might be associated with some of the proposed local community centres.

NEIGHBOURHOOD SHOPS (Map 14, *p.* 110, and Table 6, *p.* 97). None of Bedford's residential districts have ideal local shopping facilities, because in no case were shops provided as part of a coherent plan for a whole neighbourhood.

In relating shops to such a plan two conflicting factors have to be reconciled:
1. The need for shops to be as close as possible to people's homes;
2. The need for a sufficient range of trade types and for a certain amount of competition within each trade type in a single compact group.

The trend towards larger shops, which is well illustrated by the figures for Bedford's neighbourhoods given below in Table 6 (*p.* 97), makes the reconciliation of these factors more difficult, but the importance of the isolated general store revealed in the shopping survey shows how it may be done. So far as possible there should be a single local shopping centre in each neighbourhood, sited as centrally as possible, and also close to the main outlet towards the town centre, containing one shop to every 300/500 people in the neighbourhood, together with a number of isolated shops or possibly groups of two or three shops scattered among the houses so that none of the latter are more than a quarter of a mile from the nearest shop.

These principles should be incorporated in the layouts for the new neighbourhoods at Goldington, Putnoe and Kimbolton Road.

Existing neighbourhoods which will have only small or scattered additions during the next twenty years present a more difficult problem, to which no completely satisfactory solution can be found.

We propose a new shopping centre to serve most of Kempston at the junction of St John's and Bunyan Road; a small centre between Worcester and Hastings Roads for the existing Harrowden Road housing and the new Eastcotts Road estate; another for the southern part of Elstow Road neighbourhood at the corner of Mile Road and Lancaster Avenue, together with isolated shops among new houses.

Ultimately there should also be a local shopping centre for Queen's Park in the vicinity of the 'Bell' Inn, where the Western Relief Road would cross Ford End Road, and one for Black Tom at the junction of Queen Street with Park Road. These cannot, however, be put forward as proposals for the next twenty years' development, since they would involve the demolition of houses with a longer economic life.

The principles governing these decisions emerged from a detailed survey of shopping facilities and habits in the town which is fully described in Chapter 6.

PUBLIC HOUSES (Map 1, *p.* 21) shows the concentration of licensed premises in the town centre, though Bedford's outer neighbourhoods are much better provided with drinking space than those of some other towns which have grown more rapidly.

Many of the central houses are very small and outworn and a number will be demolished during the clearance of blighted areas. Fifteen new ones are proposed: at Honey Hill; in Newnham Avenue, close to the Stadium; in Kempston (three); at the junction of Harrowden and Eastcotts Roads; in Elstow Road; in the Goldington neighbourhood (five, including one hotel); in Putnoe (one); and in the Kimbolton Road neighbourhood (two). It is expected that at least two existing licences will be surrendered in exchange for every new one, so that there would be a reduction in the total number of houses during the next twenty years.

MEETING PLACES (Map 1, *p.* 21). A healthy community life depends upon an adequate number of halls suited to the needs of various organizations. The survey of clubs and associations showed that there was a

deficiency of such buildings in Bedford, particularly south of the river.

The main need is for community centres available to all organizations, and seven of these are proposed:

In Queen's Park (Old Ford End Road)
In the new Kimbolton Road and Goldington neighbourhoods
In Newnham Avenue
In Cardington Road
In Kent Avenue (to serve Elstow Road and Southend sub-divisions)
At Orchard Street in the centre of Kempston.

There is also a need for a civic Assembly Hall larger than the Corn Exchange which fulfils this function at present, and for a Community Centre to be used by the many societies which draw their members from all over the town. It is proposed that these buildings should form a group between the Central Relief Road and the Brewery on the site of the pig market south of Horne Lane. The Community Centre would provide rooms of various sizes with special facilities such as film projection equipment and a communal canteen.

A strong demand for a separate Youth Centre was expressed by a number of organizations covered in the survey of clubs, and an ideal site for this would be on the present private open space behind the Children's Home in Cardington Road. It would be available not only for all Youth Clubs, but also for such organizations as the Boy Scouts and Girl Guides. It is important that the site should be preserved as an open space and that the Youth Centre buildings should be at the edge of it. (Map 9, no. 28, opposite *p.* 74).

CINEMAS Bedford at present has four cinemas, all in the centre of the town, with a total seating capacity of about 4,000. This is one cinema seat for every fifteen people in Bedford and Kempston, a surprisingly low figure in view of the national average of one seat for eleven people, and of the large rural population visiting Bedford's cinemas.

During the proposed reconstruction of the central area two of the existing cinemas—the Plaza and the Picturedrome—would be replaced by the new cinema in the recreational centre on the south bank of the river, and there would be another new cinema in St Loyes Street. If each of these had 2,000 seats the future total in the town centre would be 6,500. At least another 1,500 seats would be needed to reach the recommended standard of one per ten persons for the future population of Bedford and Kempston alone. It is suggested that two small neighbourhood cinemas—an innovation in the town—should be built; one to serve the proposed population of 15,000 in the new Goldington and Kimbolton Road neighbourhoods, and one to serve Kempston when its population reaches the estimated 14,000. A suitable site for another central cinema would be the present bus station in the Broadway.

HEALTH SERVICES Bedford's two hospitals now form the North and South Wings of a single institution. There is ample room for the extension of the North Wing (St Peter's Hospital or the House of Industry) as far as the junction of Kimbolton and Goldington Roads without interfering with the croquet lawn or the rugby football field. This is a solution to the problem of the strategically placed but untidily developed triangle of land between these two exits from the town. The Central Welfare Clinic could also be sited there.

The only modern neighbourhood clinic is in Barford Avenue, off London Road. New ones should be associated with the proposed Community Centres at Queen's Park, Kimbolton Road, Goldington, Newnham Avenue and Kent Avenue. Kempston needs two welfare centres and it is proposed that one should be at the western end of High Street, and the other in Elstow Road.

FIRE STATION A new County Fire Headquarters is urgently needed to replace the present temporary station in the Hospital grounds in Britannia Road. It is suggested that it should be built in Kempston Road on two acres of the proposed industrial site opposite Whitbread Avenue (No. 3 on Map 11, *p.* 84). This is not too far from the town centre where some of the main fire risks are concentrated, and when the Western Relief Road crossing Kempston Road nearby is built, access to the large outlying area served from the station would be easy.

CREMATORIUM The nearest crematoria are at Northampton and Cambridge. The demand for this form of disposal is increasing and the Corporation propose to erect a Crematorium in the Cemetery. Thus it will not take any additional land that could be better used by the living.

CONCLUSION These proposals for a comprehensive improvement in urban services together with new roads, an extension of the shopping centre, and new public buildings, would not only restore the balance that has been disturbed by the changes of the last seventy years, but would also lay the basis for the future expansion of the town.

A population of 75,000 to 80,000 would enable Bedford to become a better centre of exchange in all senses of the word—not only the exchange of goods and services in the shops and businesses of the town, but also of ideas and entertainment in its cultural and recreational buildings. Bedford could support a larger and better theatre, a daily newspaper, bigger libraries and more frequent concerts. It is not rapid growth, but unplanned growth which gives rise to unbalanced development, and the carrying out of an agreed Development Plan would be the guarantee that in Bedford this would be avoided. The schools, the river, the strong agricultural interest, create a character which is sufficiently firm to assert itself over a long period of steady growth in the same way as it has done in the past. This character coupled with the careful and steady implementation of the proposals, will ensure that Bedford does not suffer from the drab commercialization that has afflicted some of the recent mushroom developments in many parts of the country.

2

Although there have been no major changes in Bedford's balance of functions since 1900, there has been a striking transformation in the physical shape of the town. But its material equipment has not yet reached the standard required to cater for its present activities

The Background

The proposals reviewed in the first chapter are based on a comprehensive survey of Bedford and Kempston which covered the present use of all land in the area, the condition of the buildings upon it, the livelihood and workplaces of the people, the amenities of the several neighbourhoods and the flow of traffic along the main roads. The more important facts are summarized in Chapters 3 to 6, which deal with certain aspects of the proposals in greater detail. We have had to concern ourselves with more than the present condition of Bedford itself. Every town has a past which must to a large extent shape its future; most towns are also linked in many ways with the surrounding countryside. This chapter, therefore, begins by considering the physical features of the Bedford district, the uses which have been made of local resources and their effects on the town. It continues with a brief history of Bedford, devoted not to outstanding buildings and events and personalities—these can be found in the guide books and memoirs—but to the town as a whole, the development of its economic functions and their physical expression in streets and open spaces, factories and railways. Finally, before we can suggest a detailed solution of Bedford's problems, it is necessary to decide in the light of past and present trends what should be the future size and character of the town. It is hoped that this chapter will help to make our proposals clear to planning students who may not know Bedford, and that Bedfordians themselves will gain a new insight into the past growth of their town and a new interest in its planned future.

THE COUNTY Bedfordshire is one of England's smallest counties, yet it does not lie wholly within any one geographical or economic region, but rather forms a sort of watershed between London, the Eastern Counties and the South Midlands. The town of Bedford is fifty miles from London—just over one hour's journey by train. This is about the limit of regular daily travel, and the town is at present a dormitory for a number of London office workers. The central government has put Bedfordshire into its Eastern Region which is administered from Cambridge, whose university also has considerable influence in the county. Bedford's 'local' evening newspaper comes from Northampton on the west, but London evening papers circulate widely in the town.

Administrative convenience rather than physical boundaries determined the size and shape of the county. For geological reasons it has remained predominantly agricultural, the successive bands of sedimentary rock which run across Bedfordshire from south-west to north-east having all been laid down later than the coal measures. The winning of brick clay and of chalk for cement works are the only important extractive industries. The manufactures of Luton, Bedford and one or two smaller towns are not based on local resources; like many of their workers these industries are immigrants to the county, depending mainly on its central position and good connections with all parts of England. Bedfordshire's affinities with several surrounding regions are emphasized by the mixture of farming types that has developed on its various soils; it has been said that 'most of the gradations from the typical arable farming of Eastern England to the dairying of the West are to be noted as one proceeds from east to west across the county'.[1]

THE BEDFORD DISTRICT Bedford's closest economic links are not those of an industrial town with its industrial neighbours, but of a market town with the surrounding countryside. As the county town it is, of course, the administrative centre for the whole of Bedfordshire. But its other urban services have a rather different sphere of influence, which does not include the southern part of Bedfordshire but extends over its eastern and western boundaries into the counties of Huntingdon, Cambridge, Northampton and Buckingham. 174,000 people live within the area coloured red on Map 4 (*p.* 40) including Bedford and Kempston.[2] Its fringes overlap the spheres of influence of Cambridge, Peterborough and Northampton, but over most of the area Bedford's influence is absolute. Smaller centres like Ampthill, Biggleswade and St Neots each have their own subsidiary sphere of influence, attracting the people of nearby villages on weekly visits. For the more important occasional outings, everybody in the district comes to Bedford. The county town itself has a 'weekly' sphere of influence which is much bigger than those of the smaller centres.

It is tempting to speak of the town's 'occasional' sphere of influence as 'the Bedford sub-region' or even 'the Bedford region', but neither would be strictly correct. On the one hand, the term 'sub-region' suggests a division of a region, but we have seen that North Bedfordshire does not belong wholly to any one region. On the other hand, a 'region' must be much more self-contained than the area served by Bedford. This area does not fit neatly into any regional pattern, and we shall speak of it simply as 'the Bedford district'.

In putting forward proposals for the planning of Bedford we must never forget that the town serves nearly twice as many people living outside its boundary as within it, that it depends upon the country folk for much of its prosperity, and that it belongs to them almost as much as to its own citizens. Bedford's sphere of influence is not likely to grow since its main competitors are also well-established centres. But its importance within the district may well increase at the expense of minor centres, and this should be borne in mind in the redevelopment of Bedford's central area.

The Bedford district includes a number of fairly well-defined physical and economic sub-divisions:

(*i*) *The Greensand Ridge*. In the south the district is bounded by the Greensand Ridge, which enters the county at Leighton Buzzard and forms a plateau four miles wide and 400 feet high at Woburn. It runs north-east through Ampthill, gradually decreasing in height and width until it descends into the valley of the Ivel. A marked characteristic of the ridge is the profusion of large country houses set in wooded parkland, one of the most famous being Woburn Abbey, the seat of the Dukes of Bedford.

(*ii*) *The Market Garden Area*. The Greensand Ridge reappears east of the Ivel between Sandy and Gamlingay, where it forms part of the second sub-division of the Bedford district. Biggleswade is the centre of one of the most intensively cultivated areas in the country. Here on the rich and varied soils derived from the deposits of the River Ivel the acreage of market gardens has increased from 8,000 in 1893 to 17,000 in 1938, and is still increasing. This type of farming has spread along the Greensand Ridge towards Ampthill, and along the Ouse Valley westwards to Willington and northwards beyond St Neots. A lot of the produce goes by road to London, whose proximity has been one of the main reasons for the intense exploitation of the area's natural assets, but vegetables are also sent by rail from Sandy to the northern towns and even to Glasgow.

(*iii*) *The Vale of Bedford*. From the steep northern scarp of the Greensand Ridge one looks across a dreary plain punctuated only by clusters of tall, slender chimneys, striking evidence of the county's most distinctive industry. Here is a deposit of Oxford clay, three to four hundred feet deep and close to the surface, and here during the last fifty years have been established some of the largest kilns in the world producing millions of Fletton bricks every week. Although the brickworks lie entirely outside the Borough, they affect the planning of Bedford in several ways. Map 4 (*p.* 40) shows that the clay workings are rapidly approaching the town from the south-west, and will prevent any extension of the urban area in this direction; they also make it impossible to build a true by-pass for through traffic on the west. The derelict 'knot holes' add another depressing feature to a rather depressing landscape, and are an ugly reminder of the lost agricultural land. If restoration is out of the question then the possibility of other uses, such as storing water for Bedford, should be investigated.

The smoke from the brickworks is blown directly over Bedford by the prevailing wind. Since the town's own industries make so little smoke, it has a right to complain about this outside source of pollution and to demand measures to reduce the nuisance.

The brickworks are the only large source of employment in rural Bedfordshire, apart from agriculture. Although a number of settlements have sprung up along the Bletchley branch of the railway—including the model village at Stewartby—about ten per cent of the brick-workers travel daily from Bedford and Kempston. The industry is at present short of labour, and its needs must be thought of in deciding Bedford's housing programme.

(*iv*) *North Bedfordshire*. North of Bedford the Oxford clay lies under drift deposits of Boulder clay, and the result is a slightly higher plateau dissected by many small streams. Mixed farming predominates in this sparsely populated area of isolated hamlets and homesteads, with few good roads and no railways. It is in these 'wilds' that the National Aeronautical Establishment is at present being constructed by the amalgamation of two war-time airfields, and it will inevitably bring great changes to the northern part of the county.

(*v*) *The Ouse Valley*. All these areas are drained by the Great Ouse, which flows from west to east across the middle of the district and then turns north towards its outlet in the Wash. Its valley forms a distinct sub-division of the district, with gravel soils of high fertility. There is a variety of farming types intermediate between the market gardening of the east, the mixed farming of the north and the dairying of the west. There are a number of large villages, like Bromham and Biddenham, growing rapidly as a result of movement out of Bedford.

THE SITE OF BEDFORD At Bedford the narrow winding valley of the Ouse opens out into a broad flood plain, and the town guards the main entrance to the western uplands. Here also is the best crossing of the river for many miles, and the extreme limit of navigation for craft of any size. These are the reasons why the Saxons founded their settlement here, and why Bedford was a defensive stronghold in the days when Saxons warred with Danes and Norman barons fought among themselves, as we know from the historic relics of the King's Ditch and the Castle Mound.

Such a site was also ideal for a market centre, and as early as the tenth century Bedford had its own Mint. It had one further advantage which determined that Bedford would become the main market for the whole district. This was its central position among the various physical and economic sub-divisions of the district—the best place for exchanging the products of different farming types. By the twelfth century a bridge had taken the place of the ford, and in 1224 the predominance of peaceful intercourse over civil war was symbolized by the demolition of the castle and the use of its stones to rebuild St Paul's Church. For 700 years its graceful spire has presided over the weekly market in the heart of the town.[3]

EARLY GROWTH The first map we have of Bedford was made by Speed in 1610, and is reproduced on page 11. The built-up area at that date forms the black core of Map 5 (*p*. 45), extending from St Peter's in the north to St John's in the south, and from Horne Lane in the west to St Cuthbert's in the east. It is clear that the large majority of Bedford's population then lived north of the bridge. There was once a market by St Mary's as well as by St Paul's, but the original settlement had been on the north bank, and it seems to have remained the more important part of the town, possibly because there was less risk of serious flooding. However this may be, the establishment of the central area north of the Ouse has had a very big effect on the subsequent growth and present problems of the town.

There was very little extension of the built-up area between 1610 and the publication of Jeffrey's map in 1765, but there was probably quite a lot of 'infilling'—increasing the density by building over the large medieval gardens. It was a period of preparation for the astonishing progress of the next two centuries. Like most commercial centres, Bedford took the Parliamentary side in the Civil War, but its part in the conflict was not distinguished; the town's proudest memory of the seventeenth century is that it gave the world (though there were those in Bedford who did their best to keep him from it) one of the most beloved pioneers of the new freedom—John Bunyan.

Curiously enough, the seventeenth-century developments that were to have most effect on Bedford's future took place in London. It was at this time that 'Damned' Barebones—one of the first speculative financiers, and as typical of one aspect of his age as Bunyan was of another—began to build on the land in Holborn that William Harpur had given to Bedford in 1566.[4] Thus began the enormous increase in value which made possible the town's later achievements as an educational centre.

There was rather more development in the second half of the eighteenth century, recorded on Brayley's map of 1807, and shown in orange on page 45. But when the first Population Census was taken in 1801, Bedford had only just under 4,000 inhabitants—about the same number as Buckingham has today. During the next fifty years the district shared fully in the national expansion of agriculture, and this was reflected in the more rapid growth of the town. Because there was no coal, however, there were few manufactures, and Bedford grew less quickly than towns that were directly affected by the industrial revolution; in 1851 it still had less than 12,000 people. The period had seen the building of one of the most distinctive and delightful features of modern Bedford—the Town Bridge, designed by the local architect, John Wing, who was Mayor of Bedford. Other additions (coloured blue on Map 5) included on the one hand the last really good domestic architecture in Bedford—the terraces in Bromham Road and the first few houses in Kimbolton Road; and on the other hand the now blighted streets of small mean houses extending west to Priory Street and north beyond Tavistock Street into the area sometimes known in the town as 'Black Tom'.[5]

The next period of growth shown on Map 5 is from 1842 to 1878, when Bedford spread slowly westwards on both north and south banks of the river towards the newly established railways that were to bring such vast changes in the functions and fabric of the town.

DEVELOPMENT OF MODERN FUNCTIONS In the last two decades of the nineteenth century, Bedford's population grew three times faster than the population of England and Wales as a whole, and increased from 19,500 in 1881 to 35,000 in 1901 (Diagram 1, *p.* 42). This growth was due almost entirely to spectacular developments in the two fields of manufacture and education.

Bedford's pioneer large-scale industry stemmed largely from its role as an urban centre for a rich agricultural area. In 1839 John Howard exhibited the first iron-wheel plough, twenty years later he completed the construction of the Britannia Iron Works, and by 1870 was employing 600 workers to make every type of plough for export all over the world. The local development of this native idea was only made possible by the building of railways linking Bedford with all parts of the country. Howard sited his works between two of the new railway lines, though it is noteworthy that water transport was used for some heavy materials throughout the century. Later industrial developments were not based on local resources, nor even in most cases on local initiative, but were due almost entirely to Bedford's good communications.

In the seventeenth and eighteenth centuries 'Bedford was the headquarters of a system of navigation . . . which supplied the county with coal, salt, iron, wine, corn and other commodities, sea-borne coal being brought from as far afield as the port of Lynn'.[6] Commercial navigation on the Ouse continued throughout the nineteenth century, but its importance was completely overshadowed by the growth of railway transport. The first train to Bletchley ran in 1846, the lines to Leicester and Hitchin were built in the 1850's, to Cambridge and London in the 1860's, and finally in 1872 the Northampton line was opened. Alongside these railways were large areas of flat land to be had at agricultural prices, an excellent proposition for firms unable to expand amidst the growing congestion of the older industrial towns. So later factories followed the example of Britannia in being established on what was then the very edge of the town. The first arrivals were Grafton Cranes at the Vulcan Works in 1883, and Allens' at the Queen's Works in 1894; the latter was to become Bedford's biggest and most famous factory (photograph on *p.* 14). The rest of the present major firms were not established until the twentieth century.

While this new function was developing in the town an old one was growing apace. Bedford is justly proud of its long history as an educational centre, but the full fruits of Harpur's bequest were not borne until after 1873, when the Endowed Schools Commissioners reformed the administration of the charity and made nearly £30,000 a year available for education in the town. The effects were striking. The number of pupils at the Grammar School (now Bedford School) grew rapidly from 270 to 800, and the new building followed, the Commercial (English) School became the Modern School, two schools for girls were founded, and grants were given to elementary education. Regulations compelled parents to live in the town if they were to send their children to these schools. 'It dawned on the retired officers and Indian civilians, with families still growing and incomes diminished, that here, within fifty miles of Charing Cross, they could find cheap and pleasant habitation and a public school education for £9–£12 per year for their sons and high school education for their daughters at the same price. They therefore flocked to Bedford.'[6] In addition to the Harpur Trust schools, the Froebel College (now Bedford Training College) was founded in 1882, and the world-famous Physical Training College in 1903. For a non-university town Bedford has a unique selection of educational establishments.

The growth of new functions was accompanied by intense building activity, and the urban area more than doubled in size between 1878 and 1900. Because the schools and the Queen's Works were sited north of the river where the shopping centre was already established, there was practically no building on the south. The development shown in yellow on Map 5 took place in a great semi-circle around the old town; on the east and north-east were the middle-class districts between de Pary's Avenue and Goldington Road, and on both sides of Castle Road; on the north the socially intermediate extension of 'Black Tom';[5] on the north-west another middle-class district—'Poets' Corner', where most of the streets bear the names of English poets; and on the west beyond the railway and the Queen's Works was the working-class area of Queen's Park as far west as the 'Bell'. Architecturally all these new neighbourhoods were undistinguished even when they were not positively ugly; whether money was lavished on decorative details, as in de Pary's ward, or standards were kept to a bare minimum, as in Queen's Park, good taste was lacking. But there was a vast difference in living conditions between the spacious tree-lined avenues that grew naturally out of the town centre on the north-east, and the tree-less gridiron of little streets isolated beyond the railway on the west. On the edge of the middle-class areas there were laid out during these years the beautiful open spaces of Bedford Park, Russell Park and the Embankment, while the Corn Exchange, Shire Hall, County Hospital and Kempston Barracks were all built during the period. Another notable event was the construction of Prebend Street bridge to relieve congestion on the then unwidened Town Bridge, and give more direct access to the Britannia Works.

By the turn of the century the present pattern of functions was established. While education and manufacture had been added, the older activities of distribution and administration had been consolidated, the County Council having been set up in 1888. In the surrounding countryside the first brick works had been founded, and the expansion of market gardening had begun. The rapid growth of population came to an end soon after 1900, and between 1911 and 1931 numbers were almost stationary at about 40,000 even though some important factories were established during the period. The apparent paradox of growing employment with a stationary population is probably to be explained by the increase of daily travel from the surrounding villages, as a result both of the absorption of country people into town jobs, and of the movement of townspeople into the countryside. The last function to develop in the town—manufacturing industry—became the most important of all, for there was no further comparable development of education, distribution or administration. Allens' had taken the only good railside site north of the river, and has remained the only large works in that part of the town. All the new factories were built alongside the railways that radiate on the south, and this became the chief industrial zone (Map 11, *p.* 84). Hence, between 1900 and 1927 —in contrast to all earlier periods—there was more development south of the river than north of it, and only small extensions were made to existing neighbourhoods on the north. Houses were built along the London, Elstow and Ampthill Roads near the new factories, and a large part of the New Town at Kempston went up during the period. The Kempston Urban District had been formed in 1896 with a population of about 4,500, which had increased to 5,500 by 1931. In that year the population of the present area covered by Bedford and Kempston was 48,000, but a number of these people lived outside the Borough boundary as it then was—in Goldington and Biddenham Turn; they were brought in by the boundary extension of 1934, which also gave Bedford large tracts of agricultural land—much of which has since been built over—in the parishes of Goldington, Eastcotts and Elstow. The area of the Borough was more than doubled, and is now 4,972 acres, but the incorporation of Kempston (1,302 acres) was turned down even though the Urban District was developing rapidly as a suburb of Bedford, its people looking to their larger neighbour for education, recreation, shopping and a large part of their employment.

Thus, although there have been no major changes in Bedford's balance of functions since 1900, there has been a striking transformation in the physical shape of the town. At the beginning of the twentieth century, Bedford was like most medium-sized riverside towns in having almost the whole of its built-up area on one side of the river barrier. Today, if Kempston be included, as it must be, more than two-fifths of the total population live on the south. This change has given rise to two of the major problems of the town:

(*i*) *the problem of cross-town communications*, particularly for people who live on one side of the river and work on the other. Bedford's predominantly radial road system was ideal for a small market town where almost all activity was in the centre and nobody lived very far from their work. It is no longer suitable for a growing industrial town where much of the employment is outside the town centre and workers may live and work on opposite sides of the town. The river is not the only barrier to cross-town communications; the railways, which were responsible for the developments on the south, have at the same time placed big difficulties in the way of urban expansion. Journeys to work in Bedford are longer and less convenient than they need be in a town of this size.

(*ii*) *the problem of neighbourhood amenities*. So long as Bedford's expansion took place on the fringes of the central area north of the river, the amenities of the town centre were available for all to use. As soon as development crossed the railway to Queen's Park a new problem arose, for it was no longer convenient to make frequent journeys to the centre. The new neighbourhoods on the south are even further from the centre than Queen's Park, yet none of them have properly developed local shopping and community centres.

While these two problems are not peculiar to Bedford, they have been made unusually serious by the special conditions of the site. The rapid growth of the town has given rise to a third major problem which Bedford shares with many similar places. When the expansion began the traditional centre was already hemmed in by residential development. Continued pressure on a limited area has led to serious congestion and confusion of land uses.

The material equipment of the town has not yet reached the standard required to cater for its present activities. Today there is an urgent need for new houses, but there is an equally urgent need for new cross-town roads, neighbourhood amenities, and the redevelopment of the town centre.

RECENT POPULATION GROWTH Contemporary opinion believed that the stagnation of numbers in the 'twenties would be permanent. Diagram 1 shows, however, that in 1931 the area entered upon a second period

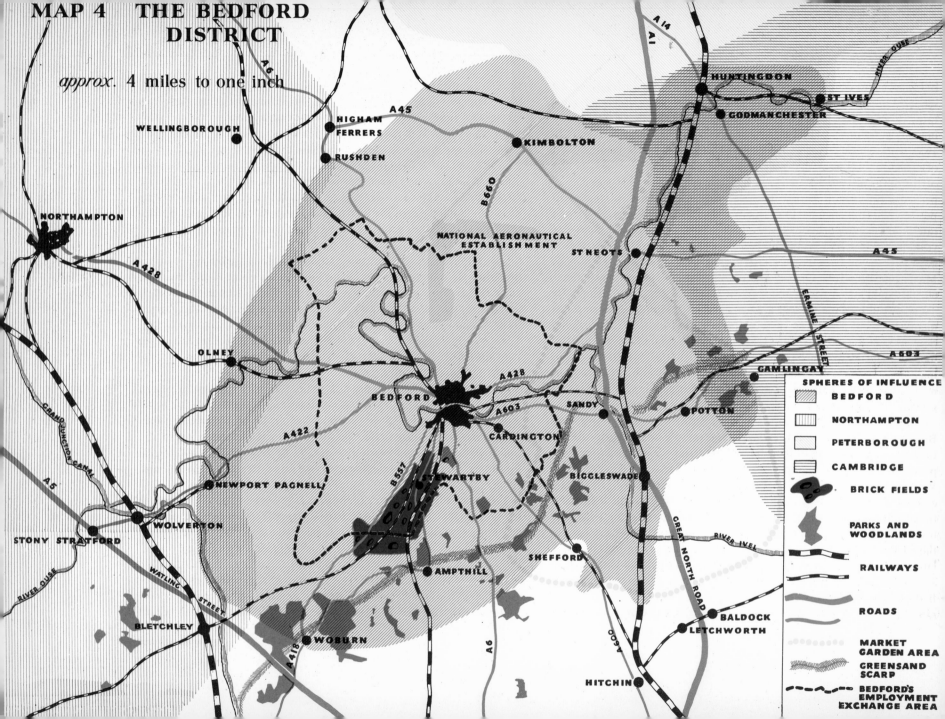

MAP 4 THE BEDFORD DISTRICT

approx. 4 miles to one inch

WELLINGBOROUGH

HIGHAM FERRERS

A45

RUSHDEN

KIMBOLTON

B660

A14
A1

HUNTINGDON

ST IVES

GODMANCHESTER

A6

NORTHAMPTON

A428

NATIONAL AERONAUTICAL ESTABLISHMENT

ST NEOTS

A45

A5

A422

OLNEY

ERMINE STREET

A603

GAMLINGAY

GRAND JUNCTION CANAL

BEDFORD

A428

A603

SANDY

POTTON

CARDINGTON

NEWPORT PAGNELL

B557

STEWARTBY

BIGGLESWADE

WOLVERTON

WATLING STREET

RIVER OUSE

STONY STRATFORD

SHEFFORD

GREAT NORTH ROAD

RIVER IVEL

AMPTHILL

A6

BLETCHLEY

A418

WOBURN

A600

BALDOCK

LETCHWORTH

HITCHIN

SPHERES OF INFLUENCE

BEDFORD

NORTHAMPTON

PETERBOROUGH

CAMBRIDGE

BRICK FIELDS

PARKS AND WOODLANDS

RAILWAYS

ROADS

MARKET GARDEN AREA

GREENSAND SCARP

BEDFORD'S EMPLOYMENT EXCHANGE AREA

of rapid expansion, and between that year and the outbreak of the second World War the population of Bedford and Kempston grew at a rate of 1·5 per cent per annum—four times the national average. The biggest recorded annual increase was 1,270 between mid-1935 and mid-1936. During the war years the population was swollen by thousands of evacuees, and was subject to abnormal fluctuations. By 1947 most of the wartime visitors had either returned to their homes or settled permanently in Bedford, and the population was found to be thirteen per cent greater than in 1939. This corresponds to an average annual rate of growth almost the same as that of the 'thirties. In the last three years numbers have not been increasing nearly so fast, but the rate of growth for the period 1947–9 was still above the national average. In May, 1950, the population of Bedford and Kempston was about 60,500 (Bedford: 51,500, Kempston: 9,000).[7]

Changes in the population of any area are determined both by natural increase—the excess of births over deaths within the area, and by migration—movements of people into or out of the area. The rate of natural increase changes very slowly; migratory movements, on the other hand, may vary considerably over quite a short period. Hence, the latter are more likely to account for sudden changes in the rate of population growth.

Until quite recently the proportionate excess of births over deaths in Bedford has been smaller than in the country as a whole, owing partly to the greater average age of its people, and partly to their social composition. We have seen that the influx of population before the first World War included a large proportion of retired Army officers, colonial administrators and the like, attracted to Bedford by the educational advantages it offered to their families. The result was that the town had proportionately more people in the older age groups and in the higher income groups than the average for the country. Such a population would not be likely to have a high birth rate, and we find that in 1920—the first year for which figures are available—the birth rate in Bedford was well below that for England and Wales. The local birth rate has remained below the national average—except during the abnormal war years—although the gap has been steadily narrowing until today there is very little difference between them.

In the 'twenties the natural increase by excess of births over deaths was about 0·3 per cent per annum, and in the 'thirties it was even lower —about 0·1 per cent. Hence the transition from an almost stationary to a rapidly expanding population was due entirely to a change in the rate of migration. Between 1921 and 1931 there was a net immigration of only about 300. The corresponding figure for 1931–39 is about 4,000 —thirteen times as many in a period of only eight years. The explanation is not far to seek. 1931 was the first year of the Great Depression, and throughout the thirties there was mass unemployment in many of our older industrial areas. By contrast Bedford was relatively prosperous. The number of workers insured at the local Employment Exchange increased by 8,000 between 1929 and 1939; the newcomers were almost equally distributed between service and manufacturing industries. Despite the agricultural depression the spread of rural bus services brought more and more country people within reach of Bedford's shops and entertainments, while the increasing importance of local government added to the numbers employed in administration in the county town. Many of Bedford's large number of middle-class residents found themselves better off during the depression as a result of the fall in prices, and this was another factor in the expansion of the service trades. Finally, the growth of manufactures themselves stimulated the growth of services. Bedford was fortunate in having a number of industries— electrical engineering and electrical apparatus, for instance—which were relatively little affected by the slump. The biggest expansion of all was in brick-making, in response to the rapid increase in the activity of the building trade, itself a national reflection of the increased purchasing power of people with secure jobs or fixed incomes. Thus, the particular combination of historical and geographical factors that determined the main functions of Bedford determined also that it should be one of the places which gained population throughout the biggest industrial crisis of modern times.

Population movements since 1939 have resulted in a further net immi-

Diagram 1

POPULATION GROWTH
1821 – 1949

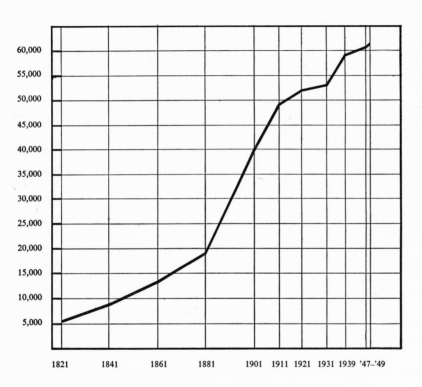

NOTES 1. The population of Kempston U.D. is included from 1901 onwards.

2. The population for 1921 and subsequent years relates to the area covered by the Borough and Kempston after the boundary extension of 1934.

3. The abnormal wartime population has been omitted.

Diagram 2

AGE AND SEX COMPOSITION
Bedford and Kempston compared with England and Wales

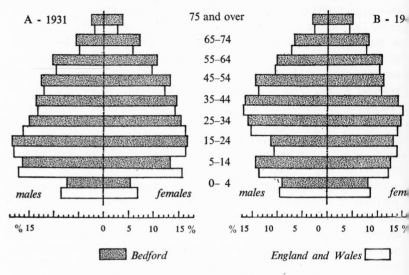

C Bedford compared with Kempston, 1947

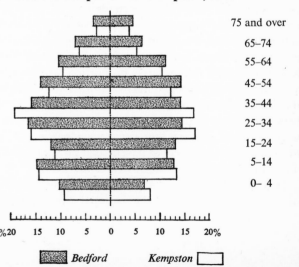

gration to the town, due to developments in all its principal functions. There was a big wartime expansion in the engineering works, and activity has remained at a high level. The new prosperity of the countryside has increased Bedford's importance as a market town, and the transfer of more local government powers to the County Council has enhanced its status as an administrative centre. The rate of natural increase during the last ten years has also been higher than at any time since the nineteenth century, owing both to the immigration during the 'thirties of younger and more prolific age and income groups, and to the national rise in the birth rate. Finally, it must not be forgotten that Bedford is still a pleasant residential town within easy reach of London, and that it has never failed to attract a number of retired persons and others who could afford to acquire a home in such a place.

AGE AND SEX COMPOSITION Diagrams 2A and 2B compare the proportions of males and females in various age groups living in Bedford and Kempston with the average proportions for England and Wales, in 1931 and 1947. The 'profile' diagram for 1931 shows Bedford falling short of the national average in the 0–4, 5–14 and 25–34 age groups, but exceeding the national average in all the others. By 1947 the pattern had changed slightly, and Bedford then exceeded England and Wales in the 5–14 and 25–34 age groups, as well as in the 45–54 and 75 and over. In the 55–74 age groups Bedford had an excess of women but a deficiency of men, while there was now a slight deficiency of both sexes in the 35–44 group. Compared with England and Wales, Bedford and Kempston had a relatively younger population in 1947 than in 1931, as a result of the immigration of young adults during the period and of the consequent increase in the birth rate. The most striking difference between the two diagrams, however, is that the excesses and deficiencies were in almost all cases smaller in 1947 than in 1931. In other words, the changes of the last twenty years have given Bedford's population a much more 'normal' age distribution.

Diagram 2C makes a similar comparison between the age structures of the separate populations of Bedford and Kempston. It shows that in 1947 the Urban District had a considerable 'bulge' in the 35–44 age group for males and in the 25–34 and 35–44 age groups for females; this is because more of Kempston's housing was built between the two wars, and occupied by young married couples who are now reaching middle age. The comparison shows that there may be big variations in population structure between different neighbourhoods of a town— due to both age and social character. Complete figures for the age composition in each neighbourhood of Bedford are not available, but we have been able to find out the proportions of children aged 0–4 and 5–18, and these are shown in Table 9 (p. 134).

In Bedford there were 117 women for every 100 men in both 1931 and 1947. For England and Wales as a whole the figure was 109 in 1931 and 112 in 1947. Thus the difference between Bedford and the country as a whole is not as great as it used to be, though the ratio of women to men is still above the national average. The greater the average age of a population the greater will be its excess of females, because women tend to survive longer than men. But this tendency does not account for the whole of Bedford's excess, for the number of females per 100 males in Bedford is above the national average in every age group from 25 upwards, though the difference is most marked among the older people. This shows that persons who settle in Bedford during their later years must include a high proportion of women.

BEDFORD TODAY AND TOMORROW The present character of the town is not the result of a conscious plan, for expansion has been allowed to take its course without any control. There is now at last an attempt to ensure that every acre is developed in that way in which it can best serve the whole community. If it is successfully carried through there will be an important difference between the changes in the face of Bedford that have been described and the equally great changes that will take place in the future. Our proposals for solving the present problems of the town should form part of a national plan which will make available the resources needed to carry them out. The details of new roads and housing estates, new public buildings and open spaces which occupy the greater part of this book must be set against the background of the future size and character of the town. We must first of all make up our minds what sort of a town Bedford should be.

Towns are almost as varied as the people who live in them; they defy classification. But from the point of view of size we may make a rough distinction between small, medium and large towns, and from the point of view of function we may contrast specialized towns with diverse towns. It is not difficult to define Bedford as a medium-sized and diverse town—not so small that its citizens have to go elsewhere for shopping and recreation, yet small enough for them to enjoy short journeys to work and easy access to the countryside. None of its functions dominates the whole community, and though manufacturing has become the most important single activity, the presence of the schools and the markets and the administrative offices has saved Bedford from becoming simply an 'industrial town'.

There is little doubt that most Bedfordians want these features preserved, but this does not necessarily imply that there should be no change whatever in the town's population or balance of functions. Character depends upon 'scale' as well as upon mere numbers, and if more people were absorbed without unduly extending the boundaries of the built-up area or destroying the intimacy of the town centre, Bedford would remain 'medium-sized'. Its balance of functions has changed in the past without radically altering its character, and could change again in the future so long as the essential mixture remained. Surveys of population and industry have shown that the recent expansion is likely to continue, and a study of the factors limiting the growth of the built-up area suggests that a further increase of population could take place without any harmful effects on the character of the town.

FUTURE POPULATION MOVEMENTS The first step in estimating the future population of any area is to determine the increase in its present numbers as a result of the excess of births over deaths. We have already seen that Bedford's age structure is now almost 'normal', and in common with the country as a whole the population will increase slowly for another ten or fifteen years, thereafter remaining almost stationary. The Registrar-General has estimated that there will be a natural increase of about 2,000 by 1971 but the average age will be higher and there will be 3,000 more 'pensioners' and 1,000 fewer 'workers' in the town. Thus Bedford—unlike some towns with a higher rate of natural increase—has no problem of finding jobs for a growing number of workers; on the contrary, it will have to attract about 500 workers from other places if the present level of employment is to be maintained.

This brings us to the main problem of our population study, for future changes in numbers will not be determined primarily by natural increase but, as in the past, by movements into and out of the area. These movements will be governed mainly by the relative number of jobs available in different districts. It has already been pointed out that people moved to Bedford in the 'thirties at a time of general unemployment because there was more chance of finding a job here than in many other industrial towns or in the countryside. A recurrence of economic depression would, no doubt, produce similar movements from the less prosperous to the more prosperous areas. But it is by no means certain that Bedford would escape so lightly from the effects of a depression in post-war conditions as it did in the 'thirties.

Full employment will not put an end to population movements, for changes in the structure of industry will in many cases entail changes in its location. But if one of the means to full employment continues to be a policy of 'taking work to the workers', wherever this is possible, then population movements are unlikely to approach the scale of the past century. This accords with the slower rate of growth and higher average age of the population, which are rapidly reducing the flexibility of its geographical distribution. At the present time the severe housing shortage is an even more powerful factor preventing movements of population. Whatever scale of internal migration proves possible and desirable, it is important that major population movements should in future be governed by conscious planning decisions as a result of further Government control over the location of industry. These decisions must

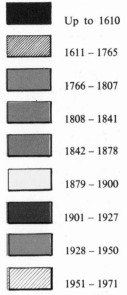

Map 5

GROWTH OF THE TOWN

■	Up to 1610
▨	1611 – 1765
▨	1766 – 1807
▨	1808 – 1841
▨	1842 – 1878
▨	1879 – 1900
■	1901 – 1927
▨	1928 – 1950
▨	1951 – 1971

As late as 1878 Bedford was a very small town and Kempston a village. Despite the rapid growth during the next twenty years most people still lived north of the river in 1901. Today nearly half live on the south, and Bedford and Kempston have merged into one urban unit. The red hatching shows areas to be developed by 1970 for housing, industry and public open space.

of necessity be taken at the national and regional levels, for they involve the balancing of considerations affecting every planning area. Local planners must, however, try to bring to light all the local considerations which may be relevant to national and regional decisions, and must insist on proper consultation in the making of those decisions.

The Board of Trade's present policy for the Bedford area is to permit the reasonable extension of existing industrial premises, but to discourage the establishment of any new works, with the exception of two already approved—the National Aeronautical Establishment at Thurleigh, and the new power station east of Barker's Lane. How much extension is considered 'reasonable' will no doubt depend upon the importance of individual firms. Bedford has a number of specialized factories turning out high-class products; most of them expect to expand production and employment during the next twenty years, in some cases on their present sites, in other cases at new sites in the area. There are at present 750 vacancies for men on the books of the local Employment Exchange, but this is far from being a full measure of the long-term needs of existing firms. No precise estimate can be made, but we may safely double the figure to 1,500. To this must be added the 500 extra workers needed to compensate for the ageing of the population, making a total of 2,000. Since it appears that there are no declining industries in the district, most of these additional workers would be immigrants for whom houses would have to be built. Workers would no doubt be attracted to Bedford from declining industries in other parts of the country, and many of the outstanding vacancies could be filled today if accommodation were available. It is reasonable to assume that an influx of 2,500 workers as a result of the extension of existing enterprises would increase the total population by about 6,000.

Turning to new enterprises, the power station is a comparatively small employer, and in any case replaces an existing works. The National Aeronautical Establishment, on the other hand, is one of the largest projects at present under construction in the country, and may eventually be the biggest employer in the Bedford district. It was originally stated that 4,000 new jobs would be created, but this forecast has recently been cut by half. The Ministry of Town and Country Planning have estimated that total immigration will now be of the order of 5,000, assuming that 500 workers are recruited locally and that service industries employ an additional 300. It seems doubtful whether local recruitment could reach anything like 500, so that total immigration may well be as much as 6,000. It is pointless to speculate about the exact number of new settlers at this stage, and sufficient to note the scale of the expected movement. The question which more than any other affects our planning proposals is whether N.A.E. workers and their families are to live in the surrounding villages or in the nearest town—Bedford. However much the villages were enlarged and improved, they could never compete with Bedford as a centre for shopping and recreation. Since most people will visit the town regularly anyway they will probably prefer to live there, providing that adequate transport to work is available. Planning proposals normally attempt to reduce daily journeys to work, but this is a rather exceptional case. Workers at the N.A.E. must inevitably travel some distance, and apart from those whose jobs compel them to live close to the Establishment, and a few others who will choose a home in one of the villages, it is thought that the majority will accept a slightly longer journey for the sake of living in Bedford. This course also involves the least interference with agriculture, and the least danger of multiplying uneconomic services. We suggest that three-quarters of the immigrants associated with the N.A.E. should live in the town, adding another 4,500 to our estimate of Bedford's future population.

Immigration to meet the needs of existing industries and of the National Aeronautical Establishment would thus provide a total of about 10,500 new settlers in the town during the next twenty years, which must be added to the estimated natural increase of 2,000. Finally, we may allow another 500 for the natural increase of the immigrants themselves, giving a minimum increase of 13,000 by 1971. We conclude that Bedford's population will rise to at least 73,500 as a result of the present policy regarding industrial location in the district. In making this estimate we have ignored the possibility that Bedford's population may also increase as a result of further immigration of retired people. Such a movement, however, might well be balanced by a reduction in the numbers at present travelling daily to Luton and London as the housing shortage is overcome.

We must now go on to question the policy itself and to ask whether the ban on new establishments and major extensions should be maintained, and why Bedford's population should not be encouraged to grow to 75,000 or an even higher figure by 1971. It is generally agreed that the population of South-East England should be stabilized or reduced; some internal migration to meet the needs of existing industries should be permitted, but it would be fatal if new industries in towns like Bedford were simply to attract the most vigorous people from the Development Areas as they did before the war. On the other hand, a redistribution of population within South-East England has been recommended in the Greater London Plan. This did not mention Bedford as a suitable reception area for dispersed industries, but we have seen that a number of factories in the town did in fact disperse themselves from London, and that the combination of advantages which drew them to Bedford still exists. The town is close enough to London for existing linkages to be maintained, but far enough away to preserve its independence of the metropolis. Bedford is ideally placed to reduce pressure on such places as Oxford, Cambridge and Luton, which are reaching the limit of economic growth. A number of excellent industrial sites are still available in Bedford and Kempston, and it is estimated that they could support an additional population of about 15,000. The needs of existing firms should, of course, be met before the introduction of new firms is permitted. Whether the new industrial sites should be taken up at all depends upon the availability of housing sites and the effect of such an expansion on the character of the town.

FACTORS IN DEVELOPMENT Even if the population were to remain stationary during the next twenty years, the built-up area of Bedford and Kempston—like that of most other towns—would have to increase. More than 5,000 people are waiting for homes, and about 2,000 would be dispersed from the outworn central neighbourhoods if blighted housing were demolished. Two groups of factors limit the ultimate growth of the built-up area—physical properties which restrict the use of land, and competing uses which may be more important than urban development. The main restrictions on development are liability to flood, clay soil and, in one area, steep slopes; the principal competing uses are agriculture and mineral working, open space and woodland, government establishments and rural amenities. All these factors have been plotted on six-inch maps covering an area within several miles radius of Bedford. The more important factors in the immediate vicinity are shown on Map 6 (*p.* 48).

The River Ouse frequently overflows its banks in the Bedford district, and as recently as 1947 a very large area in and around the town was flooded. The photograph on page 118 shows that the built-up area did not escape the inundation. The chances of a recurrence cannot be ignored, and it would be unwise to permit any further building on land affected by floods in 1947. Measures to reduce flooding throughout the course of the river are being taken and should be accelerated, but they are inevitably of a long-term character and cannot affect proposals limited to the next twenty years. Map 6 shows the extent of the 1947 floods as recorded by the Great Ouse Catchment Board; it is apparent that no more riverside land in the town is available for housing, and that the large undeveloped area in the east of the Borough is completely sterilized by the danger of flooding.

The Oxford and Boulder clays which underlie a large part of the surrounding area give insufficient support for houses with normal foundations. Some subsidence has occurred in Bedford where houses have been built on the clay. This is a relatively flexible factor, however, since the danger of settlement can be averted with some additional expense. It is clear from Map 6 that the clay covers so much of the area which is not liable to flood that if housing sites are to be found at all the extra cost must be incurred. This was recognized by the Corporation when they agreed to the building of the Goldington neighbourhood.

There are few slopes as steep as 1 in 7 in this low-lying district, and

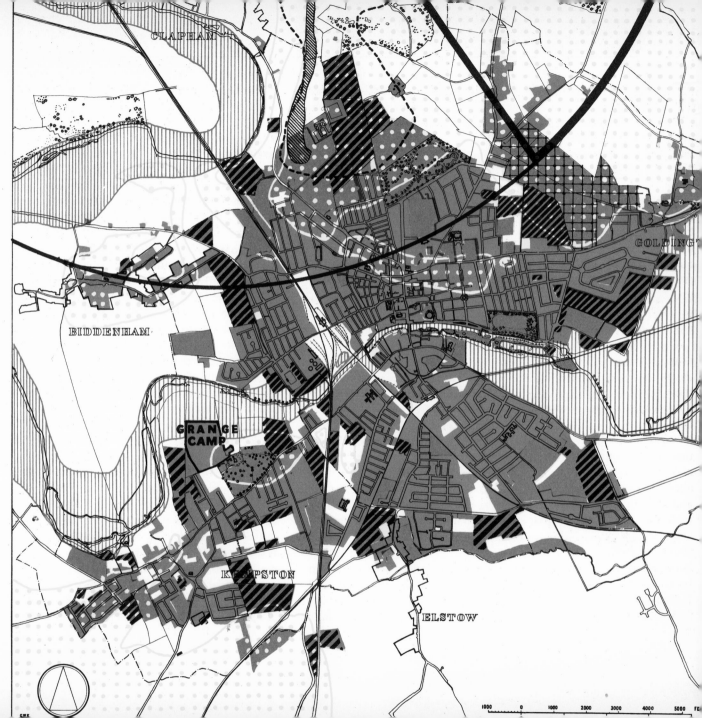

Map 6

FACTORS IN DEVELOPMENT

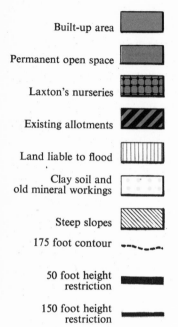

- � Built-up area
- Permanent open space
- Laxton's nurseries
- Existing allotments
- Land liable to flood
- Clay soil and old mineral workings
- Steep slopes
- 175 foot contour
- 50 foot height restriction
- 150 foot height restriction

The danger of flooding sterilises much of the undeveloped land within the Borough. Biddenham and Elstow villages must remain unspoilt, while mineral workings thwart development to the south-west. Open spaces and allotments should as far as possible be retained. The only large areas left for housing are within the Kempston Urban District and on the boulder clay north of the town. Although stronger foundations have to be provided, it is clear that Bedford cannot avoid building on the clay.

CLAPHAM

BIDDENHAM

GOLDING'

GRANGE CAMP

KEMPSTON

ELSTOW

G.W.K.

1000   0   1000   2000   3000   4000   5000   FE

the only one which will restrict urban development is the western slope of Waterworks Hill in the north of the town.

Most of the land around Bedford is used for agriculture, and much of it is intensively cultivated. It is a sound principle that as far as possible only the worst agricultural land should be taken for urban development. In Bedford's case, however, all the neighbouring land falls into the first four of the Ministry of Agriculture's ten grades, and if the town is to expand at all some first-class land must be taken out of cultivation; the distinction between the 'best' and 'worst' land in this district is largely academic. The town owes much of its prosperity to the development of agriculture, and should take as little farm land as possible for building. At the same time, the countryside looks to Bedford for many essential services, and will benefit from the planned expansion of the town. The housing of three-quarters of N.A.E. immigrants in Bedford would be less harmful to the interests of agriculture than their accommodation in rural villages.

The use of land for food production is a development factor not only in the surrounding countryside but also within the built-up area, where an exceptionally large acreage is devoted to allotment gardens. All of these have been shown on Map 6, and proposals to disturb them have only been made after careful consideration, since a large amount of labour is embodied in their soil and cannot be transferred to a new site. Nevertheless, a short journey from home to work and shops is better than a short journey to an allotment, and it is sometimes necessary to make a choice between the two. From this point of view some existing allotments would be better devoted to new roads, houses and factories, and we propose that one-third of them should eventually be taken for these uses and replaced by new allotments on the edge of the built-up area (Map 3, *p*. 29). Laxton's Nursery is an asset to the town which should remain virtually undisturbed. It would form a green wedge between the Goldington neighbourhood and the town centre, but it may be considered necessary to make an access road across part of the Nursery land.

After agriculture the most important activity in the countryside is the making of bricks from the Oxford clay south of the town. Land earmarked by the brick companies for progressive working during the next twenty years extends almost up to the Kempston boundary on the south-west, and will prevent any further extension of the built-up area in this direction. A number of abandoned mineral workings have been shown as land of low bearing capacity on Map 6; most of them could be used for housing, industry or open space.

Bedford and Kempston are fortunate in having several excellent open spaces, both public and private. Kempston Grange has recently become available for the use of the whole community through the generosity of Mrs Howard, and it is hoped that others, such as Goldington Bury, will eventually be acquired for public enjoyment. These open spaces should be preserved for all time, and they have, therefore, been shown on Map 6 as a factor restricting building development. They include the playing fields belonging to schools and factories. There are no large areas of woodland close to Bedford, but existing trees on new housing sites should as far as possible be incorporated in the layout.

Other uses competing with urban development are the civil and military establishments of the Government. The National Aeronautical Establishment will be three miles north of Bedford and, though it will have considerable effects on the growth of the town, will not directly limit its physical expansion. Height restrictions will, however, prevent the building of structures more than fifty feet high in parts of the Goldington and Kimbolton Road neighbourhoods. There is already a Royal Air Force station at Cardington, about a mile beyond the built-up area on the south-east. No height restrictions are in force, but it is not desirable that the town should approach any closer to the camp. Within the urban area is the Grange Camp at Kempston, surrounded by a black line on Map 6, which would make an excellent housing site if relinquished by the War Office.

The final factor considered in this survey was the existence of two still unspoilt villages just outside the borough boundary—Elstow and Biddenham. There is no physical reason why Bedford should not absorb these villages as it has already absorbed Goldington. But, apart from the disruptive effect on the rural communities and apart also from the historic importance of Elstow as the home of John Bunyan, both villages are valuable amenities to the townsfolk themselves so long as they remain unspoilt. No major additions should also be made to either Biddenham or Elstow, and they should be separated from the main built-up area by permanent—albeit small—green belts.

The upshot is that Bedford could expand outside its present boundary in only one direction—to the north. Concentric development is impossible because of the floodlands to the east, the brickfields to the southwest, Biddenham on the west and Elstow on the south. Development in one direction would be much more harmful to the interests of agriculture than concentric development. Furthermore, it would do away with one of the finest features of the present town—the comparatively short distance from all parts to the main centre. A survey of accessibility showed that it takes only eleven minutes to cycle from the Town Hall to the most distant points on the Borough boundary at Kimbolton Road and Harrowden Road, and only sixteen minutes to the furthest limit of the Kempston Urban District. We are proposing new roads and bridges to make cross-town journeys as short as journeys to the town centre, and we do not want to prejudice these gains by allowing the built-up area to increase unduly, particularly as the northern suburbs are farthest from the main industrial zone. It is therefore proposed that Bedford and Kempston should not expand beyond their present boundaries.

There are, however, a number of housing sites in the two local authority areas, some capable of immediate development, and others of development as soon as additions and improvements to various piped services have been made. Gas, electricity and sewerage can be provided in all parts of the area, and water can be supplied everywhere except to the upper slopes of Waterworks Hill. In view of the generous provision for allotments and open spaces, these sites could be developed at net densities somewhat higher than those of recent housing schemes in the district, and there should be multi-storey flats in parts of the central redevelopment area. A population of about 80,000 could then be housed within Bedford and Kempston. The town could grow to this size during the next twenty years as a result of industrial development by existing firms, and possibly by firms dispersed from central London. An increase of 20,000 in twenty years would be the biggest in Bedford's history. Proportionately, however, the population would expand by only a quarter; it grew by three-quarters between 1881 and 1901. The example of neighbouring Luton shows that an increase of this magnitude is quite possible, though the necessary resources would have to be made available as part of a national plan. The red hatching on Map 5 shows the ultimate extent of the built-up area and associated public open spaces if all the proposed housing sites were developed.

CONCLUSION Bedford will remain a medium-sized and diverse town even if its population reaches 80,000 through the development of manufacturing as an increasingly important function. The implementation of our proposals for new roads, for neighbourhood amenities and for an extension of the main centre would ensure that Bedford avoids the worst evils of unplanned expansion such as are to be found in, say, Luton. In our work here we have often been reminded of the pride Bedfordians have in the town, and their anxiety that its essential 'personality' shall not be lost. We are not advocating that Bedford should change its 'personality' but rather that the town should be given an opportunity to express it more fully, and that more of the citizens should have a chance to share its assets. The road proposals described in the next chapter take full advantage of the compactness of the town, and the extension of the central area proposed in Chapter 4 is designed to preserve its intimacy and charm. The neighbourhoods would be better places to live in if the proposals of Chapter 6 were carried out, and it is suggested in Chapter 7 that Bedford could make even better use of its one outstanding natural feature—the river. The last chapter proposes improvements in the appearance of the town through the more careful treatment of old buildings and the more sensitive design of new ones. Much of Bedford's townscape is monotonous and mediocre, partly due to the large areas of nineteenth-century housing set in a rather dull countryside. The contrast between the richer and poorer quarters—a feature of all English towns—is no sharper in Bedford than in most. There is a need for good planning, fine architecture and effective landscaping to correct past mistakes and redeem an unpromising site. A larger population would help to develop the town's 'personality' by providing the basis for new amenities, such as a first-class theatre and a daily evening newspaper. Bedford is no longer an exclusive educational centre, and no amount of wishful thinking will ever make it one again, but there is no reason why the county town of the future should not be an even more pleasant and prosperous place than it was in the past.

NOTES

[1] *Bedfordshire*, by C. E. Fitchitt (Land Utilization Survey).

[2] Based on a survey carried out by the Eastern Region of the Ministry of Town and Country Planning.

[3] Except during a short period in the nineteenth century when the spire was taken down to allow the tower to be raised. The identical stones were replaced.

[4] *Harpur's Bedford Charity*, by C. F. Farrar (Bedford: The Sidney Press, 1930).

[5] Bedfordians are not agreed on the exact limits of the district called after the notorious ruffian 'Black Tom' King. Some confine it to the streets north of Park Road; others use it for the whole area north of Tavistock Street between Foster Hill Road and Clarendon Street. For the sake of convenience we have adopted the wider definition.

[6] *Victoria County History of Bedfordshire*.

[7] This figure is derived from an independent population count, and is about 1,600 below the Registrar-General's latest estimate. It is believed that this is due to the exclusion of boarders at the Harpur Trust schools and of students at the Froebel and Physical Training Colleges.

Allhallows Lane   *shopping extension*

3 *" Proposals designed to solve Bedford's present and future traffic problems must be directed to three main ends—the diversion of through traffic from the central streets, the linking of the radial roads, and the improvement of circulation in the town centre "*

Roads and Railways

Traffic congestion in the narrow central streets is one of the main obstacles to Bedford's smooth functioning as a shopping and industrial centre. It is a problem common to almost all ancient market towns that are the focus of local communications and also lie on through traffic routes. In Bedford's case it is aggravated by the presence of major physical barriers in the shape of the river and the railways. The gravity of the problem was already well known to anyone who had walked, cycled or driven down High Street or St Mary's Street at almost any time between 8 a.m. and 6 p.m.; proposals for its solution, however, had to be based upon full and precise information about the pattern of traffic flows and the causes of congestion. This was obtained from a census of the origin and destination of traffic entering the town, a count of vehicles crossing the two bridges, and studies of street accidents and car parking requirements. The survey showed the need for a bold policy of constructing new roads and bridges to take much of the through traffic out of the central area altogether, and to speed the flow of cross-town traffic and of traffic which must visit the town centre. A survey of rail communications in the district has also been made, but no major changes in them are suggested during the next twenty years.

REGIONAL COMMUNICATIONS As a river crossing at the head of navigation on the Great Ouse, Bedford has always been the focus of communications in the district. It is many years now since the town ceased to be a river port, but the coming of the railway and the development of road transport have enhanced its importance as a meeting place of local and regional routes. The Town Bridge is still the most important crossing of the Ouse for several miles, while railway lines diverge from the two stations in six directions.

Map 4 (*p.* 40) shows that Bedford lies just off the two most important north-south road and rail arteries of the country. The Great North Road passes eight miles to the east at Sandy, and Watling Street eighteen miles to the west at Stony Stratford. The railways from King's Cross and Euston to Edinburgh and Glasgow follow the lines of these two roads, and can be joined at Sandy and Bletchley respectively. The north-south highway that actually passes through Bedford is officially designated the London–Glasgow–Inverness trunk road (A.6), but in fact carries little traffic to places north of Derby, and is primarily important as the main link between London and the East Midlands. So also is the town's principal railway route—the former Midland main line; but though it no longer competes for traffic from London to Scotland, the through trains that still run give Bedford direct links with the North. There are also east-west links, both by road and rail. Cross-country railways are rare enough in this country, and Bedford is fortunate to have direct lines to both the ancient University towns, though there is room for considerable improvement in the services. In general, the town enjoys excellent communications with all parts of the country, and these have been a big factor in its rapid industrial development since the turn of the century.

Two Ministry of Transport trunk roads cross at St Peter's Green— A.6 running north and south, and A.428 running east and west. The

The Bus Station was only opened in 1939, but is inadequate in size and badly sited. The bus in the foreground bears an apt slogan. 'Relief' is needed throughout the centre of Bedford, relief from a weight of traffic its narrow streets can no longer bear. A new and larger bus station in a more convenient position, with a new bridge bringing buses across the river from the south, is one of the most important proposals for giving effect to this relief. The Central Relief Road would free **St Paul's Square** (*overleaf*) from intolerable congestion.

Bedford's factories have almost as many cycle stands as workers. It is a town on wheels. Because of the outdated road system journeys to work are in many cases longer than they need be, and cyclists who are forced to pass through the town centre add to the congestion. **Allens' Bridge** is the blackest of many black spots. The Western Relief Road and the proposed cycle tracks would provide a shorter route for many of these workers, but the bridge itself should also be widened and a roundabout constructed at its foot.

importance of the first has already been mentioned; the second is part of the trunk road from Birmingham to Ipswich and links Bedford with Northampton and the West Midlands, and with Cambridge and the Eastern Counties. These roads, together with A.600—an alternative route from London via Hitchin—bring a large volume of long distance traffic right through the heart of the town. On all these five approaches between one-third and one-half of the total traffic is bound for places beyond Bedford, and is not stopping in the town. Two other first-class roads also terminate in Bedford—A.603, an alternative route from Cambridge via Sandy; and A.418, from Ampthill, Aylesbury and Oxford—but fewer than one-fifth of the vehicles entering the town on them are going through, and the proportion is even smaller on the two second-class roads—B.557 (Kempston Road) and B.660 (Kimbolton Road). Most of the traffic on the last four roads comes from the small towns and villages that look to Bedford as a centre for employment, shopping, education and recreation.

THE LOCAL ROAD SYSTEM Nine regional roads thus converge upon the centre of Bedford, the four from the north meeting at St Peter's Green, and the five from the south at St Mary's Square. The short distance between these two points, by way of High Street and the Town Bridge, is the busiest and most congested in the town. With delay and inconvenience goes danger to life and limb; more than one-fifth of the street accidents in 1949 occurred on this half-mile stretch. Diagram 3A on page 60 shows the volume of traffic on the nine approaches to the town in 1931, 1938 and 1950. On one Saturday in September 1950, nearly 26,000 motor vehicles entered or left the Borough, three times as many as in 1931 and two-thirds more than in 1938. This vastly increased volume of traffic—together with the purely internal traffic which never crossed the boundary and was not included in the figures—has to use virtually the same town road system that existed half a century ago. The only major improvement was the widening of the Town Bridge—completed in 1940 in the face of spirited opposition. It is unlikely that there will be an equally rapid growth of traffic during the next twenty years, but it is certain that the volume will substantially increase. Now is the time to plan road improvements adequate not only for the 1950 volume of traffic but for that to be expected in 1970.

The pronounced radial road pattern gives the impression of a spider with a short, narrow body and nine long, curving legs. The oddest thing about this Bedford spider is not its extra leg but the fact that it has no web. The absence of outer town bridges over the river and the railways means that all journeys between the various suburbs have to be made through the central area, adding greatly to the congestion. There is a secondary route through the town centre by way of Prebend Street Bridge, but it is not a satisfactory alternative to the High Street, nor does it make cross-town communications any more direct. Only Mile Road and Elstow Road, Kempston, on the south, and Union Street and Park Road–Park Avenue on the north, show the embryonic form of links between the various radial roads. Even the efficiency of the radial system itself is impaired by the awkward crossings of the railways, giving rise to the dangerous intersections of Elstow Road with London Road (ten accidents in 1949); Ampthill Street with St John's Street (Willmer's Corner: four accidents); Cauldwell Street with Prebend Street (Black Diamond Corner: eight accidents); and Cardington Road with St Mary's (twenty-one accidents).

It is clear that proposals designed to solve Bedford's present and future traffic problems must be directed to three main ends:
  (i) the diversion of through traffic from the central streets;
  (ii) the linking of the radial roads by putting in the outer strands of the spider's web;
  (iii) the improvement of circulation in the town centre by adding the inner strands of the web.

THE PROBLEM OF THROUGH TRAFFIC Our information about the flow of through traffic is derived from a census authorized by the Ministry of Transport and carried out by the Borough Engineer with the co-operation of the County Council on a Friday, Saturday and Sunday in September, 1950. All vehicles entering the Borough were stopped at one or other of nine points and their drivers asked where they had come from, where they were going, whether they were stopping in Bedford, and, if so, in what part of the town. The biggest volume of traffic was on the Saturday—Bedford's market day; but there was almost as much on the Friday—a typical weekday. There was remarkably little variation in the pattern of traffic flow on Friday and Saturday despite the different proportions of commercial and private vehicles. One-third of all traffic entering the town was through traffic; less than ten per cent of this was stopping in Bedford, and more than eighty per cent had come from places over ten miles away. It would benefit Bedford, and also the through traffic itself, if the latter could be diverted to by-pass roads not unduly longer than the present routes through the town. The amount of diversion which is possible in practice depends, of course, upon the actual flows of vehicles between the various entrances and exits and the feasibility of alternative lines. Diagram 3B (page 60) summarizes the main flows of traffic recorded in the census.

The biggest single flow of through traffic—almost 1,000 vehicles on Saturday and nearly 700 on Friday—was along the Bromham and Goldington Roads (A.428). But taking all roads into account there was more than twice as much traffic passing through the town centre between north and south as between east and west. The north-south flow included about 500 vehicles travelling between Clapham Road (A.6 North) and Elstow Road (A.6 South), 500 between Clapham Road and London Road (A.600), 300 between Bromham Road (A.428) and London Road, and 700 between Cardington (A.603), Kempston (B.557) and Ampthill (A.418) Roads on the south, and Bromham and Clapham Roads on the north. In all, some 2,000 vehicles could, therefore, by-pass Bedford on the west; this number will certainly grow both as a result of normal traffic increase, and of the building of the National Aeronautical Establishment north of Clapham.

Ideally, such long distance traffic should pass right outside the built-up area on the west of the S-bend in the river between Kempston and Oakley. We have searched for a road line which would achieve this aim,

but without success. Land held by the brick companies and earmarked for progressive working during the next twenty years severely hampers any westward diversions from A.6 and A.600. Apart from the enormous compensation that would have to be paid if clay extraction were interrupted, nothing should be done to interfere with the economic production of bricks so vitally necessary to the realization of this and other plans. However, in order to avoid this obstacle and still find a line no longer than the present route through Bedford, it would be necessary to build some twenty miles of almost entirely new road at a cost of more than a million pounds (Map 7, *p.* 62). Expenditure on this scale is not justified by the volume of traffic likely to use the road in the foreseeable future. We are, therefore, forced to the conclusion that Bedford cannot at present be by-passed on the west, and that some other means must be found of relieving the town centre of through traffic. The construction within the urban area of an all-purpose road which would carry both through traffic and cross-town traffic was originally suggested many years ago. This would form one of the outer strands of the spider's web, the need for which is discussed in the next section of this chapter.

First, it is necessary to consider the other flow of through traffic— that from east to west. This traffic should continue to use its present route through the town, both because it is impossible to find a satisfactory alternative line that would not be several miles longer than the present route, and because the latter is not nearly so congested as the north-south route, and is likely to become even less so when other proposals have been carried out. Bromham Road is a wide, curving thoroughfare, relatively free from accidents, except at Gallows Corner (six accidents in 1949) and at the shopping centre between Conduit Road and Union Street (nine accidents). The eastern exit by Goldington Road has a rather worse accident record, but it is wide enough to carry more traffic. The most difficult sections of the route are Dame Alice Street and St Peter's, where there were thirty-one accidents in 1949. But the diversion of a large proportion of north-south traffic away from the High Street, and the transfer of the bus station from the Broadway to

Horne Lane, would greatly reduce congestion at St Peter's Green. We propose that the shopping centre should expand westwards towards the railway station rather than northwards along Tavistock Street, so that the line of Dame Alice Street and St Peter's would be virtually the northern limit of the central area, and hence a suitable place for a through main road.

One more thing remains to be said on the subject of through traffic. It is that the Origin and Destination Census has proved conclusively that there is no case for the north-eastern or south-eastern by-passes that have been suggested at various times. Very few vehicles want to go from Goldington Road (A.428) to either London Road (A.600) or Clapham Road (A.6), while Kimbolton Road (B.660) carries hardly any through traffic. A relief road is necessary only for north-south traffic.

A WEB FOR THE SPIDER The north-south relief road would form part of a system of links between the existing radial roads. These would relieve the town centre of a large volume of traffic—particularly of cycle traffic, whose presence is a source of danger and inconvenience to itself and other road users. They would also shorten the daily journey of a large number of workers whose homes are in one part of the town and whose jobs are in another. For example, Bedford's largest works is west of the railway in Queen's Park; many of its 2,300 workers live in Kempston or in the south of Bedford, and at present have to cross the narrow Ford End Road Bridge (shown in the photograph on page 54) and pass through the town centre. So do those people who live in Queen's Park and work in the main industrial zone south of the river. Firms in the Ampthill and Elstow Roads have nearly 4,000 employees (Map 11, *p.* 84); all those who live north of the river must make their daily journey through the heart of the town. The proposed increases in the populations of Queen's Park, Kempston and Goldington, and the growth of employment in the main industrial zone, would aggravate the problem of traffic congestion if cross-town links were not provided. The outward spread of the town makes it more important than ever to keep daily journeys down to the very minimum that is consistent with more spacious planning and a higher standard of amenities. Bedford's own internal traffic, therefore, needs outer relief roads with new river crossings both east and west of the two existing bridges. We have already seen that the western cross-town link must also serve as a new route for north-south through traffic.

Two possible lines for the Western Relief Road are shown on Map 7 (*p.* 62). The so-called western by-pass suggested by the Ministry of Transport[4] takes off from A.6 south of Elstow, passes through the middle of Kempston, bridges the river by Biddenham Ford End, crosses Bromham Road at Biddenham Turn, and joins Clapham Road near Cut Throat Lane. This line has a number of serious disadvantages:

(i) As a relief road for through traffic it fails to connect with A.600, yet the Origin and Destination Census showed that almost half the north-south traffic at present passing through the town centre uses London and Harrowden Roads.

(ii) As a cross-town road it fails to join all the neighbourhoods west of the centre. It does provide a link—though a somewhat indirect one—between Ford End Road, Queen's Park, and Bedford Road, Kempston; it does not, however, solve the equally pressing problem of getting from Queen's Park to the Ampthill and Elstow Road districts.

(iii) The line passes through excellent housing sites in Kempston and Honey Hill, preventing their economical development as unified neighbourhoods, and itself using valuable housing land.

The more easterly alternative shown on Maps 7 and 8 would overcome all three major disadvantages of the Ministry of Transport's proposal. It would pick up through traffic from A.600; it would link the main industrial area along Ampthill Road with Queen's Park to the north, and Elstow Road to the south; and it would pass over no land suitable for housing. The proposed Western Relief Road would take off from the sharp turn in A.600 at Cotton End near the bottom of Hammer Hill, one and a half miles south of the Borough boundary, and proceed in a north-westerly direction to pass east of Elstow Village. Here it would be treated as a parkway separating Bedford from Elstow, and its intersections with Mile Road and Elstow Road (Diagram 4A, p. 65) have been designed so as to leave a site for a church or other public building as a terminal feature to the town. The new road would continue the line of Mile Road over the Bletchley branch of the railway and into Ampthill Road, so providing a very necessary connection between two adjacent neighbourhoods that are at present rigidly separated by the railway line. The approach to the new bridge from Ampthill Road would have a gradient of approximately 1 in 25, and while this is not ideal it can be considered satisfactory. A roundabout could be constructed at the Ampthill Road junction by the demolition of one corrugated iron shed (Diagram 4B). The Western Relief Road would bridge the main railway line south of the sidings behind Robertson's, and open up several acres of allotment land for industrial development (Map 11, p. 84). There would be another roundabout at the junction with Kempston Road by Austin Canons (Diagram 4C), which would involve the loss of one house. The road would continue over the river and through Queen's Park along the line of the Black Lane to cross Bromham Road near Biddenham Turn. The final section to join Clapham Road follows the line proposed by the Ministry of Transport.

The only serious disadvantage of the proposed line for the Western Relief Road is that it passes through the middle of the existing Queen's Park neighbourhood and crosses Ford End Road close by the very spot, namely 'The Bell Inn', where a local centre for the ward could and should be developed. Unfortunately, it would be impossible to take the new road either under or over Ford End Road; a cutting could not be made because of the danger of flooding through the drains, and a viaduct would necessitate the demolition of a large number of houses. A light-controlled crossing has been suggested (Diagram 4D) which would involve the loss of six houses, two shops, one office and part of some of the gardens on either side of the Black Lane. This would be the only intersection between the relief road and a local road in Queen's Park. The passage of the main road would complicate the eventual redevelopment of the shopping centre in Ford End Road, and would necessitate the provision of an infant school in both halves of the neighbourhood, but there is no doubt that it would also hasten the improvement of amenities in the locality and go far to end the isolation of Queen's Park from the rest of the town.

A rather difficult problem of the new road is that a large number of cyclists would want to use it at certain hours of the day, and would get mixed up with through traffic at the main junctions. We propose that the system of cross-town communications on the west and south should be completed by the construction of the four cycle ways and bridges shown on Map 8 (p. 63)—one already agreed by the Corporation from Ford End Road near the football ground to Kempston Road east of the relief road; another from Honey Hill Road to Kempston Road in the vicinity of the Grange; a third from Ampthill Road via Sandhurst Road and over the Bletchley railway to Elstow Road between Meltis and Igranic; and a fourth from Newton Road in the Elstow Road neighbourhood across the Hitchin line to Dents Road in the London Road neighbourhood. If these additional links were constructed, cycle tracks would not be necessary on the relief road itself, and the daily journeys of many workers would be considerably shortened.

The Western Relief Road would not only carry through traffic and cross-town traffic but would also bring vehicles bound for Bedford from A.600 to Ampthill Road. Another new road from the right-angle bend south of Elstow to Cow Bridge would do the same for traffic from A.6. Ampthill Road would then become the main approach from the south, and the railway bridge that descends to Willmer's Corner should be widened to fit its new function. These changes in the flow of traffic from A.6 and A.600 would confer three benefits on the town:

(i) They would free the London and Elstow Road neighbourhoods from the intrusion of long-distance traffic.

(ii) There would be a great reduction in the number of vehicles using the awkward and dangerous junction between Elstow and London Roads, which is approached from two sides over humpbacked bridges;

(iii) The southern exit from the new roundabout at Willmer's Corner would become primarily important as the approach to St John's

Station and the Eastern National Garage; vehicles bound to and from these points would no longer have to run the gauntlet of a heavy flow of traffic passing over the railway bridge.

The Western Relief Road—six miles long with three railway bridges and one over the river—would be the most important of the cross-town links, and also the only one that would carry a large volume of through traffic. Three more short strands are necessary to complete the spider's web. The first is a direct link between Goldington, where the greatest residential development is to take place, and the industrial zone south of the river, where many people from the new neighbourhood would work. The obvious line for this road is that suggested by the Borough Surveyor in 1944, and shown in the recent publication, 'Bedford—A Survey',[1] namely, a continuation of Newnham Avenue across two arms of the river (Diagram 4E), proceeding beside the Cambridge Branch of the railway to Cardington Road, and thence along the line of Rope Walk to Willmer's Corner. The intersection with Cardington Road should be designed so as to encourage traffic to enter the town centre via Willmer's Corner, which would become the main distribution point on the south of the town; a suggested arrangement is shown in Diagram 4F. Only strictly local traffic would then have to make the awkward turning at St Mary's, and the road would be made much safer for girls coming out of the Dame Alice Harpur School. It is suggested that the old name of this length of road—Potter Street—should be revived, since it would no longer be the main route to Cardington.

On the north of the town, Union Street, Park Road and Park Avenue link three of the four radial roads, and the present gap between Kimbolton Road and Goldington Road would be filled by the proposed new road from Park Avenue to Newnham Avenue.

Finally, some improvements are necessary in the existing cross-town link from Ampthill Road to Tavistock Street by way of Prebend Street bridge. If the Western Relief Road were built this route would no longer carry long-distance through traffic as it does today, but it would continue to serve vehicles travelling between the northern and southern parts of the town and wishing to by-pass the main centre. It would also remain the principal approach to Midland Road Station from north and south. The chief problems of the route are the Midland Road–Prebend Street junction and the stretch from Midland Road to Bromham Road via Ashburnham or Alexandra Roads. The proposed solution is a new link from Rutland Road across the existing Priory Street Recreation Ground to join Bromham Road opposite Union Street. At the same time the opportunity would be taken to construct a roundabout at the foot of Allens' Bridge. This dangerous junction can be improved in two stages:

(i) By the immediate acquisition of the single storey premises at the foot of the bridge to allow room for the re-alignment of the eastern approach to the bridge and the construction of a roundabout.

(ii) By setting back seven properties on the north side of Midland Road and by demolishing the house at the corner of Midland Road and Prebend Street.

The bridge itself could be improved by the construction of cantilevered footways on both sides, allowing the carriageway to extend over the full width of the present bridge.

These three new links, which have been named the Eastern, Northern and Inner Cross-Town Roads respectively, would complete a continuous ring road around the core of the town.

CENTRAL ROAD PROPOSALS On Saturday, 2 September, 1950, 6,477 vehicles crossed the Town Bridge and 4,527 crossed Prebend Street Bridge between 6 a.m. and 10 p.m. There was a peak flow in the High Street of 600 vehicles per hour, and in Prebend Street of 500 per hour. These figures are derived from a count carried out on one of the days of the Origin and Destination Census in order to discover the relation between through traffic and total traffic in the town centre. On that day about 1,000 vehicles came into Bedford from the south and went out on the north without stopping in the town, and 1,000 went through in the opposite direction. All these must have passed over one of the two existing bridges; through traffic was, therefore, just under one-fifth of

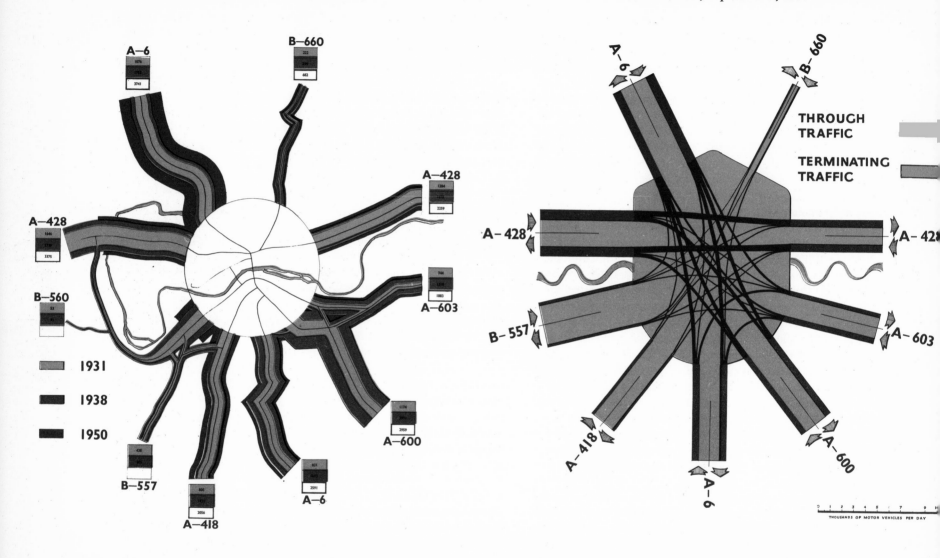

Diagram 3a   GROWTH OF ROAD TRAFFIC

Average Daily Flow 1931 1938 1950

A—6

1076
1752
3741

B—660

222
399
682

A—428

1204
1476
2259

A—428

1646
2739
3375

A—603

744
1318
1803

B—560

53
81

A—600

1174
2971
2959

■ 1931

■ 1938

■ 1950

B—557

438
855

A—418

605
1451
2056

A—6

831
1445
2591

A great increase in the volume of traffic using the same roads is the cause of today's congestion. The diagram warns us to prepare now for the increases of the next twenty years and to plan accordingly.

Diagram 3b   THROUGH TRAFFIC FLOWS

Total Volume, September 2, 1950

A—6

B—660

THROUGH TRAFFIC

TERMINATING TRAFFIC

A—428

A—428

B—557

A—603

A—418

A—600

A—6

0 1 2 3 4 5 6 7 8 9 10
THOUSANDS OF MOTOR VEHICLES PER DAY

This was the essential information needed to decide which of several proposed new by-passes was really wanted. East-west traffic cannot be by-passed, but the various north-south flows will all use the Western Relief Road.

all traffic on Prebend Street and High Street. We were not able to find out the distribution of long-distance traffic between the two bridges, but we have assumed that three-quarters used High Street and one-quarter used Prebend Street. If this was so, then at least one-quarter of all traffic on High Street would be diverted to the Western Relief Road. The total reduction of traffic over the Town Bridge would be somewhat greater, however, for a certain amount of industrial and other traffic terminating in the outer districts of Bedford would also be diverted, as well as some internal cross-town traffic. The maximum relief to be expected on the High Street as a result of these suggested changes is, therefore, about one-third of its present traffic volume. The other two-thirds could not be diverted for the simple reason that it is actually generated by the town's role as a shopping, administrative and cultural centre, and must come into the heart of the town in the course of its business. Bedford should welcome and encourage such traffic, for it is a sign of the successful performance of its main functions.

The diversion of one-third of the existing traffic would bring a considerable relief to the High Street, but it could not by itself solve the problem of congestion in the town centre. Local traffic would only have to increase by a third—which it was doing every five years or so before the war—and congestion would be as serious as ever. It is true that the number of vehicles per head is unlikely to grow so quickly during the 'fifties and 'sixties as it did during the 'twenties and 'thirties; but we must remember that in Bedford there will also be a big increase in the number of heads. Unless other measures are taken during the next twenty years, it is certain that there will be more traffic in High Street and its approaches in 1970 than there is today.

The congestion in High Street is bad enough, but the state of affairs in the narrow carriageways of St John's and St Mary's is even worse, particularly at the dangerous dog-leg intersection with Cauldwell Street and Cardington Road. Several times a week a 300-yard stream of southbound vehicles held up at this dangerous junction reaches back beyond the far side of the Town Bridge, blocking the entrance to the Embankment and even at times bringing the traffic in St Paul's Square to a standstill.

The diversion of town traffic to Prebend Street would not be a means of curing congestion. To begin with, the narrow bridge and its awkward approaches could not take a substantial permanent increase of traffic. Any reduction due to the diversion of through traffic to the Western Relief Road would be balanced by the normal increase in traffic. Prebend Street's main functions as an approach to Midland Road Station from the south, and as part of the inner cross-town link, have already been described. In any case, Prebend Street is more than a quarter of a mile west of the main shopping centre—too far to be an acceptable alternative to High Street.

The only solution lies in the bold step of building a third bridge in the heart of the town to carry a Central Relief Road to run as close as possible to the existing route. This road is the backbone of our proposals for the town centre (folding map, *p.* 74). The choice of its line has been influenced by a number of factors which are fully described in the next chapter, and will only be briefly indicated here. The road would start from Willmer's Corner, where it would collect traffic not only from Ampthill, Elstow and London Roads, but also from Cardington Road by the new link described on page 59. The roundabout at Willmer's Corner would thus become the main distribution point for all vehicles from the south giving them the choice of proceeding through the town centre either by St John's and High Street or by the new Central Relief Road. It would follow the line of the King's Ditch, passing the sites proposed for a flatted factory and the agricultural markets. Picking up traffic from Kempston at Cauldwell Street it would pass the new College of Further Education and cross the Ouse by a new bridge from Holme Street to Batts' Ford. On the north bank it would run between the new County Hall and the new Assembly Hall, following the line of River Street, with the new bus station on the right. From Midland Road to Bromham Road it would be a broad boulevard with two carriageways on the lines of Hassett Street and Gwyn Street, dividing the westward extension of the shopping centre from the new residential development in Greyfriars.

The construction of the Central and Western Relief Roads would not

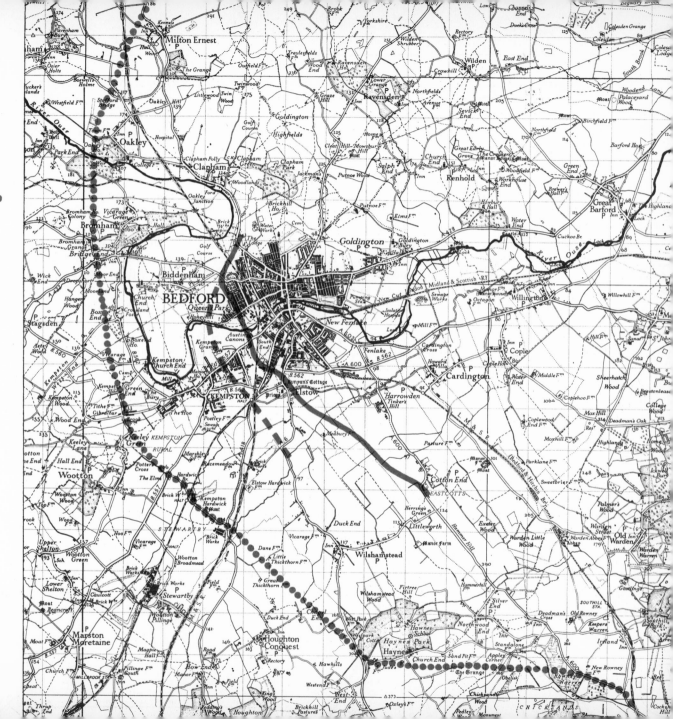

Map 7

ALTERNATIVE
NORTH-SOUTH ROADS

Only possible line
for outer western
by-pass of Bedford
and Kempston

Inner western by-
pass suggested by
Ministry of Transport

Western relief road
proposed in this
book

1 ¾ ½ ¼ 0   1   2 MILES

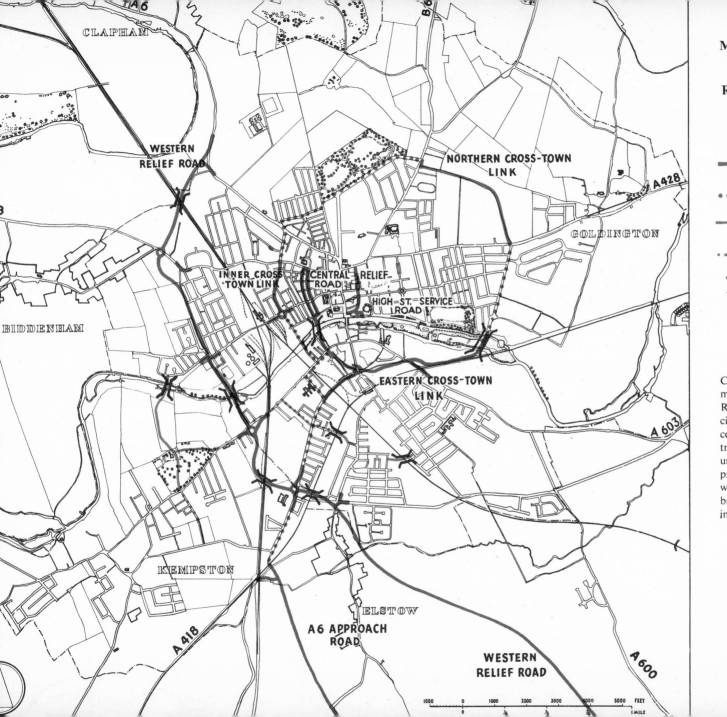

CLAPHAM

WESTERN
RELIEF ROAD

NORTHERN CROSS-TOWN
LINK

GOLDINGTON

A428

BIDDENHAM

INNER CROSS
TOWN LINK

CENTRAL RELIEF
ROAD

HIGH ST. SERVICE
ROAD

EASTERN CROSS-TOWN
LINK

A 603

KEMPSTON

ELSTOW

A6 APPROACH
ROAD

A 418

WESTERN
RELIEF ROAD

A 600

Map 8

ROAD PROPOSALS

Proposed roads

Existing roads, to form part
of new major routes

Proposed cycle and
pedestrian ways

Existing roads to form part of
new cycle and pedestrian ways

Proposed bridges over
rail and river

Congestion in the town centre is the
major traffic problem. The Central
Relief Road would improve
circulation around the shopping
centre, and much of the through
traffic and cross-town traffic would
use the Western Relief Road. The
proposed cycle and pedestrian ways
with their river and railway
bridges would make an early
improvement in journeys to work.

1000   0   1000   2000   3000   4000   5000   FEET

0   ¼   ½   ¾
                                        1 MILE

leave High Street 'high and dry'. On the contrary it would be better able to concentrate upon its function as the main shopping street. Its present intimate character should not be lost, even if the buildings are gradually set back to a new building line. At present the carriageway is only twenty-five feet wide and the pavements eight feet. The absence of cycle racks and the limitations of unilateral parking, add to the inconvenience of shoppers. The eventual building line should give ample room for pavements with cycle parks and for cars to wait on both sides of the road. But it would be many years before this could be done.

The north-south relief road is by far the most important of our central road proposals; by duplicating High Street on the west, where the principal new developments are suggested, it would make the biggest contribution to circulation in the town centre. But it is also necessary to make certain road improvements in that part of the town centre that lies east of High Street. There are three problems:

(i) to relieve congestion in Mill Street by providing an alternative route from Castle Road to the west;

(ii) to improve circulation at the head of the bridge by finding a substitute for the present awkward and dangerous turning on to the Embankment.

(iii) to gain access to the rear of the High Street shops and to the new car parks serving this side of the shopping centre.

The basis for a solution of all three problems would be to make a new outlet from High Street opposite the south side of St Paul's Square. The new road would pass through seriously blighted property to the south of Castle Lane and would then branch into two, a northern arm going to Ram Yard by the existing stretch of Castle Lane which passes Bennett's Clothing Factory, and a southern arm passing east of the Town and County Club to the Embankment. The first 100 yards of the Embankment would be closed to motor traffic, and the place where the beauty of the Town Bridge and the river can be most enjoyed—the pavement beneath the bow windows of the Swan Hotel—would be freed from the dangers of inturning vehicles. From Ram Yard the northern arm of the proposed new road would pass through four domestic properties to Mill Street, up Duke Street and across the present vicarage garden to Lurke Street. Along the line of this road sites are suggested in Chapter 4 for car parks to accommodate nearly 500 vehicles. It is suggested that the junctions of Howard Street with Mill Street and of Lurke Street and Castle Lane with High Street should be closed to vehicular traffic, but not before the implementation of the rest of the scheme. The northern outlet from the new car parks would be by way of St Cuthbert's Street to an improved junction with St Peter's (Map 9).

The east-west route through the town centre would be greatly improved by a direct link between the new bus station in Horne Lane and Midland Road railway station. But this cannot yet be put forward as a definite proposal since it would involve the demolition of a large number of houses with more than twenty years' economic life.

THE BUS STATION As an important district centre Bedford is the terminus of a large number of bus services from the surrounding countryside. During one week in the summer of 1950, 91,000 people came into the town by bus;[3] bus traffic is a major source of congestion in High Street and St Paul's Square, particularly on market days. The photograph on page 54 is convincing evidence of the need for a new bus station. The present 'station' in the Broadway is a small deep opening only 65 feet by 120 feet. The buses discharge from this recess into the neck of the awkward jun ctionbetween A.6, de Pary's Avenue and Foster Hill Road. Its situation at the northern extremity of the shopping centre causes considerable inconvenience.

It has been suggested that the best course would be to build a second terminal in the Cauldwell Street area to take all south-bound buses, while the existing station in the Broadway continued to deal with buses departing in other directions. Apart from the great disadvantages to the transport undertaking of operating services from two terminals, this suggestion would not meet the needs of the majority of bus passengers who want to be carried right into the heart of the town where lies their business or pleasure. We cannot support proposals that would cure

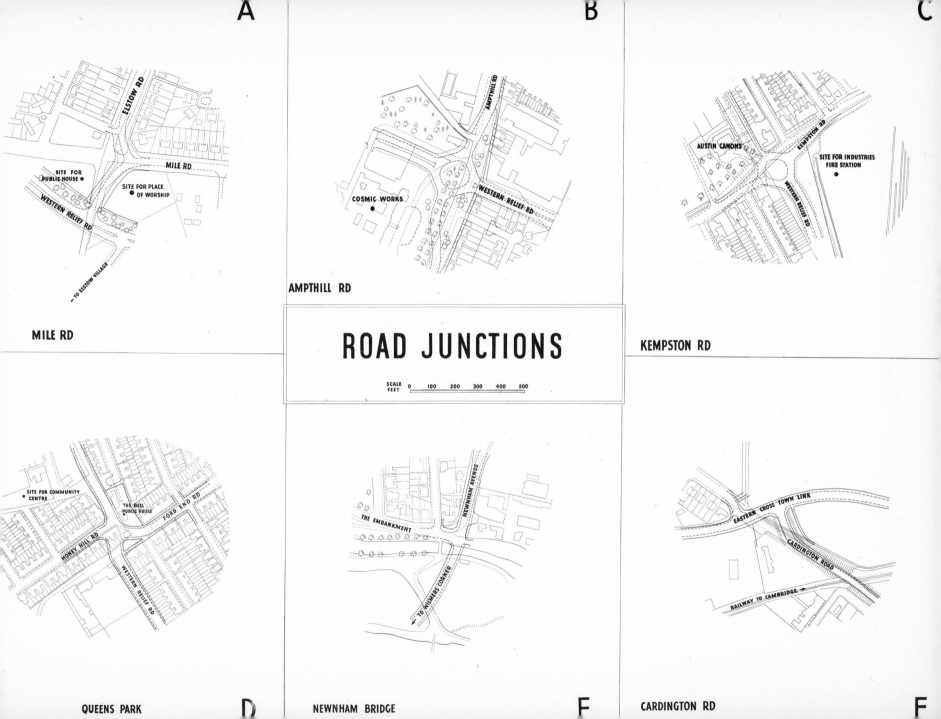

A

MILE RD

ELSTOW RD
MILE RD
SITE FOR PUBLIC HOUSE •
SITE FOR PLACE OF WORSHIP •
WESTERN RELIEF RD
← TO ELSTOW VILLAGE

B

AMPTHILL RD

AMPTHILL RD
WESTERN RELIEF RD
COSMIC WORKS •

C

KEMPSTON RD

AUSTIN CANONS
KEMPSTON RD
SITE FOR INDUSTRIES FIRE STATION •
WESTERN RELIEF RD

ROAD JUNCTIONS

SCALE FEET
0   100   200   300   400   500

D

QUEENS PARK

SITE FOR COMMUNITY CENTRE •
THE BELL PUBLIC HOUSE
FORD END RD
HONEY HILL RD
WESTERN RELIEF RD

E

NEWNHAM BRIDGE

NEWNHAM AVENUE
THE EMBANKMENT
TO WILMERS CORNER

F

CARDINGTON RD

EASTERN CROSS TOWN LINK
CARDINGTON ROAD
RAILWAY TO CAMBRIDGE →

congestion only at the expense of the efficient functioning of the town. The present bus station, besides being intolerably overcrowded, is in the wrong place, and the problem would not be solved by building a second bus station also in the wrong place. Moreover, the removal of the bus station from the Broadway would simplify the problem of designing a roundabout at this junction and so eliminate a serious source of danger (Map 9, *p.* 74). The proposed Central Relief Road would clearly provide the ideal location for a new bus station; it should be built in Horne Lane on the site of the two market yards on either side of Gravel Lane, in a central position between St Paul's Square, the new administrative centre south of Commercial Road, and the new shops north of Midland Road. Most of the town services would then pass by the bus station. It would also be quite near to the main railway station; we do not think it is desirable to site the country bus terminus in the immediate vicinity of Midland Road Station because the majority of passengers are shoppers who want to step straight from the town centre into the bus queue.

The maximum number of departures from the present bus station in any one hour is thirty.[2] To this must be added the services run by Birch Bros and other independent operators, and an allowance for a future increase in traffic. It seems likely that the new Bedford Bus Station should be big enough to handle at least fifty departures per hour. The size of site necessary to accommodate this load would depend upon the type of design adopted, but a rough comparison with some existing bus stations in North-east England suggests that an area of about one and a half acres would be required.[3] The proposed site is about sixty yards by a hundred yards and should provide room for arrival and departure platforms, parking space for idle vehicles, a light maintenance shed, offices, waiting rooms and a restaurant.

THE RAILWAYS Bedford is not a major railway junction, but it is an important minor centre, and the railways occupy a considerable amount of land—about 140 acres in the Borough alone, nearly as much as is taken up by manufacturing industry. A large area behind Robertson's factory was once used as a ballast hole and is now devoted to the new

technique of prefabricating sections of track for quick replacement of the permanent way. The railways have been largely responsible for the changes in Bedford's functions during the last century and have determined the direction of industrial and residential development, but at the same time they have aggravated the major problem of cross-town communications. Bedford is already a town of hump-backed bridges, but we are forced to suggest a number of additional ones in order to completely overcome the railway barriers. They are vastly preferable to the level crossings that encumber many another town on a flat side.

Bedford's rail communications are good, and while they could be improved by the amalgamation of the two stations at Midland Road, the necessary capital expenditure would not be incurred during the next twenty years. The distance of the stations from the main centre is not exceptional for a town of this character, and the present inconveniences would be greatly reduced by road improvements such as the new links to Willmer's Corner and the road from Midland Road to Bromham Road. The westward extension of the shopping centre would bring it closer to the main railway station. If the population grows beyond 75,000, additional sidings may be necessary, and these could be provided behind the existing electricity works. We have had several cordial discussions with officials of British Railways who are in agreement with proposals affecting railway land, and are ready to co-operate in the re-siting of the agricultural markets west of Melbourne Street.

CONCLUSION The Central and Western Relief Roads with their new bridges over the Ouse are the two most drastic schemes in the proposals. They are also the most important. The two roads are in no sense alternatives. Both are necessary if Bedford's communications are to correspond to its future size and functions. The present system of radial roads converging upon a single 'spine' was ideal for a small market town; it should now be adapted to the changes in character and growth of population during the last fifty years. Bedford is still expanding and the road proposals outlined above are the foundation of its plan of expansion.

NOTES   [1] *Bedford—A Survey*, a report by the Council of Social Service (1950).   [2] Figures by the Eastern National Omnibus Company Limited.   [3] By courtesy of the Peterlee Development Corporation.   [4] Since the time of writing the final draft of this report this proposal has been officially abandoned.

4 *" The rate of renewal and repair in the old centre has been greatly outpaced by the demands put upon it by the growth of Bedford's industries, business houses and administrative offices, and the traffic that serves them. The gradual overhauling of the whole central core is a formidable but necessary task "*

The Town Centre

The road proposals are as crucial to the future of the central area as to that of the town as a whole. The Western Relief Road, described in the last chapter, would take all the north-south through traffic from the centre of the town; it amounts to one-third of the total flow. In the centre itself the proposals would provide a new spine to the old town and a new framework within which its life could flow. The suggestions for the extension of the shopping centre and for new civic buildings, car parks, factories, markets and warehouses, fall into place within this arterial framework, which consists of the three major proposals already described in Chapter 3. These are:

1. The new river bridge and Central Relief Road from Willmer's Corner to Bromham Road (*p*. 61).
2. The High Street Service Road from St Paul's Square to Lurke Street via Castle Lane and Duke Street (*p*. 64).
3. The western stretch of the Inner Ring Road linking Prebend Street Bridge ('The Green Bridge') with Union Street and Clapham Road (*p*. 59).

The High Street from St Peter's Green to St Paul's Square is the well-established hub of a wide district. But the rate of renewal and repair in the old centre has been greatly outpaced by the demands put upon it by the growth of Bedford's industries, business houses and administrative offices, and the traffic that serves them. The gradual overhauling of the whole central core is a formidable but necessary task.

To achieve this any form of dry dock technique, in which part of the town's functions are suspended for a time, is out of the question.

Drastic shifts of existing uses from one part of the town to another could not be paid for and must be avoided. The pattern and structure of the town is set, and even though Bedford doubles its 1931 population, the future centre is bound to respect the form from which it originally sprang. Fortunately, over a reasonable period of time, there are no insuperable difficulties in rendering the town centre healthy and efficient. In itself the convenient inter-relationship of shops, business and administrative buildings assists the solution; but within this compact core the arrangement is chaotic, and the prevalent mixture of conflicting land uses cramps the buildings and handicaps their efficiency. Many are blighted and nearing the end of their economic life, and their circulation both within and without is congested. Though a master-plan can be formulated to re-order the detailed uses to which land may be put, it is only by skilful estate management over many years that the process of sorting out and re-establishing displaced and blighted property can be achieved.

In simplest terms, the proposals for the central area are fourfold:

1. To maintain the main shopping centre where it is and extend it to the west (5), and at the same time to relieve it of through traffic and provide adequate car parks (4).*
2. To open up fresh stretches of both northern and southern river embankments for gardens, civic buildings and places of recreation (15), (18), (19), (22), (25).
3. To redevelop areas of blighted housing between Midland Road and Bromham Road (5) and behind Tavistock Street (1).

---

* **NOTE:** Throughout this chapter the figures given in parentheses relate to Map 9 opposite page 74.

4. To re-locate displaced offices, workshops, warehouses and administrative buildings that must be in the town centre on sites designed to enhance their function (3), (7), (27), (29), (31), (32).

THE EXTENSION OF THE SHOPPING CENTRE Bedford's shopping centre has the advantage of being compact, grouped round a central core of ten acres consisting of the three street blocks lying between St Paul's Square and Dame Alice Street, High Street and Harpur Street. From here it extends eastwards for a short distance down St Peter's Street and westwards down Midland Road. In Midland Road the large stores attract many customers. This compactness, however, is somewhat lost in the sprawl of shops along Tavistock Street to the north-west and St John's to the south, and any further expansion of the shopping centre must try to avoid aggravating this trend. Bedford cannot escape the necessity of providing more central shops for the growing population, and of catering for the ever increasing numbers of shoppers who come in from the villages.

The ideal site for the expansion of the shopping centre without losing its intimacy and compactness is provided by a parcel of land cleared of slum housing in Allhallows Lane, now used as a car park (5). This lies immediately north of Midland Road and west of Harpur Street, an area into which the shopping centre is already tending to expand.

Whenever expansion comes it will not be before its time, since the premises in the High Street have long been seriously congested, many are ill arranged and exposed to heavy fire risks, and there is an urgent demand for alternative central premises for those retailers who cannot be allowed to extend on overcrowded sites.

There are four reasons why the site selected for the expansion of the shopping centre is the most suitable for its purpose:

  (i) It would bring the main shops closer to the railway station (X)
  (ii) It would keep the shopping centre south of Dame Alice Street and St Peter's, the main east-west road through the town.
  (iii) It lies north of the river, where the main centre has always been.

(iv) It is an area of blight that is already partly cleared; it can, therefore, be commenced almost immediately, and continued without interruption.

But this extension of the main shopping centre must also be related to the traffic circulation, for the two problems are interdependent. The proposed new Central Relief Road should serve the new shopping area without passing directly through it. The use of Gwyn Street and Hassett Street, which bound the proposed shopping extension on the west, would provide an ideal solution. The location of the new bus station, discussed in Chapter 3, on this central road to the south of Midland Road and conveniently near the new shopping extension, also gives a better point of connection for passengers coming from south of the river, from the High Street shopping area and from the station.

In considering the extent of floor space provided by these new shops, what we mean by 'the central shopping zone' must be defined. We have taken the boundaries of this to be: (1) from Tavistock Street where it joins Harpur Street to St Peter's on the north; (2) a line drawn down the centre of Howard Street to The Embankment on the east; (3) St Paul's Square and Horne Lane on the south; and (4) River Street and Gwyn Street, Bromham Road, St Loyes and Harpur Street on the west.

TOTAL FLOOR SPACE	Ground Floor	Other Floors	Total
Main existing Shopping Centre	509,453	423,097	932,550
New Shopping Extensions	110,150	109,850	220,000
Less shops displaced	48,428	17,211	65,639
Effective additional space	61,722	92,639	154,361
Percentage increase	12%	22%	17%
SHOP FRONTAGE			
Main Shopping Centre	7,361 feet		
New extensions	2,509 feet		
Less shops displaced	203 feet		
Effective additional frontage	2,306 feet		
Percentage increase	31%		

As can be seen from these figures within this area there are approximately 932,550 square feet of floor space used by retail trade, and 7,360 feet of shop frontage. The proposals to extend the shopping centre to the west of Allhallows Lane would increase the floor space by seventeen per cent and the shop frontage by thirty-one per cent.

The principles of planning this shopping area would be to provide:

(i) pedestrian access only to the main shop frontages;

(ii) car parking and service access to the rear of all shops;

(iii) the freeing of the shopping area from other uses.

The shops themselves would be arranged to face on to a courtyard where pedestrians could circulate freely and no traffic could enter; where prams could be left and bicycles parked without interfering with access to the shops. Service roads and entrances and ample car parks should all be placed on the outside of the courtyard shops. The inner concourse would be quiet, and could accommodate a discriminate variety of trees and flowers and an open air café.

Once access has been gained from Harpur Street to Church Square it would be possible to proceed at an early date with the extension of this shopping centre over the cleared land in Allhallows Lane. It is proposed to continue this westwards over the remainder of the blighted properties in Thurlow Street and Greenhill Street until it fronts Gwyn Street. Apart from service vehicles using James Street, it is undesirable that any traffic should turn into this new centre from Midland Road whence pedestrian access only is to be given down Allhallows Lane. Pedestrians only would also enter from Harpur Street adjacent to Messrs Canvin's premises, and from St Loyes Street through Dane Street. Vehicles would turn into the shopping centre from St Loyes Street down Allhallows Lane and from Gwyn Street into Greenhill Street. Car parking accommodation would be provided in Greenhill Street and Gwyn Street for approximately 280 cars (4A-E).

The extension of the shopping centre westwards would increase the local traffic on Midland Road, and this would accentuate the present need for widening the narrowest portion by setting back the frontages of the shops on the south side, immediately west of the Modern School. The premises involved comprise Nos. 2 to 14a (9).

THE EXISTING SHOPPING CENTRE The new shopping extensions would supplement the existing centre based on the High Street, but would in no way displace it. The need in the old centre is, over a period of time, to remove the worst features of congestion and rearrange the confused admixture of land use.

The two most congested building blocks are bounded by High Street, Lime Street, Harpur Street and St Paul's Square; they are divided by Silver Street (6), (10). Here the total floor space inside the buildings exceeds the area of the block by more than one-third. The floor space index, obtained by dividing the interior floor space by the area of the site, is 1·42 for the northern block, and for the southern block 1·36.

This index is not unduly high, but the distribution of floor space within the blocks is unsatisfactory because modern buildings have crammed themselves into a honeycomb of former small residential plots, leaving light wells, alley ways, service accesses and street widths of inadequate size and disjointed arrangement.

With the same relationship of inner floor space to site area it would be possible to rearrange the accommodation to provide for efficient and easy flow of pedestrian, goods and vehicular traffic in and around each building, and at the same time give adequate daylight, safety against fire spread, eliminate accident points and reduce the nuisance of noise.

However, on the ground of cost, a comprehensive scheme for this is not yet contemplated, but during the next twenty years there will doubtless be opportunities for the Corporation to purchase a number of premises on the interiors of these blocks, premises now mostly used for storage. In this way inner circulation space could be opened up to give service access to shops which should remain the predominant use in this area. A suggestion for one of the blocks is shown on Map 9 (No. 10).

CAR PARKING Congestion in the town centre is much aggravated by the inadequacy of car parks and, although it is not considered essential to rule out all parking in streets, the provision of enough parking places is one of the major proposals in this report.

A survey was undertaken on Saturday, 21 October, 1950. 1,074 cars were parked, 370 in public parks and 704 in the streets. This total represented one car to every seven feet of shop frontage. The full capacity of the existing public car parks alone allows for only one car per twenty feet of shop frontage. The proposed car parks are listed as follows and shown on Map 9. The principal existing parks in St Loyes, Allhallows Lane and the Cattle Market would be built on, and St Paul's Square has not been included because it is not available on Saturdays.

In the shopping centre:

4A	In Greenhill Street	130	
4B,C,D	In three parks in the centre of the boulevard between the parallel carriageways of Gwyn Street and Hassett Street	126	
4E	A further park between Allhallows Lane and Gwyn Street for	24	
			280 cars

Elsewhere:

4F	East of High Street, once the semi-blighted property has been cleared, accommodation in Howard Street (on its west side) can be found for	56	
4G,H	On the east side of Howard Street and on either side of the proposed northward continuation of Duke Street to Lurke Street, a large park can be sited, after clearance has taken place, for	248	
4I	A southward extension of Ram Yard over part of Castle Lane clearance area would permit parking space for	162	
	Thus, the ultimate extent of new car parking places for the High Street area would be for		466 cars

Further parks are suggested:

Adjacent to the proposed bus station	100	
In the curtilage of the proposed riverside site for the County Council Offices and Library	121	
		221 cars
On the south side of the river and Town Bridge the chief parking area would be in Duckmill Lane, where the proposed new recreation centre, described below, would permit the accommodation of some		276 cars
		1,243 cars

The Ministry of Town and Country Planning's handbook on central areas recommends that parks should be provided on a basis of one car per five feet of shop frontage. We have, however, aimed at the provision of a standard of public car parks close to the shops on the north side of the river to accommodate about one car per ten feet of shop front, holding that some of the side streets could and should still be used for cars to wait in; but should a higher standard than this be required, underground or multi-storey parks would have to be considered, though in a town of Bedford's size their cost and inconvenience would be unlikely to warrant them.

If the total capacity of public car parks is to be raised even to one car per ten feet of shop frontage, no less than seven acres of costly central land must be set aside for this purpose, and it is considered impracticable to use more of the clearance area than this.

Altogether in the town centre 1,243 cars could be parked, which would increase the existing accommodation threefold. A reasonably generous spacing per car has been suggested to permit the planting of trees, which not only give valuable shade in the summer but clothe with life the arid deserts of concrete presented by most municipal car parks.

THE USE OF THE RIVERSIDE Undoubtedly the most attractive feature of Bedford is its magnificent river, which flows through the heart of the town. The Council as well as private individuals have seized many opportunities of adding to the attractiveness of this natural amenity. A two-mile stretch of the river is used for boating, and a mile-long parkway and pleasantly planted embankment—the town's most attractive open space—provides the setting for the most important event of the year—the Regatta.

It is the purpose of these proposals to make still greater use of the river, and gradually to give the western stretch between the Town Bridge (20) and Prebend Street (21) as dignified a setting as that to the east. Already the plans for the College of Further Education in Cauldwell Street (23) will assist towards this end, but we propose that when the adjacent blighted property in Great Butts Street and Little Butts Street

The need to duplicate the spine of the town arises from the revolution in methods of transport and the growth of business, shown by the contrast between **High Street in 1900** and **the same street in 1950.** New car parks are needed as well as new roads. Charming survivals of an earlier era, such as **Rose Yard** should be given a new function as a means of access to the car parks serving the High Street shops.

The huddle of little houses in **Greyfriars Walk** is just around the corner from the elegant **Regency Terrace in Bromham Road.** They were built within a few years of each other and both are falling into disrepair. But while the former should be pulled down as soon as possible, the latter should be carefully restored. Bedford has not so many examples of first-class domestic buildings that it can afford to permit the deterioration of such architectural features and their defacement by commercial additions.

Map 10

BLIGHTED HOUSING AND BUILDINGS OF INTEREST

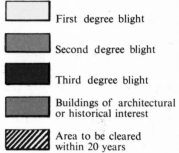

First degree blight

Second degree blight

Third degree blight

Buildings of architectural or historical interest

Area to be cleared within 20 years

There are comparatively few houses in Bedford at the end of their economic life. Even so, it is doubtful whether all the dwellings in the three classes of blight can be demolished during the next twenty years. All the yellow and blue areas would be cleared, together with those purple areas that are needed for the extension of the town centre. The map also shows in red those buildings which should as far as possible be preserved because of their aesthetic quality or historic interest.

CLAPHAM

GOLDINGTON

BIDDENHAM

KEMPSTON

ELSTOW

1000   0   1000   2000   3000   4000   5000 FEET

0   ¼   ½   ¾   1 MILE

(25) has reached the end of its economic life the area should be left open as a further amenity to continue the attractive riverside walks and as a site for an Art gallery. Similarly, on the north side of the river the proposed reconstruction of the municipal offices, the building of a new Assembly Hall at Batts' Ford (18), and the erection of new County Offices on the site of the old Cattle Market (19) would do much to add to the civic dignity of the town centre. On the east of the Town Bridge the major proposal is to improve and reconstruct the Duckmill Lane area as an entertainment centre, with a new covered swimming bath (22C), theatre (22B) and cinema (22A), as described below; close by would be the proposed youth centre on the south side of Cardington Road (28) at the rear of the Howard (Dr Barnardo's) Home.

THE ADMINISTRATIVE CENTRE The existing advantage of compactness in one of the main functions of the town is well illustrated by the present administrative centre, grouped around the south and west sides of St Paul's Square. The Town Hall and Municipal Offices (13), the County Offices and Law Courts (17) are here, and the Police Station and Borough Engineer's Office extend westwards from this main block down Horne Lane (14). The Corn Exchange (11), which is used for the town's civic receptions and concerts, is also in St Paul's Square, on the north side. Apart from the Shire Hall and the Corn Exchange, none of these premises were originally designed for the purposes they now serve. Space is so limited that recently established departments, such as the County Planning Office, have had to 'spill over' into improvised accommodation in the already overcrowded High Street. There is also a serious inadequacy of car parking space.

Were it not for the existence of Wells' Brewery (16), the municipal buildings could have extended westwards along the river front—a fitting place for a civic centre. Though it is hoped that the brewery, occupying nearly two acres on the north bank of the river, could ultimately be shifted to a site on the outskirts of the town, this move is not considered timely within the period covered by this report. In view of the obsolete nature of most of the administrative buildings, a combined policy of re-conditioning, extension and rebuilding on new sites is suggested. A scheme to retain both the county and town buildings in St Paul's Square was prepared before the war, and was the subject of a competition. This proposal could not be put into effect without adding to the congestion in the square, and without completely destroying its character. In any case, it is doubtful whether those who initiated the competition and provided the programme of accommodation had foreseen the increase in the work that local government would have to do. The chief merit of the pre-war scheme was that the buildings, though somewhat crammed on to the St Paul's Square site, were carefully related to the river front, and this principle of combining civic buildings with water front is adopted in our present proposals, though on more spacious sites.

MUNICIPAL BUILDINGS It is suggested that the municipal offices (14) should remain on their present site but should undergo an extensive remodelling process—opening up more of the northern bank of the river, and replacing with new offices the former Girls' Modern School and other makeshift premises that are now used. The present Town Hall with its adjoining rooms has already become, in effect, quite a successful central community centre. It is suggested that it should be left free to develop further as part of this desirable and much-needed amenity.

THE PROPOSED ASSEMBLY HALL A hall to seat from 1,000 to 1,500 people is much needed in Bedford. The Corn Exchange, where many excellent concerts are given and which was used by the B.B.C. during the war, seats only 750. The population of the town and district has long overgrown this limit of seating space, and further growth makes imperative the need to earmark a site for such a building, even if circumstances do not permit it to be built at once. The suggested site (18) is also on the north bank of the river, immediately west of the brewery (16) and flanking the new bridge on the side opposite to the proposed County Buildings.

THE COUNTY COUNCIL OFFICES It is suggested that the new site should be on the north river bank, where the old Cattle Market still

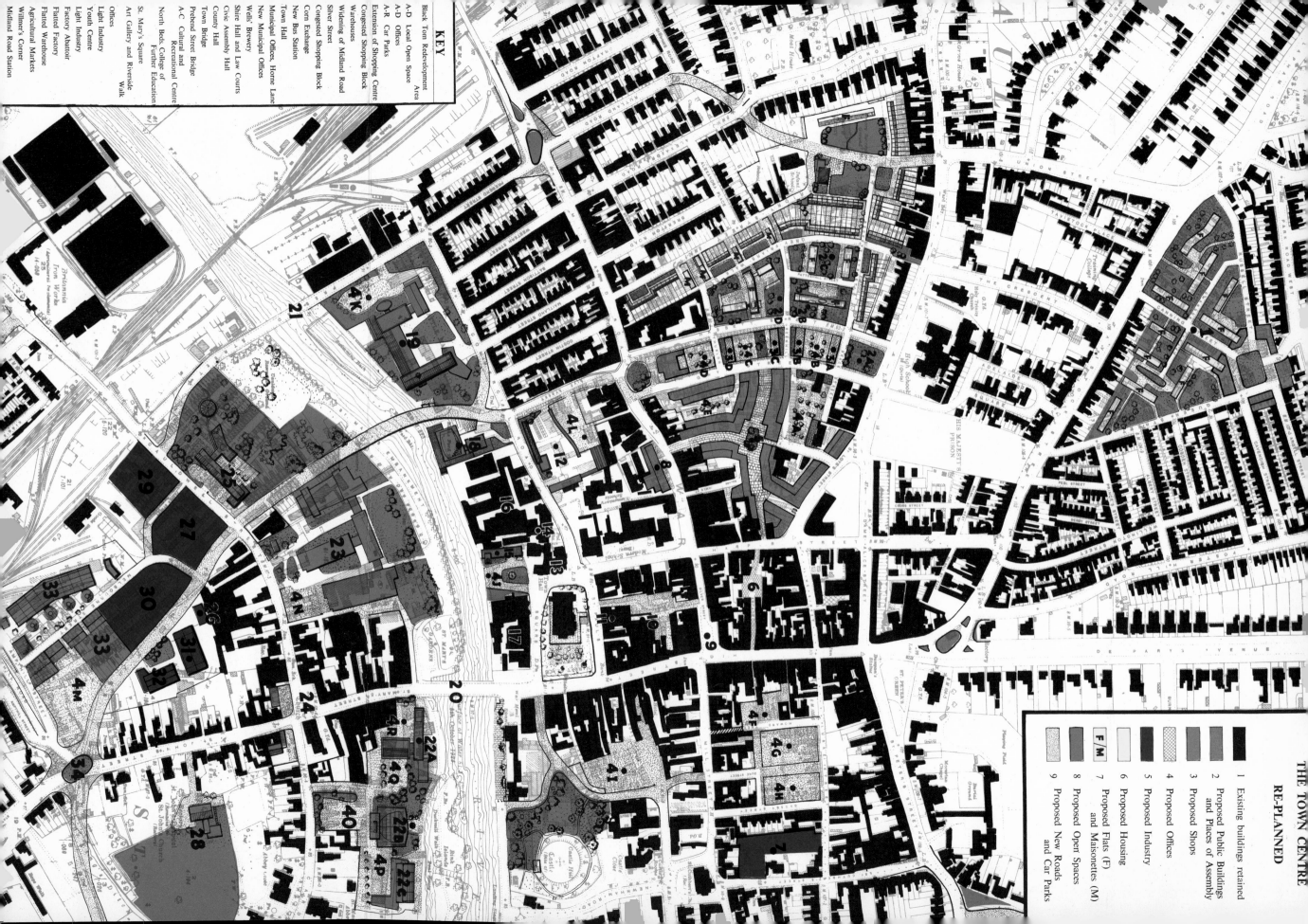

THE TOWN CENTRE
RE-PLANNED

KEY

Black Tom Redevelopment
Area
A–D Local Open Space
A–D Offices
A–R Car Parks
Extension of Shopping Centre
Congested Shopping Block
Warehouses
Widening of Midland Road
Silver Street
Congested Shopping Block
Corn Exchange
New Bus Station
Town Hall
Municipal Offices, Horne Lane
New Municipal Offices
Wells' Brewery
Shire Hall and Law Courts
Civic Assembly Hall
County Hall
Town Bridge
Prebend Street Bridge
A–C Cultural and
Recreational Centre
North Beds. College of
Further Education
St. Mary's Square
Art Gallery and Riverside
Walk
Offices
Light Industry
Youth Centre
Light Industry
Factory Abattoir
Flatted Factory
Flatted Warehouse
Agricultural Markets
Wilmer's Corner
Midland Road Station

1 Existing buildings retained
2 Proposed Public Buildings
   and Places of Assembly
3 Proposed Shops
4 Proposed Offices
5 Proposed Industry
6 Proposed Housing
7 Proposed Flats (F)
   and Maisonettes (M) **F/M**
8 Proposed Open Spaces
9 Proposed New Roads
   and Car Parks

exists, though now used primarily as a fair ground and a car park for the market. This large area in Commercial Road (about 5½ acres) has remarkable potentialities for the development of its extensive river front of 170 yards (19). The Ouse itself is now obscured by storage depots and the unsightly screens round the town bathing place—an untidy and obsolete establishment. All these buildings should be cleared, and new baths built on the Duckmill Lane site (22C). If the County buildings were placed here, not only would they have room for extension but they would occupy one of the best riverside sites in the town, and would contribute greatly to the civic interest and dignity of this central waterfront. The buildings should include all County Departments, Committee Rooms and Council Chamber, and the County Library, totalling altogether 75,000 square feet. Their arrangement should ensure that the river is seen between and through them. It is suggested that the block which fronts on to the river might be raised on columns with covered circulation space between them. This County Centre would have the added advantage of proximity to the main entrance to the town centre over the proposed new bridge at Batts' Ford; it would be quite close to the railway station and almost next to the proposed new bus station, and it would have ample accommodation for car parking (121 cars).

THE LAW COURTS The Law Courts are at present in the middle of the County Offices, but it is not proposed that the former should be moved. The present County Architect's and Surveyor's Offices, as well as what is not required by the Law Courts, could be used and let out as professional offices, for which there is a demand in the St Paul's Square district.

ST MARY'S STREET AND THE DUCKMILL LANE RECREATION CENTRE The south bank of the river has long been used as a place of recreation with its café, picture theatre and boathouses. It is proposed to extend this area to include all the properties in Duckmill Lane, Bedesman's Lane and Bedesman's Place with the exception of Messrs Randall's shop and warehouses. The recreation centre would eventually extend as far south as Cardington Road, from which cars would enter. This is made practicable by the proposal to divert the western end of

Cardington Road along the line of Rope Walk to Willmer's Corner, thus freeing the dangerous cross-roads at St Mary's of a large stream of traffic. The southern riverside embankment would continue to be for pedestrians only, and the buildings could comprise a cinema, restaurant and café with small dance halls and boat-houses (22A), a theatre (22B), and a covered swimming bath and one open bath (22C). St Mary's Abbey and house No. 26 on the north side of Cardington Road would remain. With the exception of a small group of cottages (Nos. 2 to 8 Cardington Road), the rest of the houses between St Mary's Church and these buildings would be cleared to provide access to the site and car parks for about 276 cars.

The safety of pedestrians and traffic at the St Mary's cross roads should be further improved by the widening of Cauldwell Street on the south side, providing better sight lines at the junction. It is not proposed to place a roundabout at this point. A careful tree planting scheme for this part of the town is essential.

THE YOUTH CENTRE The want of central premises for young people is much felt in Bedford, as was emphasized in a number of the 106 completed replies to the clubs questionnaire. There would not be room for this on the Duckmill Lane Recreation Centre site, but an ideal site presents itself nearby on the glebe land behind the Howard (Dr Barnardo's) Home (28). This triangular site, which is now partly cultivated, comprises about four acres and is bounded by the King's Ditch on the south-east, and St John's Church and Rectory on the west. This field could accommodate a hall, committee rooms, canteen and changing rooms and a sports field. It adjoins the inner ring road, and is 150 yards from the proposed new swimming baths and the Rink Island boat-houses. The buildings should be erected on the perimeter of the site so that it is preserved as far as possible as an open space.

INDUSTRY There would be nearly 180,000 square feet of industry displaced by the new proposals. This excludes the industrial buildings that, over the course of time, will have to be cleared from the present shopping area surrounded by Howard Street, Harpur Street, Dame Alice Street, St Paul's Square and Castle Lane. It is suggested that industrial sites in the centre of the town should eventually become available in the area covered by Cauldwell Place and Farrer Street (29) (90,000 square feet), and that a four- or five-storey flatted factory of 50,000 square feet (discussed below) should be built on the triangular site of about 60,000 square feet, immediately east of the proposed Central Relief Road from Willmer's Corner (31). Anything between 100,000 and 200,000 square feet of floor space would be available on these new sites. A further site for light industry is suggested south of the Cambridge railway line and north of Fenlake Road, which could be used for a second flatted factory were there the demand. The site is 2½ acres, or approximately 100,000 square feet, in area.

THE PROPOSED FLATTED FACTORY Apart from providing premises for those factories displaced by clearance, there is also the need to overcome the severe shortage in Bedford of industrial premises for small businesses starting up or expanding. It is, therefore, suggested that the Corporation should consider at an early date the building and maintenance of a flatted factory to let at an economic rent.

There are advantages of such a project in Bedford, with its variety of small industries scattered over a somewhat compact central area.

First, a maximum amount of floor space on one site could be provided so that as many displaced firms as possible could be rehoused in the central area; secondly, an economical provision of piped services is made possible; thirdly, a communal canteen, rest rooms and other amenities could be provided; fourthly, as an architectural feature, the building would have advertisement value for firms and for the town; last, and perhaps most important, it would provide the key to the reconstruction of the central area as the place of easy transference from existing premises.

However, not all businesses could be carried on in a flatted factory—those requiring specialized buildings, e.g. corn millers, and those using heavy machinery are excluded. Others may be unwilling to rent premises

and share amenities, and would prefer their own buildings either in the centre or on the outskirts of the town.

Those wishing to go to the outskirts are provided for in the proposals outlined in Chapter 5, and those requiring central sites would be accommodated in the Farrer Street-Pilcroft Street area after the clearance of blighted houses.

In order to estimate the likely demand for floor space in a flatted factory, a questionnaire was sent to ninety-five small firms in the central area. A number of others were interviewed in the course of the main industrial survey. Warehouses as well as workshops were included, since storage space for wholesale businesses might be provided in a flatted warehouse. Fifty-three replies were received and analysed as follows:

PREFERENCES OF CENTRAL AREA BUSINESSES

	No. of Firms	No. of Employees	Present Floor Space	Floor Space Required
Would welcome space in flatted factory	15	250	82,600	85,000
Wish to remain in town centre, but NOT in flatted factory	28	650	213,300	Not known
Would prefer to move to outskirts	10	110	46,500	Not known
TOTAL	53	1,010	342,400	Not known

Among those who were interested in the project were manufacturers of clothing, underwear, mineral water, guns, furniture and electrical apparatus, as well as those running workshops for repairs of furniture and reconditioning of car engines.

Of the fifteen firms willing to consider moving to a flatted factory only seven would actually be affected by the proposals for clearance in the town centre. They require about 30,000 square feet. This in itself would hardly be enough to justify the building of a flatted factory; however, many of the firms who occupy part of the other 150,000 square feet of industry to be disturbed, and who did not reply to the questionnaire, would no doubt welcome the opportunity of renting space in a flatted factory when forced to vacate their present premises. There would also be a demand from new firms and firms unable to expand on their present sites.

Flatted factories do not, however, provide a complete solution to the problem of industrial location in the central area. Measured in floor space, just under a quarter of all central industry covered by the results is willing to consider space in a flatted factory, about half as much would prefer a site on the outskirts of the town, and the remaining two-thirds want to stay in the central area in its own premises.

It is important that space in the flatted factory should be available before the start of the demolition in blighted areas so as to make the transfer of industry as quick and painless as possible. It is, therefore, necessary to find a vacant site in a suitable location, and the piece of land at the back of St John's alongside the projected Central Relief Road is ideal for a flatted factory.

Here a four- or five-storey flatted factory served by large lifts could be built with a floor space of 50,000 to 100,000 square feet. There would be many problems in its detailed design that could only be solved by discussion with the firms likely to take space in it. It is important that the probable rent should be estimated as soon as possible.

Before putting forward this solution to the problem of small central industries, the new flatted factory in the Goudsesingel at Rotterdam was visited and discussed with the Architects, Van Tijen and Maaskant. Here are forty industries, averaging 2,000 square feet each, producing machinery, clothing, hats and plastics. There are 550 workers (335 male and 215 female); they average thirteen per firm, and occupy approximately 150 square feet of floor space each (see illustration, *p.* 132). We have also compared our own suggestions with those of the County Borough of West Ham for a similar project.

WAREHOUSING The warehousing displaced by the present proposals amounts to about 149,015 square feet. Two types of warehousing are under review:
  (i) stock room accommodation;

(ii) storage space independent of retail trade.
The first class is accommodated within the new shopping centre. The second class, it is suggested, could be accommodated on three sites:
  1. The site north of Willmer's Corner where a flatted warehouse could be erected adjacent to the flatted factory (32).
  2. The light industrial site in Fenlake Road, mentioned above as a possible alternative site for a flatted factory, would also accommodate warehouses.
  3. An area of about $1\frac{1}{2}$ acres on the east side of Gadsby Street, part of which is covered by housing that would be scheduled for clearance in due course (7).

THE AGRICULTURAL MARKETS Several interviews have been held with the regional staff of British Railways concerning the possible use of railway land for the re-siting of the Agricultural Markets which would be displaced by the proposed Bus Station.

A satisfactory site is that which backs on to the goods yard between Ampthill Street and Cauldwell Street and lies immediately west of Melbourne Street, but this site is not likely to be available at an early date (33).

A practical suggestion would be to accommodate the cattle market on the fair ground site in Commercial Road until such time as the new County Offices are erected here (19). By then, the blighted housing in Pilcroft Street and Melbourne Street should have been cleared, and the whole of this area, together with the triangular site which backs on to the goods yard, would be available for the markets, abattoir (30), cold store and car park (4M).

It is considered that the markets should remain as close to the town centre as possible, but that they should not occupy land which could be put to more profitable use. The St John's site satisfies these conditions, and is close to the main traffic distribution point at Willmer's Corner.

CENTRAL HOUSING AREA The Greyfriars area west of Hassett Street and east of Priory Street is one of the most blighted in the town.

Here, on nine acres of near slum property, 850 persons will be displaced from 250 dwellings, but it is possible to rehouse them all in the same area in blocks of flats and maisonettes. At the same time the public gardens around the flats would help to make good the present deficiency of local open space (2).

The Priory Street playground, which would be traversed by the proposed inner cross-town road, would be slightly enlarged to provide an equivalent amount of open space, around which dwellings would be grouped. This arrangement also allows a larger Primary School site than that envisaged by the County Education Committee. The existing school would be retained on a portion of this site.

It is not likely that the blighted dwellings will be cleared all at once, but the new plan is so arranged that the present street pattern is unchanged, apart from the extinction of minor streets, such as Roise Street. This means that new housing units can be built as and when the blighted property is cleared, each unit ultimately taking its place in the final scheme.

A similar arrangement has been followed in the Chandos Street/Canning Street area, where 300 persons are to be displaced through blight, and 600 are to be accommodated, mostly in flats (1).

THE ASHBURNHAM ROAD AREA The residential district that lies east of the station and west of Priory Street was developed in the third quarter of the last century, and consists of middle-sized and large houses with their own gardens built for the wealthier Victorian citizens. Gradually this area has deteriorated. A growing number of the houses are being sub-divided into flats, and some are let as lodgings to the detriment of the area as a whole. If the area is not to suffer further loss of character and rateable value it must be saved by a policy of gradual and positive development.

In this the Corporation have themselves taken the initiative by commissioning a rebuilding scheme in Ashburnham Road on a site at present occupied by eight four-storey Victorian terrace houses and their gardens. All but one of these dwellings are let as lodgings. The scheme provides

for the obsolete terrace to be cleared, and for the erection in its place of a multi-storey block of flats (see illustration on *p.* 132).

The scheme provides fifty-four flats altogether, eighteen with two bedrooms and thirty-six with one bedroom. They are not intended for families with children, but are to supply the need of those who work in the schools and offices of the town, and are either single or have no families.

It is suggested that over a period of years this area should gradually be the subject of careful redevelopment and planting, so that this formerly pleasant and convenient neighbourhood may provide the amenity and enjoyment that its central position warrants.

CONCLUSION We have now outlined the proposals for the centre of the town, and it remains to assess the amount of disturbance to owners and occupiers that the implementation of these proposals would involve. In making these calculations we have had the advantage of the special survey of floor space in the central area of the town, carried out by the students of the Durham University School of Town and Country Planning on behalf of the County Planning Committee, and we are indebted to Mr E. Sterne for the loan of this work.

In all the areas of clearance, both north and south of the river, that would fall ripe for redevelopment within the approximate period of twenty years, there are about 1,400 hereditaments of all uses that would be directly affected by the proposals. These premises comprise varying amounts of floor space for the following categories of use:

	Square Feet		Square Feet
Residential	1,040,715	Places of Assembly	20,050
Shops	145,330	Two Cinemas	16,600
Industry	177,790	Boat-house	5,800
Storage	149,015	College of Further Education	1,600
Offices	20,775	Commercial Road Baths	3,650
Public Houses	32,865	Cattle Market	15,000
Garage Space	43,910	Miscellaneous	10,000

TOTAL: 1,683,100 *Square Feet*

It will be noted that the total floor space of shops displaced throughout the whole of the town centre (145,330 sq. ft.) is over twice the amount of floor space displaced in the area where the main shops are to be extended (65,639 sq. ft.), shown on page 68. Fortunately, these extensions take place over land that is primarily occupied by blighted housing, and therefore the actual amount of retail trade displaced is exceptionally small for so central an extension.

The 177,790 square feet of industry will find adequate space for its ultimate re-location on sites already mentioned, both in the central area and on the outskirts of the town.

The same applies to the warehouse accommodation of 149,000 square feet that would be involved in the ultimate clearance.

So far as the remainder of the uses are concerned, we are satisfied that these proposals not only provide adequate room for the re-location of uses displaced, but also allow for considerable increases in floor space, should this be desired.

The detailed list of hereditaments affected by these proposals has been submitted to the Town Clerk.

It is clear that positive planning will involve an intelligent policy of estate management. Once the Council have decided upon the staging of their programme, every endeavour should be made to achieve satisfactory negotiations with individual landowners in such a way that alternative accommodation is made available before the actual clearance takes place. The building of a flatted factory in advance of the clearance is the sort of positive measure that we have in mind.

Since, however, a considerable population will move to the outskirts of the town, it is anticipated that some of the strictly local services, e.g. the shops and public houses, would seize the opportunity of moving with them. It is clear that a sustained attempt to reduce a large measure of chaos and muddle to a degree of order and efficiency is bound to tax to the utmost the capacity of any individual, committee or official charged with the responsibility of estate management of a long-term project of this size; and, if the Council's policy is that of planning by lease control, the scope of this responsibility becomes even greater.

The new bridge at Batt's Ford and the proposed civic buildings

5 *" Bedford's industrial expansion has been continuous and has not yet come to an end. The town is ideally placed to receive factories dispersed from central London and these should be encouraged to take up any industrial sites not needed by existing firms "*

Work

The people of Bedford earn their living in about as big a variety of ways as can be imagined in a town of medium size. This is due to its wide range of functions as a centre for distribution, administration, education and manufacture.

Bedford cannot be called an 'industrial town', yet manufacturing is today its most important single function, and more than half the population depends directly or indirectly upon the prosperity of its factories. We can speak truthfully of this fact being 'revealed' by our survey, because the stranger does not associate Bedford with manufacturing industry. One reason for this is that most of the big firms in the town make capital goods, industrial equipment of one sort or another, which, although absolutely vital to the production of consumer goods, do not themselves come directly to the notice of the buying public. Another is that manufacturing is still a comparatively new function, having developed almost entirely during the last seventy years. Bedford remained a quiet country town throughout the early years of the nineteenth century, when the national pattern of industrial location was largely established. Its factories mostly belong to the later era of dispersal, when the country towns—particularly those with good communications—were found to have advantages that had long been lost in the older manufacturing centres. Many local firms are still expanding, and a number of excellent industrial sites are available. We propose that $115\frac{1}{2}$ acres of undeveloped land and three acres to be cleared of blighted housing should be reserved for industry. The first claimants on these sites should be existing firms wishing to build new or additional premises, but it is

unlikely that these will take up the whole of the available area. Bedford is a suitable place to receive factories dispersed from Central London under the Greater London Plan.

The increasing importance of manufactures has not been and will not be at the expense of other forms of employment. As a result of changes in the structure of local government, more and more people are occupied in administration in the county town; as a service centre for the surrounding countryside, Bedford's importance relative to that of the smaller centres is constantly growing. The building of the National Aeronautical Establishment north of the town will increase the number and variety of jobs in the district.

THE SURVEY Our study of livelihood and workplaces began with an analysis of the official statistics; in this we had the assistance of local officials of the Ministry of Labour and National Service, and of the Factory Inspector. The County Planning Officer had already circulated a questionnaire to thirty-five of the larger employers, and we were able to study the thirty replies he received. This information was supplemented by personal interviews with principals of a further thirty-nine firms. Together the two enquiries covered nearly every firm with twenty or more employees, and a few smaller ones. It was, of course, impossible to obtain first-hand information from every employer; there are more than 400 'factories' alone, but many of them are small workshops attached to retail premises. A special questionnaire was sent to ninety-five small manufacturing and wholesale businesses in the town centre which were likely to be affected by redevelopment, and fifty-two replies were received. For the story of industrial growth we were able to draw upon an unpublished thesis by Mr R. J. Harper, *The Manufacturing Industries of Bedford and their effect on the Town*, and in formulating our proposals we have had the benefit of consultations with the local committee of the Federation of British Industries.

INDUSTRIAL STRUCTURE This analysis is based on the statistics of employed persons insured at the local Employment Exchange, which covers not only Bedford and Kempston but also the greater part of Bedford Rural District and a small corner of Ampthill Rural District. The exchange serves 80,000 people, of whom a quarter live in the countryside. Map 4 (*p.* 40) shows that this area is smaller than the 'Bedford district' described in Chapter 2. It is much more closely linked with Bedford, which is the only town in the area and far and away the most important centre of employment. Apart from workers in agriculture and brick-making, almost all employed persons in the area work either in Bedford or Kempston. Village craftsmen and shopkeepers are mostly self-employed persons who are not included in the statistics. The figures relate to July, 1948, but we know from the survey of firms that there have been no major changes in the industrial structure during the last three years. We regret, however, that we have not been able to make use of more recent statistics; the needs of social and economic research were apparently omitted in the re-organization of the national insurance scheme. Unless this defect is remedied, planning authorities will find it impossible to fulfil their statutory duty to keep the survey up-to-date.

Diagram 5 shows how the industrial structure of the Bedford area compares with that of Great Britain. Employment is divided into twenty-four broad categories. First come the industries which take wealth directly from the land—agriculture and mining. Nationally these two groups are about equally important, each having just under five per cent of all employed persons. Locally, on the other hand, agriculture has ten per cent of all employed persons, while in the second group

there are only a handful of workers in gravel pits. The contrast is due entirely to the geology of the county, with its rich soils but lack of coal-bearing strata. Such mineral wealth as the district possesses is reflected in the third employment group—manufactures closely based on mining products, in this case bricks. Bedford has four times the national proportion—the biggest excess for any industrial group. Brick-making is the most distinctive industry of the county and—apart from agriculture—the only major source of employment in the rural areas.

The factory industries are divided into thirteen groups which together account for two-fifths of Bedford's workers. But in all except two of them the local proportion falls short of the national average. The two exceptions are engineering, the biggest single source of employment in the Borough itself, and food, drink and tobacco manufactures. A further analysis of the manufacturing industries is given in a later section.

Next come the basic services of building, public utilities and transport, in which there is little difference between the local and national proportions. It is clear that Bedford is not one of the main centres of communications. On the other hand, its function as the market town for a wide area is shown by the excess proportion in distribution. This would be more striking if self-employed persons were included in the statistics, but the figures are unfortunately not available. It is not surprising to find that employment in insurance, banking and finance falls short of the national average, for though Bedford is a local centre for these services, national employment in them is heavily concentrated in London. The fourth biggest excess—after bricks, agriculture and engineering —is found in public administration and defence; Bedford has a number of national and local government offices, there are important R.A.F. establishments in the district, and the Bedfordshire and Hertfordshire Regiment has its headquarters at Kempston Barracks. The last two groups of miscellaneous services show little variation between the local and national proportions.

In general the diagram shows that the district has what may be called a healthy 'industrial profile'. True, the nose (engineering) has a tendency

Diagram 5

INDUSTRIAL STRUCTURE 1948

BEDFORD COMPARED WITH GREAT BRITAIN

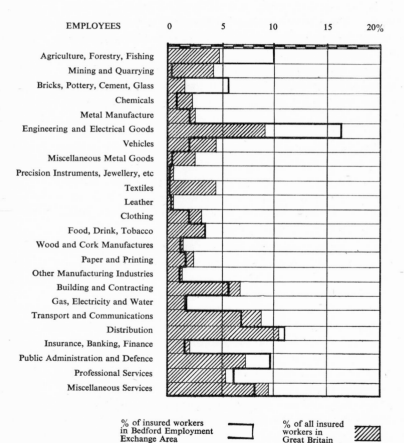

EMPLOYEES   0   5   10   15   20%

Agriculture, Forestry, Fishing
Mining and Quarrying
Bricks, Pottery, Cement, Glass
Chemicals
Metal Manufacture
Engineering and Electrical Goods
Vehicles
Miscellaneous Metal Goods
Precision Instruments, Jewellery, etc
Textiles
Leather
Clothing
Food, Drink, Tobacco
Wood and Cork Manufactures
Paper and Printing
Other Manufacturing Industries
Building and Contracting
Gas, Electricity and Water
Transport and Communications
Distribution
Insurance, Banking, Finance
Public Administration and Defence
Professional Services
Miscellaneous Services

% of insured workers in Bedford Employment Exchange Area   % of all insured workers in Great Britain

Diagram 6   GROWTH OF EMPLOYMENT 1929 – 39 – 48

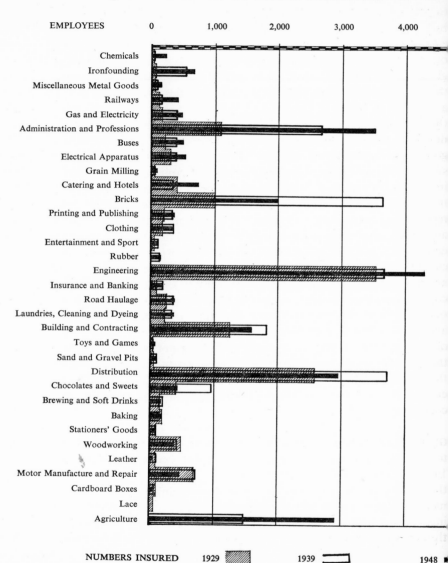

EMPLOYEES   0   1,000   2,000   3,000   4,000

Chemicals
Ironfounding
Miscellaneous Metal Goods
Railways
Gas and Electricity
Administration and Professions
Buses
Electrical Apparatus
Grain Milling
Catering and Hotels
Bricks
Printing and Publishing
Clothing
Entertainment and Sport
Rubber
Engineering
Insurance and Banking
Road Haulage
Laundries, Cleaning and Dyeing
Building and Contracting
Toys and Games
Sand and Gravel Pits
Distribution
Chocolates and Sweets
Brewing and Soft Drinks
Baking
Stationers' Goods
Woodworking
Leather
Motor Manufacture and Repair
Cardboard Boxes
Lace
Agriculture

NUMBERS INSURED   1929   1939   1948

to protrude, but it is well balanced by a strong brow (agriculture and bricks) and a firm chin (service industries). When we consider the employment structure of Bedford and Kempston apart from the rest of the exchange area, however, the protruding nose assumes much greater significance, for while nearly all the factories are located within the town, the balancing occupations of brick-making and agriculture are outside it. Although there is a considerable variety of firms among the engineering and other manufacturing industries, we have already noted the tendency to concentrate on the making of durable capital goods, which have always suffered most severely from the downward swing of the trade cycle. The proportion of Bedford's workers engaged in making capital goods is somewhat greater than that of all workers in the country; this may mean that in any future depression unemployment in the town is likely to be relatively more severe than in the country as a whole. Such a recession would prevent the realization of the aims embodied in our planning proposals. There is little that local planning can do to guard against this danger. We can—and do—recommend that any new industries that may be introduced should, as far as possible, be consumer goods industries that will be less affected by ups and downs of employment. But there is not much scope for further diversification, and it can at best be regarded as no more than a palliative. As pointed out in the Barlow Report,[1] the cure lies in the field of national rather than local planning, but it is necessary for the local planner to state that the implementation of his proposals depends upon the stability of employment and this can only be attained through the action of the central authorities.

GROWTH OF EMPLOYMENT Diagram 6 gives the main changes that took place in the industrial structure of the district between 1929 and 1948. They are based on a more detailed industrial classification than the profile diagram, and show that there was a steady growth of employment in almost every industry, both manufacturing and service. An interesting exception is the wood-working group which lost numbers throughout the period. The most spectacular changes were in brick-making, which more than trebled its employment between 1929 and 1939—the period of the great building boom; lost a high proportion of its workers during the war; and by 1948 had only recovered to a little more than half its 1939 level. The proportionate distribution of workers between different industries has altered very little since 1929. Engineering appears to have lost ground slightly, but if ironfounding and miscellaneous metal industries are included there has been little change. Together the group employed about a quarter of all insured workers in both 1929 and 1948. The only significant increase was in administration and the professions, which more than trebled their numbers between 1929 and 1948, and doubled their proportion of the total insured population. The same thing was happening all over the country. By and large, the industrial structure of the district had already assumed its present shape by 1929. The formative period was the closing decades of the nineteenth century and the opening years of the twentieth, when the ancient functions of administration, distribution and education were consolidated and extended, and the new function of manufacturing added. But the figures tend to conceal a long-term trend towards the increasing importance of manufacturing industry, which is to be measured not simply by the numbers employed in the factories themselves but by the proportion of those in the service trades who owe their jobs to the prosperity of the factories. This relationship cannot easily be disentangled from the complex industrial structure of the Bedford district, but we can be certain that the proportion has grown.

JOBS FOR WOMEN AND YOUNG PEOPLE The variety of jobs in the area applies to women as well as men. The ratio of employed women to employed men for the whole exchange area is just below the national average of 50:100. Since the exchange area includes most of the Bedford Rural District, where there is very little employment for women, the female:male ratio for the town itself is, of course, somewhat higher. If employment in agriculture and brick-making is omitted, the ratio for the exchange area is 58:100, and this can be taken as a fair approximation to the ratio for Bedford and Kempston.

Map 11

INDUSTRY

Engineering

Other basic industries

Residentiary industries

Factories to be moved

Works sports field

Proposed industrial site

Proposed sports field   P

SIZE OF FIRMS
(No. of employees)

under | 20– | 50– | 100– | 200– | 500– | 1000– | over
20 | 50 | 100 | 200 | 500 | 1000 | 1500 | 1500

Most of the big works are sited by
the railways south of the river. This
would remain the principal industrial
zone and its communications
with all other parts of the town
would be improved by new roads
and cycle tracks bridging the river
and railway barriers. Nearly all the
land suggested for industrial
expansion is in this main zone, but
there are also sites for female
employing factories adjoining the new
Goldington neighbourhood, and for
a flatted factory in the town centre.

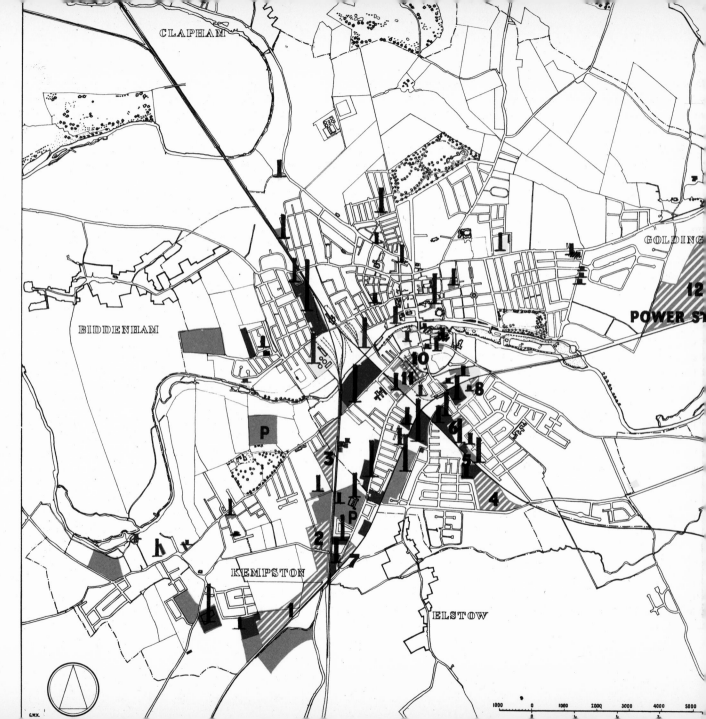

CLAPHAM

GOLDING

12
POWER ST

BIDDENHAM

KEMPSTON

ELSTOW

G.W.K.

1000   0   1000   2000   3000   4000   5000

Table 3: EMPLOYMENT OF WOMEN AND YOUNG PEOPLE

Showing all industries with 100 or more females, or in which females are 25 per cent or more of the total labour force, and all industries with fifty or more juveniles (persons under eighteen) or in which juveniles are 10 per cent or more of the total labour force. Girls under eighteen are included both as women and young people.

INDUSTRY OR OCCUPATION	WOMEN 1—Nos. insured 1948 2—% all workers in each industry 3—% all insured females			YOUNG PEOPLE 4—Nos. insured 1948 5—% all workers in each industry 6—% all insured juveniles		
	1	2	3	4	5	6
Retail Distribution (non-food goods)	1,168	57	9·8	277	13	12·6
Local Government	1,005	35	8·4	74	3	3·4
Education	994	69	8·4	—	—	—
Catering and Hotels	753	71	6·3	—	—	—
Non-resident Domestic Service	696	94	5·8	—	—	—
Agriculture	673	19	5·7	190	5	8·6
National Government	546	71	4·6	—	—	—
Chocolate and Sweets	485	74	4·1	—	—	—
Electric lamps	443	66	3·7	85	13	3·9
Medical and Dental Services	437	76	3·7	—	—	—
Retail Distribution (food)	430	44	3·6	90	9	3·9
Electrical Engineering	418	32	3·5	97	8	4·4
Resident Domestic Service	406	96	3·4	63	15	2·9
Marine Engineering	287	12	2·4	168	7	7·6
General Engineering	261	16	2·2	68	4	3·1
Laundries	239	83	2·0	—	—	—
Tailoring	211	86	1·8	65	26	3·0
Post Office	165	28	1·4	51	9	2·3
Insurance and Banking	152	29	1·3	—	—	—
Printing and Publishing	151	34	1·3	49	11	2·2
Wholesale Distribution (non-food goods)	133	49	1·1	—	—	—
Dressmaking	116	91	1·0	35	28	1·6
Hairdressing	116	66	1·0	27	15	1·2
Rubber	100	61	0·8	—	—	—
Underwear	70	95	0·6	9	12	0·4
Miscellaneous Electrical goods	43	88	0·4	—	—	—
Mica	23	77	0·2	4	13	0·2
Law	67	59	0·6	20	17	0·9
Cleaning and Dyeing	69	59	0·6	13	11	0·6
Ice Cream	11	55	0·1	4	20	0·2
Cardboard Boxes	19	51	0·2	—	—	—
Entertainments	56	48	0·5	27	23	1·2
Crayons	50	48	0·5	28	27	1·2
Miscellaneous Metal goods	74	46	0·6	19	12	0·8
Accountancy	27	45	0·3	8	13	0·4
Miscellaneous Business and Professions	35	43	0·4	—	—	—
Canvas goods and Sacks	10	42	0·1	—	—	—
Retail Distribution (sweets and tobacco)	48	39	0·5	—	—	—
Toys and Games	17	35	0·2	6	13	0·3
Religion	8	31	0·1	—	—	—
Baking	73	30	0·6	27	11	1·2
Wholesale Distribution (food)	16	25	0·1	—	—	—
Building	—	—	—	135	8	6·1
Garages	—	—	—	55	14	2·5
Boot repair	—	—	—	10	11	0·5
Electrical contracting	—	—	—	10	11	0·5
Batteries	—	—	—	3	12	0·1
TOTAL (above industries)	11,101	—	93·9	1,717	—	77·8
TOTAL (all insured workers)	11,947	33	100·0	2,204	6	100·0

It is not possible to calculate the proportion of Bedford's female population who are gainfully occupied, because we do not know how many of the employed women actually live in the town; quite a number of them travel daily from surrounding villages and small towns, and since Bedford has proportionately more females in every age group than Great Britain, the numbers at work are probably not exceptional. What is surprising in a town of medium size is the wide range of opportunities open to women.

It is natural, of course, to find a large number of jobs for women in an administrative, distributive and educational centre, but Table 3 shows that in Bedford these are supplemented by a large number of jobs in manufacturing industry as well. The latter accounts for nearly a quarter of all employed females, and of the twenty-four industries each employing more than 100 women, nine are factory trades. It is clear that no one industry dominates the field of female employment. The biggest single employer of women—retail distribution of non-food goods—has less than ten per cent of all insured women. Distribution as a whole employs 1,779 women, but this is only fifteen per cent of the total.

The biggest factory trade in Table 3 is the manufacture of chocolates and sweets, which was also one of the first female employing industries to arrive in the town; it was established in 1912 to draw on the pool of female labour resulting from the development of the engineering industry. Three-quarters of its employees are women. It has been followed by electric lamp manufacture, and branches of the rubber and clothing industries, in all of which women are more than two-thirds of all employees. Table 3 shows a number of smaller industries which rely largely on female labour and, though each employing only a small number, help to add to the variety of opportunities in the district. Meanwhile, the engineering industries themselves have taken on more and more women. The proportion rose from twelve to seventeen per cent between 1929 and 1948, and engineering now has about 1,000 women, over eight per cent of the total.

With so many industries competing for women workers, there is a severe shortage in Bedford. One means of overcoming this is by operating four-hour shifts. It has not been possible to find out the number of part-time workers among the female insured population, but it is known that there are a large number in a variety of occupations. Every firm tries to avoid having part-time employees; nevertheless, the extra cost of doing so must be borne if factories are to be kept fully manned. There is evidence that a majority of part-time workers are drawn from the immediate vicinity of the place where they work. Planning proposals can, therefore, further the use of this valuable labour reserve by siting predominantly female employing industries on the edge of residential districts, as well as by setting aside land for the building of day nurseries and nursery schools. Factories to employ women should be steered to the new industrial sites at Goldington and Chantry Avenue, Kempston, and nurseries should be built at an early stage in the development of the new estates. Although there are at present nearly 400 vacancies for women in the Bedford exchange area, there is likely to be a case for the expansion of female employment during the next twenty years to give jobs to the families of workers at the National Aeronautical Establishment, which will employ mainly men. The biggest manufacturer of underclothing in Bedford has plans for building a new factory to employ about three times his present numbers, and this appears to be a suitable firm to absorb any surplus female labour which may arise.

Table 3 also shows that there is a wide range of opportunities for young people in the industries of the district. At the same time there is no industry which places undue reliance on the employment of juveniles giving rise to the danger of 'blind alley' jobs. The highest proportions of young people—slightly more than a quarter—are found in clothing and crayon manufacture, and these are mainly girls. The Youth Employment Officer has stated that there is little difficulty in finding openings for school-leavers with various aptitudes and preferences. A number of the larger firms in Bedford are noted for their training and educational schemes.

BASIC AND RESIDENTIARY INDUSTRIES There is another way of analysing the employment statistics. We may make a useful distinction between those trades and occupations which directly satisfy the needs of the local population, and those which 'export' their products to other districts. Professor Sargant Florence has called the former 'residentiary' industries,[2] since their local and regional distribution tends to be proportional to that of the total population. They stand in sharp contrast to 'basic' industries which are the foundation of a district's economic life because they pay for the 'imports' which it cannot produce for itself. The distinction is not clear cut, and different sections of the same industry may be both basic and residentiary. In Bedford, for instance, the principal basic industry is engineering, but some of the small engineering workshops are engaged exclusively on service work for the local population, and are, therefore, residentiary. Most residentiary industries are, of course, service trades in the strict sense; they do not make goods. But there are important exceptions such as bakeries, sawmills, corn mills and so on, whose market is confined to the town and its immediate sphere of influence. Tables 4 and 5 show Bedford's basic and residentiary industries respectively, and give the most complete picture possible from official statistics of the industrial structure of the town. A large number of separate industries are represented, some of them by only one or two firms.

Map 11 (p. 84), shows the principal areas of land occupied by 'factory' industries. The engineering and electrical group has been distinguished by a separate colour since it is of such dominant importance in the local economy. The remainder have been divided into basic and residentiary. The vertical bars ('candlesticks') show the approximate size of each enterprise in terms of numbers employed. Note that there is a very great variety in the size of firms as well as in their processes and products.

MANUFACTURING IN BEDFORD We have already mentioned two reasons why the stranger does not associate Bedford with manufacturing industry; there is a third. The town is not a recognized centre for any particular trade (its only 'traditional' industry—lace making—has practically died out), nor does it form part of any of the great industrial complexes like the Black Country. Bedford's manufacturers do not in general use local raw materials or sell their products in a local market. Although about two-thirds of the factory workers are in the engineering and electrical group, Bedford does not concentrate on any distinct branch, and there is very little 'linkage' between the different works. It is a town of independent, specialized firms with world-wide trade connections.

There are, of course, a number of old-established businesses of the sort one expects to find in a thriving market town—several corn millers and manufacturers of fertilizers and canvas goods—but together they account for but a small proportion of industrial employment. It is true that Bedford's first large-scale manufacturing industry, the Britannia Works, resulted largely from the town's function as an agricultural centre. But, although ploughs and other implements are still made in Kempston by an offshoot of Howard's original enterprise, the liquidation of the latter in the early 'thirties seems to symbolize the present lack of connection between the products of Bedford's industries and the town's immediate hinterland.

The development of manufacturing as a principal function has been described in Chapter 2. The example of Allens' in moving out of London to this convenient country town was followed during the next fifty years by such firms as Meltis, Hairlok, British Mica and Weaver's. Others, like Igranic, Robertson's and Sterling were founded either by Bedfordians or by engineers who had worked in the town, and who knew of its excellent communications and suitable sites. These were the two factors mainly responsible for the rapid industrial expansion, but there were also other advantages—relatively low costs and good living conditions, cheap education for the sons and daughters of employers and white collar workers, and a pool of surplus labour in the surrounding countryside. All but the last of these factors still operate today; Bedford's industrial expansion has been continuous and has not yet come to an end. The sites chosen by the long succession of industrialists who have established works in the town have had an immense influence on the present pattern of land use.

Table 4: BASIC INDUSTRIES

BASIC INDUSTRIES[1] (arranged in descending order of location quotients[2])		1—Location Quotient[2] 2—Number of insured workers 1948 3—% all insured workers 4—Number of firms with more than 20 workers			
		1	**2**	**3**	**4**
CT	Marine Engineering	16·2	2,283	6·3	1
MA	Bricks	14·5	1,986	5·5	3
GKL	Electric lamps	8·9	596	1·6	1
XE	Chocolates and sweets	6·2	656	1·8	1
TK	Stationers' goods (crayons)	6·0	104	0·3	1
CN	Electrical engineering	4·3	1,280	3·5	2
CE	Ironfounding	3·8	717	2·0	1
CDL	Locomotives	3·2	154	0·4	1
ZTA	Agriculture	2·3	3,593	9·9	—
CDX	General Engineering	1·4	1,679	4·6	8
SP	Sand and gravel pits	1·3	44	0·1	—
HE	Toys and games	1·0	48	0·1	1
WS	Other dress industries (corsets)	1·0	39	0·1	1
KA	Rubber	0·8	159	0·4	1
FBP	Pharmaceutical preparations	0·8	42	0·1	1
KBL	Leather	0·8	63	0·2	1
GKB	Batteries	0·7	24	0·1	1
VXM	Canvas goods and sacks	0·7	24	0·1	1
WB	Dressmaking	0·7	127	0·4	1
WH	Underwear	0·7	74	0·2	2
ZTB	Forestry	0·6	22	0·1	—
TBC	Cardboard Boxes	0·6	37	0·1	1
FBC	Heavy chemicals[4]	0·6	204	0·6	1
EBF	Furniture and woodworking	0·5	137	0·4	2
WA	Tailoring	0·5	246	0·7	1
GWZ	Miscellaneous metal goods	0·4	160	0·4	2
WXM	Boot and shoe manufacture	0·3	85	0·2	1
MF	Non-metalliferous mining manufactures (mica)	0·2	30	0·1	1
GKZ	Miscellaneous electrical goods	0·2	49	0·1	—
DAM	Motor manufacture	0·1	63	0·2	1
	TOTAL	—	14,839	41·0	40

Source: Ministry of Labour

NOTES TO TABLES 4 AND 5

1 The distinction between basic and residentiary industries is described on page 87, but it is not clear cut. Some industries (e.g. engineering and printing) have sections falling into both groups. Considerable research would be necessary to distinguish them, however. In these tables each industry has been allocated to that group in which the greater part of it would fall.

2 THE LOCATION QUOTIENT (also known as the Location Coefficient or Location Factor) is a convenient method of measuring the extent to which a district specializes in particular industries. It is obtained by dividing the percentage of the occupied population of the district engaged in any one industry by the percentage of the total occupied population of Great Britain engaged in that industry. A quotient of 1·0 shows that the locality has exactly the same proportion of its workers in the particular industry as the country as a whole. A quotient of more than 1·0 for an industry therefore indicates a degree of specialization by the district in that industry.

The location quotients for the basic industries (column 1 of Table 4) range from 16·2 to 0·1, showing that there are some industries in which Bedford contributes a significant proportion of the total national output, and others in which the local contribution, though important in the town, is of little national account. The local importance of a particular industry is measured not by its location quotient but by its percentage of the total occupied population in the district (column 3).

The location quotients for the residentiary industries (column 3 of Table 5) range only from 0·3 to 2·2. Most of them are near to 1·0—i.e. the local and national proportions are similar, showing that Bedford is a centre for the provision of many local services. There is no rigid relationship between the numbers employed in an industry and the quality of service provided or the size of area served; nevertheless, the variations in the location quotients for the residentiary industries show that Bedford is a more important centre for some services than others. A full analysis of these variations and a comparison with other towns would be interesting and useful, but there was unfortunately neither the time nor the resources to carry it out.

3 Water is supplied by the Corporation and the employees of the undertaking are therefore included in ZK.

4 Including the hydrogen plant at Cardington R.A.F. Station as well as the fertilizer factory.

Table 5: RESIDENTIARY INDUSTRIES[1]

GROUP AND INDUSTRY		1—Number of insured workers 1948 2—% all insured workers 3—Location Quotient[2]			GROUP AND INDUSTRY		1—Number of insured workers 1948 2—% all insured workers 3—Location Quotient[2]		
		1	2	3			1	2	3
Manufacturing						ZEM	Industrial materials and machinery	70	0·2	0·4
DAR	Garages	402	1·1	1·1		ZEF	Wholesale food	64	0·2	0·3
WXR	Boot repair	92	0·25	1·25		ZEG	Retail food	967	2·7	0·8
XD	Grain milling	132	0·4	2·0		ZEN	Wholesale non-food	269	0·7	0·6
XAL	Baking	241	0·7	0·8		ZEP	Retail non-food	2,061	5·7	1·5
XHC	Milk products	20	0·1	0·5		ZET	Sweets, tobacco, newspapers	123	0·3	1·0
XKB	Brewing	179	0·5	1·25	*Business*				
XKZ	Soft drinks	18	0·1	0·5		PH	Insurance, banking, finance	522	1·4	0·7
EA	Timber	241	0·7	1·75					
TEN/ TEZ	Printing and publishing	450	1·2	0·8	*Administration*				
						ZH	National government	1,775	4·9	1·4
Building and Contracting						ZK	Local government	2,904	8·0	2·2
AB	Building	1,620	4·5	0·8					
AP	Electrical contracting	94	0·3	1·0	*Professions*				
AC	Civil engineering	173	0·5	0·6		ZMA	Accountancy	60	0·2	0·7
						ZME	Education	1,443	4·0	1·7
Public Utilities						ZML	Law	113	0·3	1·0
ZAG	Gas	215	0·6	1·0		ZMD	Medicine and dentistry	574	1·6	0·8
ZAE	Electricity	362	1·0	1·4		ZMR	Religion	26	0·1	1·0
ZAW	Water[3]	—	—	—		ZMZ	Other professions	82	0·2	0·3
Transport and Communications					*Miscellaneous*				
RE	Railways	866	2·4	0·9		ZPA	Entertainment	117	0·3	0·4
RH	Buses	575	1·6	1·1	ZPB/				
RMF	Taxis and private hire	56	0·15	1·0	C/E		Sport and betting	47	0·1	0·2
RMG	Road haulage	367	1·0	1·1		NS	Catering and hotels	1,056	2·9	0·8
RXP	Post office	593	1·6	1·1		NXL	Laundries	288	0·8	1·1
RXS	Storage	32	0·1	1·3		NXO	Cleaning and dyeing	117	0·3	1·5
						ZSH	Hairdressing	177	0·5	1·7
Distribution						PDR	Resident domestic service	425	1·2	1·2
ZEC	Coal, builders' materials and agricultural supplies	312	0·9	1·3		PDN	Non-resident domestic service	742	2·0	1·3
						ZSX	Other services	113	0·3	0·4
					TOTAL		21,175	58·6	—

Source: Ministry of Labour

THE SITING OF INDUSTRY Most of Bedford's major works lie alongside the railway lines but, with one or two important exceptions, few of them have private sidings. The main reason for their location seems to have been the availability of large areas of flat land; being less attractive for residential development, railside sites may have been cheaper than sites elsewhere. At the same time, it is possible that when the earlier factories were built the rapid development of road transport was not foreseen, and firms expected to make more use of the railways than they have in fact done. One of the sawmills, for instance, moved to a railside site soon after the first World War, with the intention of building a siding; they found that it was cheaper to buy a fleet of lorries. But in other cases—the printing works in Poets' Corner, for example, which is several feet above the level of the main line—the presence of the railway was obviously not a factor in location. One of the biggest firms in Bedford has railway tracks on two sides of its factory, yet all goods enter and leave the works by road. Whether having sidings or not, however, it is a good thing for the town that industry should be sited beside the railways, insulating the latter from residential areas, and ensuring that in many cases only one side of a factory is adjacent to houses. We recommend that most of the undeveloped land alongside the railways should be reserved for industry, and nearly all the proposed industrial sites are in this position. Curiously enough, there are at least two firms in the town (the fertilizer works and one making trailers) which would like their own sidings but are at present without rail access; both will probably move to new premises during the next twenty years, and should have first preference in the allocation of sites where sidings can be provided.

Most firms took advantage of the wealth of land on the outskirts of the town and acquired large sites. They built spaciously, and as a result working conditions are in many cases above the average. Several firms have playing fields adjacent to the works. In most cases they have also been able to expand on their original sites, or to acquire additional sites nearby. An exception to this is Allens', whose second factory (the Biddenham Works) is unfortunately sited in what will soon become the very centre of a housing estate. Some firms own patches of undeveloped land alongside their works; such land is often neglected and untidy, and while it is right that these spaces should be reserved for future expansion, they should in the meantime be laid out as playing fields or cultivated as allotments. There are one or two good examples which might be generally followed. Tree planting is needed around some of the town's factories as well as along many of its roadsides, not only to hide industrial scars from such amenities as the river walks, but also to make the factories themselves more attractive places to work in.

Nearly all the available land was in the south-west quadrant bounded on the north by the river and on the east by London Road, and the factories were built beside the three railway lines and four main roads which traverse this area. The location of the main industrial zone in the south-west has not given rise to any smoke nuisance because most of the works use electric power; the absence of factory chimneys distinguishes Bedford from many an older industrial town. The position of the industrial zone has given rise to one major problem, however; despite considerable residential development on the south during the last fifty years, many workers still live north of the river and will continue to do so. The road pattern has not yet been altered to accord with the new shape of the town; no two points in Bedford are very far apart as the crow flies, but journeys to work are in many cases much longer than they need be in a town of this size. The proposed cross-town roads and cycle tracks, described in Chapter 3—the 'spider's web' bridging the river and railway barriers—would be a great boon to Bedford's industrial workers.

Convenience of travel between home and workplace is one of the objects of planning, but it must as far as possible be combined with a wide choice of jobs within easy reach of everybody. In a medium-sized town these two objects are best achieved by concentrating industry in one zone and improving cross-town communications rather than by attempting to introduce factories into every neighbourhood. Most of the proposed new industrial sites form logical extensions of the existing main industrial zone.

PROSPECTS AND PROPOSALS The Bedford district has been one of the most prosperous in the country since the end of the war. There have been consistently more than five times as many vacant jobs as unemployed workers, and there is no evidence of the possible contraction of any of the major industries. There are at present about 750 vacancies for men and an equal number for women and young people. These do not provide a measure of the total additional requirements of existing firms during the next twenty years. Some, even among the larger ones, expect to double their employment; others protest that it is impossible to make any reliable estimate of future numbers. In the absence of a national economic plan the second view must be considered more realistic, and we accept the fact that no accurate estimate can be made. We can be certain, however, that if a high level of productive activity is generally maintained in the country, Bedford's employment will continue to grow. In estimating the minimum population to be expected in 1971 (Chapter 2), we have assumed that 1,500 more men, i.e. twice the present number of vacancies, will be employed by existing industries, though the total might well be larger. Female and juvenile workers have been ignored in making this calculation, since they must mainly be drawn from the families of adult male immigrants.

Most firms can expand on their present sites but a few wish to build entirely new premises on larger sites, some require new sites for extensions, and others will be moved during the comprehensive redevelopment of parts of the central area. It is estimated that existing firms will require about forty acres during the next twenty years. If the more optimistic forecasts of increased employment are realized, this total might be higher. It has, therefore, been necessary to consider carefully how much land in the area could be made available for industry.

Despite the difficulty some firms have encountered in finding suitable sites, there are about 115½ acres of undeveloped land that would be better devoted to industrial development than any other use. This total includes ten sites which are described below; there is also the site of the new power station and one of the clearance areas in the town centre which is suggested for industry. The twelve sites are numbered on Map 11.

1. *Chantry Avenue, Kempston.* This is the largest single site, comprising forty-seven acres alongside the main line and the Bletchley branch. It is not central in relation to the urban area as a whole, but is well placed to attract workers from Kempston, where the population may increase to almost twice the present numbers.

2. *Spring Road.* Two sites of nine acres in all between Springfield House and the railway.

3. *Western Relief Road.* Two sites of sixteen acres in all adjacent to the main railway line and the proposed new trunk road. Two acres at the Kempston Road end may be needed for a new fire station.

4. *Mile Road.* An extension of the main industrial zone along the Hitchin railway, eighteen acres already owned by the Corporation and earmarked for development as a trading estate.

5. *Newton Road.* A railside site of one and a half acres in the main industrial zone, suitable for a small factory.

6. *Willmer's Field, London Road.* A site of five acres already allocated to the sawmills moving from St Mary's to make way for the College of Further Education.

7. *Ampthill Road.* Another small site (three and a half acres) opposite Elstow Road, Kempston, in an area already mainly industrial.

8. *Fenlake Road.* Two and a half acres of land beside the Cambridge railway.

9. *Goldington* (Twelve acres). A site that should be used mainly for female-employing industries to draw on the large population who would live in the adjacent new neighbourhood.

10. *St John's—Central Relief Road.* A site of three acres suitable for a flatted factory and warehouse to accommodate small firms moved during the comprehensive redevelopment of the central area (Chapter 4).

11. *Pilcroft Street—Central Relief Road* (Five acres). An area of blighted housing to be cleared during the next twenty years, which should be reserved for small businesses which need to be near the centre of the town, but which are not suitable for a multi-storey building. It is sug-

gested that about two acres of this site be used for the new agricultural markets, abattoir and associated car park.

12. *Barker's Lane.* The construction of a new power station on this eighty-acre site has already begun.

It appears that existing firms will require only about forty acres of the 112½ available, leaving aside the central redevelopment and flatted factory sites which have already been discussed in Chapter 4. There would remain some seventy acres which could be developed for new industry. This is roughly equal to the area at present occupied by the five largest firms in Bedford who together employ more than 5,000 workers. The average number of workers per acre is thus about seventy, which is the ratio used by the Board of Trade in planning new trading estates. Floor space per worker varies very widely between different firms, but the larger and more diverse the development the more likely it is to approach to the average of seventy. Since Bedford should attract light consumer goods industries, the number of workers per industrial acre would probably be high. The town is ideally placed to receive factories dispersed from central London under the Greater London Plan, and these should be encouraged to take up any industrial sites not needed by existing firms.

But even if this policy were adopted by the Government it is unlikely that the whole of the land considered suitable for industry would be taken up. The limiting factor is the extra population that can be housed in the area. 5,000 more workers in the town would mean an additional population of between 12,000 and 15,000, over and above the increase due to the National Aeronautical Establishment and the immediate needs of existing industries. This would bring the total population up to nearly 90,000. It was suggested in Chapter 2, that Bedford's population should not grow beyond about 80,000, so not more than one half to three quarters of the land proposed for industry is likely to be needed. On the other hand, the space per worker may increase substantially as a result of improvements in technique over the next twenty years, and existing firms may well need room for physical expansion even if their employment does not greatly increase. It would be wise to maintain this reserve of suitable sites in the main factory zone so as to avoid any possibility of future industrial sprawl.

Manufacturing industry is one of the foundations of the town's life, but its fortunes cannot be decided simply by suggestions for changing the use of land. The industrial proposals have been made as flexible as possible, so that Bedford may readily take up any part it is called upon to play in the process of implementing a national plan.

REFERENCES
[1] *Report of the Royal Commission on the Distribution of the Industrial Population* (H.M.S.O) 1940.
[2] "*English County*" and "*Conurbation*" (Surveys by the West Midland Group).

New municipal building   *St Paul's Square*

6

" Neighbourhood amenities cannot be planned simply by dividing a town into areas of equal population, but must take account of the physical and social characteristics of its different parts "

Neighbourhoods

We now turn from considering the town as a place to work in and consider it as a place to live in. In planning an area it is first of all necessary to provide for the efficiency of the main functions by which its people earn their livelihood, and then to provide for the improvement of the environment in which they spend their leisure. Both sorts of proposals should, of course, be carried out together. The proposals for new roads and industrial sites and for the redevelopment of the town centre are designed to secure the future of Bedford's main functions, so that the town may be able to support the additional amenities demanded by its citizens.

Some of the new amenities, like the proposed cultural and recreational centre on the south bank of the river, would draw people from all over town, and indeed from much of the surrounding countryside. They have already been described in Chapter 4. But many amenities, such as schools, shops, public houses, churches, allotments and playing fields, are distributed throughout the town, each group serving only the people living in a particular district. These are neighbourhood services, and in order to assess the adequacy of their present provision and make proposals for future additions it is necessary to divide the town into smaller areas and consider each of these separately. The neighbourhoods are the catchment areas for the various services provided outside the town centre; they are the immediate environment of people's homes.

There is no clear distinction between the various neighbourhoods of a town as there is between town and countryside. A medium-sized town, in particular, can be more easily seen as a social unit than any of its separate neighbourhoods. The truth of this would probably be recognized by most Bedfordians, whose loyalty is, and should be, to the town as a whole. Yet at the same time, the physical barriers of the river and the railways, and the social contrast between the different districts, have given rise to fairly well defined neighbourhood units. In dividing up the town for the purpose of survey, an attempt was made to group together streets with similar types of houses, whose residents tend to use the same shops and other local services, and the same routes to other parts of the town. These divisions necessarily had to be made before the surveys were carried out, but their correctness was in general confirmed by the survey findings, and in particular by the conclusions of the shopping survey—the most detailed investigation it was possible to carry out. Not all local services can be supported by the same size of population, so that one set of neighbourhood divisions is inadequate for this type of analysis. The town was, therefore, split into eight neighbourhoods with sixteen sub-divisions. Their boundaries are marked on Maps 1 (*p.* 21), 3 (*p.* 29), 12 (*p.* 101) and 14 (*p.* 110), which show the existing and proposed provision of the principal neighbourhood services. Map 12 also shows the boundaries of the municipal wards; it will be seen that there is little relation between wards and neighbourhoods, and that their boundaries only coincide when they follow rigid physical barriers. Nevertheless, the informal discussions we were privileged to have with the Aldermen and Councillors representing each of the Borough's seven wards, laid the basis for the subsequent detailed investigation of each neighbourhood.

The populations of the eight neighbourhoods range from 1,750 to 17,000, but all except two have between 5,000 and 9,000 people. The exceptions are Goldington—the old village and a few modern streets nearby—which was considered as a separate neighbourhood because of the considerable new developments proposed there; and Cauldwell-Kingsbrook—comprising most of Bedford south of the river—which had to be treated as a unit for certain purposes, though it also has four clearly defined sub-divisions. Queen's Park and Goldington were not sub-divided, and of the sixteen sub-divisions of the other neighbourhoods twelve have between 2,000 and 5,000 people. Three are smaller—Austin Canons, the group of isolated streets on the Bedford-Kempston boundary; Wendover Drive; and Harrowden Road—and one is larger—London Road. If the future populations envisaged in our proposals were achieved, three more neighbourhoods—Black Tom-de Pary's, Goldington, and Kempston—would have more than 10,000 people, but the remainder would be more or less unchanged. There would be even greater variation between the sub-divisions than there is today. This variation emphasizes the fact that neighbourhood amenities cannot be planned simply by dividing a town into areas of equal population, but must take account of the physical and social characteristics of its different parts. For this reason it is probable that the municipal wards, which must be roughly equal in size, can never correspond exactly with the neighbourhoods; but when the wards are re-shaped as a result of the growth of the town, the opportunity should be taken to bring the two units more into line.

The main proposals for neighbourhood development have already been summarized in Chapter 1, where the principles governing the planning of amenities in outer districts were discussed. The remainder of this chapter is devoted first to a more detailed description of some of the neighbourhood surveys and their main conclusions, and then to a discussion of the character and problems of each of the seven outer neighbourhoods and their sub-divisions, and the improvements proposed during the next twenty years. Neighbourhood 8—the town centre—has already been fully dealt with in Chapter 4. It has not been possible to quote all the relevant facts and figures in the text and frequent reference should be made to the maps, and to the Tables which are to be found on pages 134–5.

EXISTING HOUSING Housing is the basis of the neighbourhoods, and the housing survey was designed to find out as much as possible about the state of existing dwellings in the town. This could not be done on a house-to-house basis, so the whole area was divided into 'street-units', within which housing conditions were as homogeneous as possible. Large and complicated streets were split into smaller units. For each street-unit the following information was collected:

(i) number of dwellings;
(ii) their age, type and condition;
(iii) number of habitable rooms;
(iv) number of persons aged 0–4, 5–18, and 19 and over;
(v) area of street-unit.

Accommodation (rooms per acre) and population (persons per acre) densities were then worked out. Houses were classified into ten types, mainly according to their means of access and size of garden, e.g. terraced houses with no secondary means of access and those with a common yard were regarded as two separate types; so were semi-detached houses with front gardens of more and less than ten feet in depth. Houses were also classified into five grades of condition, based upon the state of structure, sanitation, daylighting and damp-proofing. Houses in bad and poor condition could not be brought up to a reasonable standard even if much money were spent on them; those in fair condition might be improved by such measures as the addition of bathrooms, but should be demolished where the density is too great; those in good and very good condition are considered satisfactory. The assistance and advice of the Borough's Chief Sanitary Inspector (F. C. Haynes, Cert.R.San.I., M.S.I.A.) and his staff were sought and freely given in the course of the field survey. The information was mapped on the 1/1250th scale, and coded on survey cards for electrical tabulation. This was carried out by the Tabulating Research Centre (Director:

John P. Mandeville, A.M.I.Mech.E.), and the tables provide a permanent record of housing conditions in the district.

The primary object of the housing survey was to find out how many dwellings could be considered 'blighted', i.e. at or near the end of their economic life, or for some other reason requiring to be demolished. In order to determine priorities for clearance, and to make proposals capable of adjustment to national economic conditions, three degrees of blight were distinguished:

1. All dwellings in bad condition (i.e. ripe for demolition), and those in poor condition (i.e. approaching the last stages of decay) wherever the accommodation density is more than 120 rooms per acre.
2. The remaining dwellings in poor condition, and any others without secondary means of access.
3. Dwellings in fair condition, but built at a density of more than 120 rooms to the acre.

Street-units affected by the three degrees of blight are coloured yellow, blue and purple respectively on Map 10 (*p. 73*), and those areas which it is proposed to clear during the next twenty years are hatched in a black line. It will be seen that all dwellings in the first two degrees of blight are suggested for demolition, but only those in the third degree that lie in areas needed for new buildings as part of the comprehensive redevelopment of the town centre. Proposals for clearance cannot be based simply on the condition of housing, but must also take account of the other problems of the town. For this reason it is proposed to demolish the Pilcroft Street area, which should become part of the main central industrial zone, earlier than the Queen Street area, which will remain residential even after eventual redevelopment. The clearance and redevelopment of all areas of third degree blight should be undertaken as soon as the more urgent cases have been dealt with.

There are 463 dwellings with a population of 1,681 in areas of first degree blight; 478 dwellings with 1,602 people affected by the second degree of blight; and 1,184 dwellings with 3,470 people affected by the third degree. Of the last group it is proposed to demolish 359 houses with a population of 1,217. In all, 1,300 dwellings and 4,100 people would be affected by the proposals. About 2,350 people could be re-accommodated in cleared areas devoted to residential development, leaving a net 'overspill' of some 1,750 to be found homes elsewhere (*Table* 9).

NEW HOUSING SITES The principles governing the choice of new housing sites have been described in the section on Factors in Development in Chapter 2 (*p.* 47). The proposed sites are shown on Map 12 (*p.* 101), together with the residential density (persons per acre) at which it is suggested they should be developed. These densities take account of the condition of the site and of the existing provision of open spaces and other amenities in the vicinity. The population that could be accommodated on each site is shown in Table 9 (*p.* 134).

ALLOTMENTS The survey of allotments was carried out with the co-operation of Major A. E. Frost, B.E.M., the Borough Allotments Manager, but it covered privately held allotments as well as those owned by the Corporation, and, like all the other surveys, included Kempston as well as Bedford, in so far as this was possible without the assistance of the Urban District Council. The principal conclusions and the proposals based upon them have already been described in Chapter 1 (*p.* 26), and little need be added here. The existing allotments are scattered throughout the town, and in suggesting new allotments on the outskirts to replace those taken for other uses an attempt has been made to preserve a balanced distribution. Neighbourhood standards per head of population have not, however, been calculated. Allotments are neighbourhood amenities in the sense that they draw tenants from areas smaller than the whole town; but they do not need to be distributed so evenly in relation to the population as do shops and open spaces, because allotment holders are a small proportion of the population, because it is easier for men to travel to an allotment than for housewives to take small children to shops and playgrounds and because the journey has to be made less frequently. The suggestions that result from applying this principle are shown on Map 3 (*p.* 29) and Table 1 (*p.* 27).

SHOPS The survey of retail trade, covering the provision of shops throughout the town and the shopping habits of the population, was designed to test the adequacy of the existing facilities and to serve as a guide to the number and location of shops on new housing estates. The shops in each neighbourhood were analysed according to trade type, and an attempt was made to distinguish those which formed part of local shopping centres from those which could more properly be regarded as isolated. Map 14 (*p.* 110) shows the main shopping centre and its sub-centres, the neighbourhood centres and the isolated shops. Circles of radius one quarter of a mile have been drawn around each of the local shopping centres to give a rough idea of their accessibility from different parts of the neighbourhood. We were not able to find out the exact catchment areas of each group of shops, i.e. precisely where their customers came from, but the local Food Office gave us the number of sugar registrations for central and isolated shops in each neighbourhood, and it was assumed that most people do their daily and weekly shopping in the area where they buy their sugar.

The most striking fact shown by the survey was the immense variation in the proportion of people in different neighbourhoods who were registered at their local shops. This varies from less than five per cent in Goldington to 100 per cent in Queen's Park. The figure for each sub-division of the town is given in Table 6. In some cases the explanation of these figures was obvious. For instance, the present Goldington neighbourhood is very small and has only six shops. De Pary's and Rothsay Road, with bigger populations, have even fewer shops, but this is clearly due to their relatively wealthy residents and to proximity to the central area. In these two neighbourhoods shopping provision broadly corresponds to the need, and there is no demand for additional shops. In other cases, the variations raised interesting problems. Why, for instance, do less than half the people of the Elstow Road sub-division shop in their own district, whereas more than three-quarters of those in Southend and London Road shop in their's? The social character of all three areas is very similar, and they are about the same distance from the town centre. The contrast is not due to differences in the total number of shops in relation to the population, for while there is one shop to every hundred people in Southend there is only one to every three hundred in London Road, and the ratio for Elstow Road is 1:323. Nor is it due to the date of development of the neighbourhoods. It is true that Southend was built largely before 1920, and that this also applies to some other areas with a high proportion of home shoppers, like Queen's Park and Castle Road, but it does not apply to London Road, which belongs almost entirely to the inter-war period. So does Elstow Road, though it is actually the older of the two. The two factors which seem more than any others to determine the usage of local shops are the variety of trade types and the convenience of access to the centre from all parts of the neighbourhood. Thus, while London Road has a compact group of shops at the town end of the main road with eleven trade types represented in all, in Elstow Road most of the shops are isolated and there are only eight trade types. Southend's local centre in Ampthill Road is not quite as compact as that in London Road, but is much more so than Elstow Road, while it includes no less than twelve trade types.

Two planning conclusions have been drawn from this analysis:

(i) That there is a need for a local shopping centre in Elstow Road (below, *p.* 109).

(ii) That shopping provision in the new neighbourhoods should be based broadly on that of London Road, which illustrates the trend towards larger shops, the need for a compact centre close to the main line of communication, and the importance of the biggest possible variety of trade types in one group.

This is not to say that existing retail trade provision in the London Road area is adequate. The shops are too far from the geographical centre, and there are very few isolated shops. The survey has shown the importance of isolated general stores—as distinct from other isolated shops—even in neighbourhoods with well developed shopping centres. In Castle Road and Queen's Park, for instance, between twenty-five and thirty per cent of the total sugar registrations are at isolated shops. There is no doubt that the corner shop plays an important part in the

Table 6: NEIGHBOURHOOD SHOPPING FACILITIES AND HABITS

NEIGHBOURHOOD	NUMBER OF SHOPS		PERSONS PER SHOP	NUMBER OF GROCERS		REGISTRATIONS PER GROCER		% OF POPULATION REGISTERED IN THEIR OWN NEIGHBOURHOOD			NUMBER OF TRADE TYPES
	Centres	Isolated		Centres	Isolated	Centres	Isolated	Centres	Isolated	Total	
	1	2	3	4	5	6	7	8	9	10	11
1—QUEEN'S PARK { Ford End Road	38	25	74	8	8	264	163	40·8	25·1	106·5[1]	13
Iddesleigh Road	15			3		700		40·6			9
2—BROMHAM ROAD	64	25	69	3	6	730	122	35·6	11·9	47·5	19
3a—BLACK TOM	7	62	71	5	15	234	184	24·3	56·0	80·3	15
3b—DE PARY'S	—	2	1,942	—	2	—	619	—	31·9	31·9	1
4—GOLDINGTON	—	6	290	—	1	—	75	—	4·3	4·3	3
5a—ROTHSAY ROAD	—	1	2,119	—	1	—	818	—	38·6	38·6	1
5b—CASTLE ROAD	30	27	77	4	10	854	217	63·4	31·7	95·1	15
5c—WENDOVER DRIVE	5	—	261	1	—	1,200	—	91·9	—	91·9[2]	5
6a—SOUTHEND	23	16	101	7	5	286	206	51·0	26·3	77·3	12
6b—ELSTOW ROAD	10	4	323	2	6	270	264	11·9	35·0	46·9	9
6c—LONDON ROAD	17	6	306	8	3	640	113	72·8	4·8	77·6	11
6d—HARROWDEN ROAD	—	9	166	—	2	—	183	—	24·5	24·5	7
7a—OLD KEMPSTON	29	12	83	3	2	343	197	30·2	11·6	41·8	16
7b—NEWTOWN	31	20	78	5	7	430	424	63·0	87·0	150·0[3]	16
7c—AUSTIN CANONS	—	7	91	—	1	—	118	—	—	18·5	4

Table 7: SHOPS IN THE TOWN CENTRE AND THE OUTER NEIGHBOURHOODS

	DISTRIBUTION OF SHOPS								REGISTRATIONS AS % OF POPULATION
	FOOD		OTHER GOODS		SERVICES		TOTAL		
	No.	%	No.	%	No.	%	No.	%	
Town Centre	119	33·1	261	66·1	98	47·4	478	49·9	449·0[4]
Outer Neighbourhoods	241	66·9	134	33·9	109	52·6	484	50·1	67·6
TOTAL	360	100·0	395	100·0	207	100·0	962	100·0	104·8[4]

[1] Includes some people from Neighbourhood 2.
[2] Includes some people from Neighbourhood 4.
[3] Includes some people from Neighbourhoods 6a and 6c.
[4] Includes 3,000 people from outside Bedford and Kempston who are registered in the town centre.

Sources: Local Food Office and Field Survey.

social life of the neighbourhood, and its omission from recent housing estates is one of their more serious defects. A third conclusion drawn from the shopping survey is that isolated shops or small strictly local centres should be provided within a quarter of a mile of every house that is built during the next twenty years, and, wherever possible, in existing areas where the need has been overlooked.

While there are too few shops in the newer neighbourhoods, there are too many in the older ones. No provision for retail trade was made when they were built, so most of the shops are converted houses and do not form coherent groups. In Queen's Park, for instance, there are two distinct and independent shopping centres, although the neighbourhood would be better served by one centre with fewer, larger shops forming a compact and continuous group. The case of Black Tom is even worse, for only one very small centre has emerged at all, and there are no less than sixty-one isolated shops. The trend towards larger shops will inevitably affect these old neighbourhoods as well as the new ones, but new centres cannot be provided during the next twenty years because their construction would involve the demolition of houses which have not yet reached the end of their economic life. Kempston, with a very similar need, is in a rather more fortunate position, and a new centre could be built (p. 111). The ultimate goal of concentrating shopping facilities at convenient points in Queen's Park and Black Tom as well should be kept in mind, so that expensive piecemeal alterations of existing shops can be avoided. This is the fourth and last conclusion from the shopping survey.

PUBLIC HOUSES After shops, the most common social buildings in the neighbourhoods are public houses. It is said that fifteen per cent of the total population of most towns are to be found there on a Saturday night, and they are, therefore, most important community buildings. The survey of licensed premises was carried out by Messrs J. W. Hammond, Chartered Architects and Surveyors, of Romford, who are consultants to the Bedfordshire Brewers' Association. The proposals, described in Chapter 1 (p. 32) and in the neighbourhood sections below, broadly follow the recommendations made in their report. The existing and proposed provision is shown on Map 1 (p. 21).

There are 109 public houses in Bedford and Kempston—one to every 550 people. This is a much greater provision than in many towns of this size, but is not exceptional in an established market town. More than half the licences are in the town centre, and many of the houses are very small by modern standards. In the outer neighbourhoods there is one for every 1,000 people, but there are considerable variations in the standard of provision between different neighbourhoods. Proposals for the new residential areas are based on one licence to between 1,500 and 2,500 people according to the character of development. Most of the new public houses would be small and medium-sized rather than large, and could preserve the intimate character that is a feature of some of the best existing houses in the town. At the same time, hotels to serve the whole town are suggested at Honey Hill, Newnham Avenue, and Putnoe Farm.

Fifteen new sites are proposed in all. There would be a reduction of about the same number as a result of the proposed clearance of parts of the town centre, and it is likely that a number of additional licences in the central area would eventually be surrendered. The future Bedford can expect to have fewer and better licensed houses, with only about a quarter rather than a half of them in the town centre.

CLUBS AND SOCIETIES Voluntary organizations play an important part in the social life of any town and they are much in evidence in Bedford. In order to make every allowance for their requirements questionnaires were sent to 184 organizations. 121 replies were received, of which fifteen stated that the questions did not apply to their society.

The main conclusion, confirmed by other investigations in the town, was that there is a need for more and better meeting places, both in the central and in the outer areas. These needs would be met by the proposed community centres listed in Chapter 1, and by the proposed central Assembly Hall described in Chapter 4. A site has also been suggested for the Youth Centre that was requested in a number of the replies.

QUEEN'S PARK Neighbourhood 1 is the most clearly defined in the town, but does not include the whole of the Queen's Park Ward. The streets north of Winifred Road have a different social character from the rest of the ward, and are oriented about Bromham Road. They have, therefore, been included in Neighbourhood 2.

Queen's Park owes its development to the establishment of Allens' Works opposite the main railway station in 1894 (photograph on *p.* 14). Within six years new streets extended as far west as the Bell Inn, whose name may recall the famous bell—still to be seen at the gate of the Queen's Works—which was installed because the residents of Bedford objected to a common hooter.

Queen's Park was Bedford's first industrial suburb, and was made all the more distinctive by its isolation beyond the railway; it is said that for many years the new district was known in the town as 'Devil's Island'. The neighbourhood is no longer exclusively linked with Allens', which has become Bedford's biggest factory and draws workers from all over the town, while the people of Queen's Park journey to jobs in every area. Yet it remains as isolated as ever; the long, narrow Ford End Bridge, with its dangerous approaches, is still the only outlet to the shopping centre and to most other parts of the town. The improvement of communications is Queen's Park's most urgent need; it would be met by the construction of the Western Relief Road and the two cycle tracks and bridges to Kempston. The Corporation are already going ahead with the first cycle bridge, agreed after considerable pressure from residents in the ward. Allens' bridge should also be improved by the addition of cantilevered footpaths on both sides, and by the construction of a roundabout at the Midland Road end (Chapter 3).

Most of Queen's Park was built before 1918, but there were later additions north and west of Honey Hill Road. Its residential density of fifty persons per acre is exceeded only in the central area and Black Tom. The earliest development is uniformly dull in appearance—late Victorian bye-law streets, with large bay windows but very small gardens. The first tree planting has only recently been carried out and much more should be done. Honey Hill Road, for instance, is at present one of the most monotonously oppressive in the town, but a few trees would do much to make up for the lack of imagination of its builders. Few of the houses have fixed baths, but all are structurally sound and cannot yet be considered blighted. The further expansion of Queen's Park to the west is limited by the need to preserve the pleasant field walks between Bedford and Biddenham, and there should be no building west and north of Allen Park. The suggested sites on its east and south sides could accommodate another 1,500 persons, bringing the future population of the neighbourhood to about 6,250.

These people will continue to form one of Bedford's most self-contained communities, needing not only improved communications with the rest of the town, but also better amenities within their own neighbourhood. The present recreation ground and river walk provide only two acres of open space per thousand people, one of the lowest standards in the town. It would be increased to 3·2 per thousand for the future population by the extension of the river walk; the development of Cox's Pits; and the provision of a small park west of the new Secondary Modern School in the green wedge between Queen's Park and Biddenham. The standard would still be one of the lowest in the town; but it would be above the recognized minimum of three acres per thousand. The neighbourhood has access to pleasant open country, and a delightful rural riverside. In the Lido at Honey Hill it also possesses an important potential amenity. Suggestions for the further development of this great asset are made in Chapter 7.

At present the only sports fields in the neighbourhood are the twenty acres of Allens' Recreation Ground. It is proposed to provide 1·9 acres per thousand people at Cox's Pits and in the green wedge south of Biddenham Turn. This is a low standard, but if Allen Park is included it rises to six acres per thousand. It is understood that Allens' field is not used exclusively by the firm's own employees so the proposed overall provision can be considered adequate.

The area has sixty-two acres of allotments. Those behind the gas works would remain undisturbed, but the six acres at Cox's Pits are suggested for adults' sports fields, and the nineteen acres at Winifred

Road for a new Secondary Modern School and Roman Catholic Primary School. Thirty-two acres of new allotments could be developed at Honey Hill. The school would be centrally placed in the neighbourhood alongside the Western Relief Road. Infants' schools should be provided on both sides of the new road, so that the younger children would not have to cross the stream of traffic (Map 3, *p.* 29).

The isolation of Queen's Park was emphasized by the shopping survey. It is the only neighbourhood where the shops have more sugar registrations than the total population, no doubt because some of the people north of Winifred Road shop in Queen's Park rather than in Bromham Road. Another interesting fact emerged: there are about the same number of registrations in Iddesleigh Road and Ford End Road, though one has twice as many grocers as the other. These two parallel streets are virtually independent centres, even though they are only two hundred yards apart. Most people tend to go to the nearest shops, although Ford End Road has a slightly higher status with more shops and a greater variety of trade types. Nearly all the shops are in converted houses, and some of them have had a precarious existence. As in most other local 'centres' in Bedford, the shops are not arranged in coherent groups. Queen's Park could support one large local shopping centre, but not more than one. The best site for it would be just east of the 'Bell' —the present bus terminus and the point where the Western Relief Road would cross Ford End Road. This would have better access than either of the existing shopping streets from most parts of the neighbourhood, including the proposed new extensions to the west. Such a centre should eventually be built, but it will not be possible to demolish the houses in the vicinity during the next twenty years.

A number of clubs and societies in Queen's Park have halls which are used by other organizations, but, if the community spirit that exists in the neighbourhood is to be fully expressed, there is a need for a meeting place independent of any particular group, but available to all. We propose that a community centre should be built on the site of the two small factories in Old Ford End Road. Neither of these businesses is suitable for a residential area, and both wish to build new premises on one of the industrial sites described in Chapter 5. The present welfare centre is inadequately housed in the Co-Partners' Hall, and a new one should be associated with the proposed community hall.

There are five public houses in the neighbourhood—one to every 1,000 people. This relatively high ratio is due to their small and intimate character, a feature which should be copied in new neighbourhoods. One additional licence is recommended at Honey Hill. It should be a large hotel near the river, serving the whole town as well as the proposed new housing in its immediate vicinity.

BROMHAM ROAD Neighbourhood 2 includes several rather scattered residential areas tributary to Bromham Road. The largest is Poets' Corner, the popular name for the roads running up to Clapham Road, and the neighbourhood also includes the northern end of Queen's Park and Biddenham Turn. Sub-division 2(b) consists of the streets east of the station, which look to Midland Road rather than Bromham Road. The neighbourhood is covered by parts of three wards: Harpur, Castle and Queen's Park.

It is a mainly middle-class area of large houses; apart from the fine Regency and early Victorian terraces in Bromham Road, nearly all are detached and semi-detached villas, nineteenth century on the east of the railway and inter-war on the west. In Poets' Corner many houses have now been converted into flats; a number are also used by students at the Physical Training and Froebel Colleges—both of which are in the neighbourhood—and by boarders at the Harpur Trust Schools. The playing fields of these establishments enhance the pleasant living conditions in a part of the neighbourhood where few improvements are needed.

Near the station are a number of boarding houses, and some of the older dwellings in the area are beginning to decay. The residential density of Sub-division 2(b) is seventy-five persons per acre, against only twenty-three per acre in Sub-division 2(a). The proposed demolition of seven houses in Ashburnham Road and their replacement by a block of multi-storey flats would begin the necessary process of re-

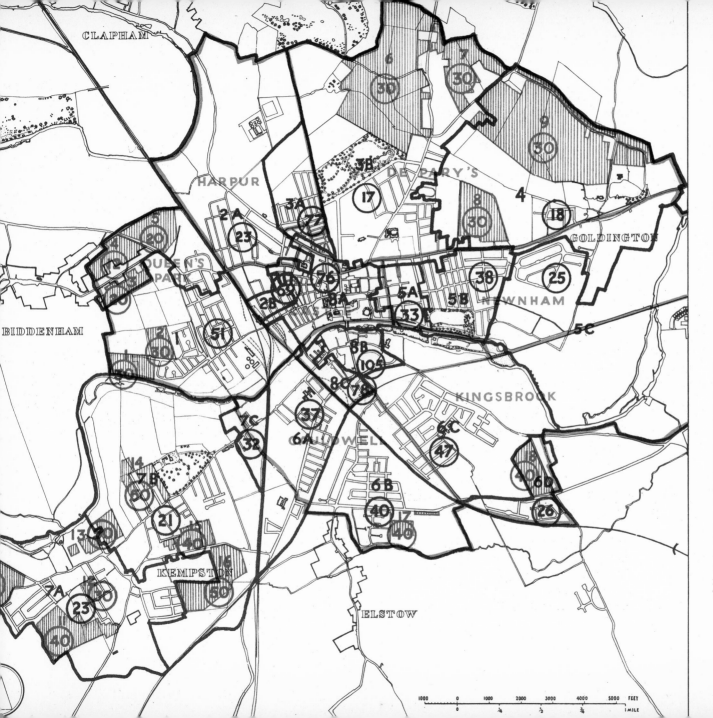

Map 12

HOUSING SITES AND RESIDENTIAL DENSITIES

Proposed housing sites

Ward boundaries

Neighbourhood boundaries

  Present neighbourhood densities (persons per acre)

  Proposed densities of new development (persons per acre)

Map 6 (page 48) shows the factors that were taken into account in selecting areas for future residential development, and this map shows the proposed housing sites that emerged from that study. Existing residential densities in each neighbourhood are given, together with those suggested for the new estates, bearing in mind the present and proposed provision of schools, open spaces and other amenities. The map also shows that there is very little correspondence between the existing ward boundaries and the neighbourhoods distinguished in the survey. The red numbers refer to the list of housing sites in Table 9, column 5, p. 134.

habilitation. There is a small area of blight in Tavistock Place, but half the displaced population could be re-accommodated on the site. Sites for further private development are available on either side of Bromham Road in Evan's Field, Biddenham Turn and Day's Lane. The first would involve the extinction of nine acres of allotments, but they are on heavy clay land that is not easily worked.

There is adequate open space on the edge of the neighbourhood, but a need for additional playing fields.

There are more people in this neighbourhood than in Queen's Park, but they do not form a coherent community, partly owing to the physical isolation of the various divisions, and partly owing to their social character. Slightly less than half the population are registered at the local shops in Bromham Road. These are in any case almost an extension of the town centre, where many people from the neighbourhood shop. Those in Sub-division 2(b) use Midland Road, which has been included in the town centre, and a few from the Queen's Park end shop in Iddesleigh Road. The only two public houses in the neighbourhood are both on the edge of the central area, but there does not appear to be a demand for any additional licensed premises. Nor is a neighbourhood community and welfare centre considered necessary.

BLACK TOM—DE PARY'S The grouping of these two districts as Neighbourhood 3 will no doubt shock many Bedfordians, for they present the greatest contrast in the town. Northwards from St Peter's Green at the top of the High Street run two parallel but unconnected streets—Foster Hill Road and de Pary's Avenue. The one gives access to an area of tightly packed terraces with no gardens or very small ones, and a density of seventy-seven people to the acre—the highest in the town; the other is one of a number of broad tree-lined avenues with large villas and spacious gardens, and a density of seventeen—the lowest in the town. In sub-division (a) there are no less than sixty-nine shops for less than 5,000 people; in sub-division (b) only four for nearly 4,000. The two have only one thing in common: they were both largely built during the second half of the nineteenth century. But the reason

for grouping them together is that they share the same major open space—Bedford Park. In all other respects the two sub-divisions have been separately considered.

Bedfordians are not agreed as to the exact limits of the area called after 'Black Tom' King. Some say that the name was first given to the huddle of little streets south of Park Road West, built before 1840. Others confine it to the later development of the 1890's reaching up to the slopes of Cemetery Hill—though it is said that this part was once known as Klondyke, because it was built at the same time and went up just as quickly. Some local people refer to the whole area as 'Black Tom', and in the absence of agreement, and for the sake of convenience, we have adopted this practice. Sub-division 3(a) is shared by Harpur and de Pary's Wards.

Nearly all the houses south of Park Road and west of Foster Hill Road fall into one of the three degrees of blight, but during the next twenty years it is only proposed to clear those in the first and second categories, where the structure is definitely outworn. These comprise eighty-nine houses in Chandos Street and Canning Street with 300 people. By building a group of multi-storey flats it would be possible to re-house 600 people on the site. No attempt should be made to reduce the residential density in Black Tom, which is close both to the central area and to the finest park in the town. The whole area south of Park Road should eventually be re-developed at a high density, making provision for small communal gardens and possibly tennis courts.

Despite the very large number of shops (the number of registrations per grocer is less than half the average for the town), one-fifth of the population shop outside the neighbourhood—probably in Tavistock Street, which, like Midland Road and Bromham Road, functions both as an extension of the town centre and as a local centre. There are no chemists in the whole of Black Tom, but there are two in Tavistock Street. Sixty-two of the sixty-nine shops are isolated, the only recognizable 'centre' being the group at the top of Queen Street. But by no means all the isolated shops are general stores; many of them can be regarded as forming frustrated centres which have never reached maturity because shops could only be provided in converted houses, and compact grouping was impossible. The neighbourhood could be adequately served by half the number of shops if most of them were concentrated in a convenient centre. The Queen Street group already forms the nucleus of such a centre; it should be enlarged when the whole area south of Park Road is eventually re-developed.

De Pary's sub-division has been the most select residential quarter of Bedford since the end of the nineteenth century, when it was built to house the families drawn into the town by the development of the Harpur Trust schools. The mellow spaciousness of the well-planted streets is enhanced by the presence of Bedford School, with its broad playing fields, as also of the Rugby Ground and Bedford Park. The latter is shared with Black Tom, and would also serve the proposed new estates in Kimbolton Road and Cave's Lane, but the Park would still provide 3·3 acres of open space for every thousand of the combined future population.

Despite the open development in de Pary's there is a serious lack of public playing fields in both sub-divisions of Neighbourhood 3. Bedford Park provides only 1·1 acres per 1,000 people. No fields can be found in the immediate vicinity of the existing built-up area, but sixty acres should be provided in the new community north of the Park and west of Kimbolton Road to serve the whole neighbourhood, giving a population standard of four acres per thousand (Map 3, *p.* 29).

Like Poets' Corner and Biddenham Turn, de Pary's has many people with cars and telephones who prefer to shop in the town centre. Although the two grocers in the sub-division have 1,200 customers, two-thirds of the population shop elsewhere.

There are three possible housing sites on the edges of the neighbourhood—Cave's Lane, Waterworks Hill and the area north of Putnoe Lane. The allotments in Cave's Lane form a natural extension of Bedford's present main private housing area, and could accommodate about 1,400 people. Even at the proposed density of thirty persons per acre a large part of the area could remain cultivated as private gardens, since no other buildings or open spaces are wanted on the site. A new

Secondary Modern School is proposed north of the Cave's Lane site to serve both de Pary's and the Newnham neighbourhood south of Goldington Road.

The eastern slope of Waterworks Hill, extending across to the western side of Kimbolton Road as far as the Borough boundary, is the finest housing site in Bedford, both in its attractive physical features and views over the Ouse valley, and in its proximity to the Park and the town centre. All sections of the community should have an opportunity of living here, and houses should, therefore, be built both by the Corporation and by private developers. This area and the Putnoe site on the eastern side of Kimbolton Road could together accommodate 7,400 people. Many of these would no doubt be workers at the National Aeronautical Establishment, who would find this the most convenient part of Bedford to settle in. The two sites should be developed as a self-contained residential unit, with a local shopping centre of fifteen to twenty shops, three public houses, a community and welfare centre, and two or three churches, and they might also include a small cinema such as is planned for Goldington, and their public playing fields would also serve the existing parts of Neighbourhood 3.

There is very little industry in either Black Tom or de Pary's but complaints have been directed against the smoke nuisance from the chimneys of the hospital and the laundry, and the noise and smell of one of the bakeries.

GOLDINGTON Neighbourhood 4 consists mainly of undeveloped land to the north of the picturesque village of Goldington at the eastern extremity of the Borough. The village has a population of about 1,750 people, and its chief feature is a large rectangular green bounded on three sides by fine trees and on the south by the main road to Cambridge. To the north are the Hall and eighteenth-century Bury, whose presence has safeguarded this typical Bedfordshire village against the tide of the town's eastward extension. Between the Green and Laxtons' Nurseries on the west some mediocre housing has sprung up, but fortunately much of this development is masked by the trees.

The proposed new neighbourhood shown on the folding map of Future Land Use lies north of the Green and behind the grounds of the two great houses which it is proposed should be put to use as public gardens and social centres. Nine-tenths of the site is west of Church Lane—the remaining twenty-three acres are to the east and north-east of the church. A population of 7,000 could be accommodated on these 233 acres, giving an overall density of thirty persons to the acre.

The site is a somewhat featureless expanse of arable and grazing land, extending as far north as the Borough boundary; it is rectangular in shape, a mile long from east to west and a quarter of a mile wide, with a handful of trees towards its southern boundary. There are gently undulating slopes and a long, shallow valley extending across the south. On the crown of the site in the north-west corner the landscape is relieved by the well-wooded garden and entrance drives of Putnoe Farm. Apart from three long, straight hedges that traverse the site from north to south and three small ponds, there are no other features of interest.

Inasmuch as the site is unrestricted by natural features, it offers freedom of approach in the field of architectural design; but the lack of interest in the site itself would need to be offset by interesting arrangements of dwellings and community buildings, and a skilful handling of planting and landscape. However, the whole neighbourhood is ideally orientated, with long, sunny slopes. The one restricting feature—the clay subsoil—would mean incurring the expense of specially constructed foundations; but the siting of houses economically along the length of the contours would help to avoid unnecessary digging.

As regards arrangement of buildings, the design aims at providing an interesting variety of house types, taking maximum advantage of the sun and the slight slopes. Because of the absence of woods and good hedgerows, careful attention has been given to the few interesting features that exist—the trees, ponds, natural terraces and hedges. The streets are laid out informally on a broad grid, but it is intended that each street should be designed as an entity in itself, obtaining a contrast between open and enclosed spaces by the grouping of the buildings in crescents, terraces and squares, or as detached units. The dwellings should be freed from the sterilizing tyranny of the building line, and enhanced by the planting of trees and shrubs.

With such a large new population some thirty-three acres of open space should be provided for parks and adults' sports fields. In addition to these, there would be two Junior Schools and one Secondary Modern School, which together comprise a further thirty-four acres. This considerable acreage enables open space to be handled in the best way—namely, by arranging a free flow of green right across the site, and using this flow as both the link and the buffer between the residential enclaves which make up the whole scheme.

An eighteen-acre plateau in the centre of the site is suggested for the main playing fields, from which broad green ways would flow east, west and south, linking up with the farm and its gardens and with the school sites. Smaller green ways would run from north to south on the eastern part of the estate, and end in the grounds of Goldington Hall.

These green ways would provide safe journeys for children to school and for toddlers to their nursery schools, which are all sited on these inner parkways—a feature which provides play spaces freer than the garden and safer than the street.

The shopping centre would be the focal point, situated on the main east-west estate road opposite the point where an approach road from the town centre could join it. Here would be a cinema, bank, branch library, clinic and community centre. A church, a public house and the secondary school complete this forum, and there is an existing group of trees and a pond.

There would also be two small strictly local shopping centres—one a quarter of a mile north and one a third of a mile east of the main centre; similarly placed are sites for two other places of worship and three more public houses. It is suggested that the present farm house might ultimately be used as a residential hotel.

The whole scheme would have about 2,000 dwellings. Roughly a tenth of these would be flats or maisonettes, and about a quarter privately built houses. At the rate of 300 houses per year it would take seven years to complete the scheme—but to this might have to be added at least one year's delay for the installation of the sewerage scheme and water supply. Meanwhile, the possibility of serving the neighbourhood with hot water from the cooling system of the new Power Station in Barker's Lane should have careful consideration.

Until a new sewer is laid, the Corporation could only proceed with the eastern part of the neighbourhood, the subject of a detailed layout approved by the Council, but private development is possible in the west.

The detailed scheme is shown on Map 13 (*p.* 107) and comprises the layout for the first 401 houses in the new neighbourhood. About 300 of these could be serviced by existing sewers and water supplies. Nine house types have been included in the layout in order to get architectural variety and also to give good orientation for the living rooms of every dwelling. In all cases the stores are incorporated in the main body of the house, and are not placed in separate 'barns' at the rear. This means that a number of the two-bedroom dwellings could have a third bedroom added above the store.

The density of this part of the estate averages between thirty-five and forty persons to the acre, i.e. eleven to twelve houses to the acre.

The main features of the scheme are:

1. The vista from west to east, culminating in the west front of St Mary's Church in front of which would be a green surrounded by three-storey terraced houses or flats.
2. The open space system leading from the school site in the north down to Cricket Lane; a second green is formed at the southern end of this slope, and contains a site for a church and shops.
3. Old people's dwellings have, for the most part, been grouped near the shops, but have also been placed amongst the houses in other parts of the estate, and have been used to mask the return ends of street blocks which often open up untidy views over back gardens and fences. In addition to the better architectural appearance of this treatment, it contributes towards the attainment of a higher density.

4. A small group of old persons' dwellings has been planned to form an open square in the paddock adjoining the garden of Goldington Hall. This links on to the main estate development by a short length of road. A nursery school site is also suggested on the north-east corner of this paddock.
5. A site for three blocks of flats is provided in this scheme on the highest point of the site. These could comprise a further forty-two dwellings.

In general, this plan seeks to exemplify the principles of layout already described. A number of the front gardens would be left open and maintained by the Corporation. The houses themselves have been arranged for the most economical foundation work, with a minimum of cut-and-fill, and their frontages run parallel to the contours wherever practicable. The same considerations have influenced the planning of the roads. Similar principles should be followed in the layouts for the other new housing estates suggested in the proposals, with modifications to suit the special conditions of each site.

NEWNHAM Neighbourhood 5 includes all the area east of the town centre between Goldington Road and the river, comprising the whole of Newnham Ward and a small part of Castle Ward. The whole neighbourhood is oriented about the central spine of Castle Road with its frequent bus service, but it falls into three distinct sub-divisions:

(a) The area of large houses between St Cuthbert's and Bushmead Avenue, laid out by Wade Gery of Bushmead Hall. This was built at about the same time as de Pary's, and has a very similar character as a select residential area on the edge of the town centre, with the Embankment providing a feature corresponding to Bedford Park.
(b) The area from Bushmead Avenue to Newnham Avenue, developed over the whole period from 1880 to 1930, and consisting largely of the smaller type of owner-occupied house.
(c) The pre-war and post-war estate around Wendover Drive, which has its own small shopping centre.

The whole neighbourhood has a density of thirty-four persons per acre, and the houses are very evenly spread throughout. There is a small number of blighted houses in The Grove, but the displaced population could be rehoused on the same site. No further new housing is possible because the whole of the undeveloped area to the east of Newnham Avenue is liable to flood. Indeed, as Map 6 (*p.* 48) shows, a number of the existing streets were flooded in 1947. A large site to the east of Barker's Lane is being used for the new electric power station. It is appropriate that this should be put on land unsuitable for housing.

There is very little industry in Newnham, and most of the people work outside the neighbourhood. But it cannot be considered solely as a residential area, for it contains one of the town's major assets—the Embankment Gardens. Most Bedfordians and nearly all visitors to the town find their way into Newnham neighbourhood to enjoy this finely laid out and planted urban riverside. Because of this, there is a need for increased car parking facilities near the Embankment.

The Embankment and the adjoining Russell Park give the neighbourhood 3·5 acres of open space per thousand population, but, as in the rest of the town, there are not enough adults' sports fields. Those in Russell Park and Newnham Avenue provide only two acres per thousand. The deficiency cannot be made good within the neighbourhood, because the only available land is the allotments on the site of the old sewage works, which are among the best in the town. A small strip of these allotments would have to be given up for the proposed church and community centre in Newnham Avenue, and for an entrance to the playing fields which are to be developed as a Stadium for the whole town. The proposed new road and bridge continuing Newnham Avenue over the river and on to Willmer's Corner would give access to the Stadium from the south of the town. While many people from other neighbourhoods will then come into Newnham for its special facilities, the deficiency of sports fields in the ward itself will have to be made up by travelling to Goldington, or crossing the bridge to the wide expanse of Cardington Meadows.

As in other neighbourhoods, it was found that while Newnham could be taken as a whole when considering the provision of allotments and open spaces, shopping habits were very different in each of the three sub-divisions. Like nearby de Pary's, sub-division 5(a) (Rothsay Road) has no local shopping centre; indeed, there is only one shop, at which two-fifths of the neighbourhood's population are registered. This is a slightly higher figure than in de Pary's, even though the neighbourhood is closer to the central area. In sub-division 5(b), on the other hand, no less than ninety-five per cent of the population shop locally. Castle Road has a greater variety of trade types than any other centre in the town, and it is also the most conveniently placed in its neighbourhood, every house being within a quarter of a mile of the shops. When sub-division 5(c) (Wendover Drive) was developed beyond Newnham Avenue, the estate builders left four sites for a group of twenty shops at the focal point of the neighbourhood where the bus service now terminates. Five of these shops have been built and taken up by a grocer, a butcher, a chemist, a newsagent and a radio and cycle dealer. The grocer's registrations amount to ninety-two per cent of the population of the neighbourhood, but it is known that some of his customers live in Goldington, where he delivers. The population will not increase, since all the undeveloped land in the sub-division is liable to flood; it is suggested that only five more shops should be built and that the remaining two sites should be used for houses.

There are eight licensed houses in the Newnham neighbourhood, one of which—the Embankment Hotel—serves the whole town and many of its visitors. Provision for the local population is adequate, but there should be an additional licence in Newnham Avenue to serve visitors to the Stadium and the riverside.

CAULDWELL—KINGSBROOK Nearly a third of the population of Bedford and Kempston live in Neighbourhood 6, which includes almost all of the Cauldwell and Kingsbrook Wards, except those parts which fall in the central area and the three streets in Neighbourhood 7. It also includes a small part of the Kempston Urban District at the southern

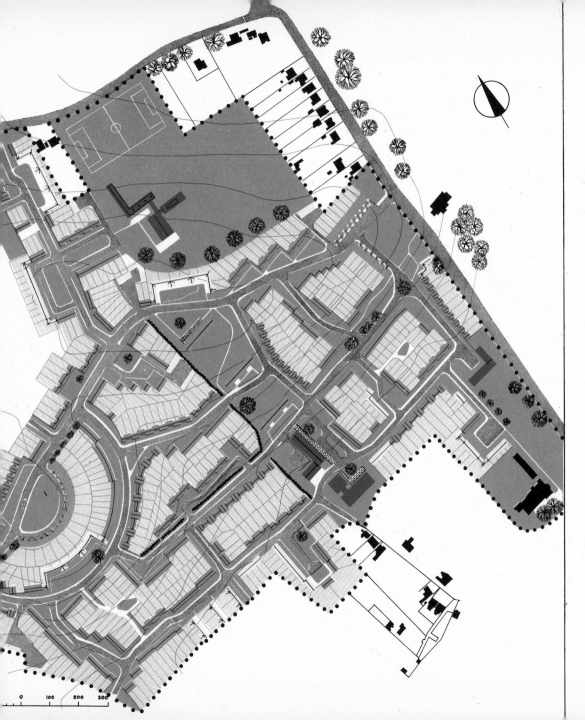

Map 13

**GOLDINGTON:
SUGGESTED LAYOUT FOR PART
OF NEIGHBOURHOOD**

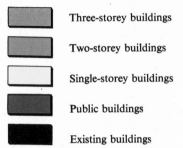

	Three-storey buildings
	Two-storey buildings
	Single-storey buildings
	Public buildings
	Existing buildings

This plan shows a layout for the first 560 dwellings in the proposed Goldington Neighbourhood. About 300 of these could be serviced by existing sewers and water supplies.

Note the contrasting elements in street design, and the way in which the arrangement makes the most of the natural features of trees and slopes on the site. A number of front gardens would be left open and maintained by the Corporation.

Eleven house types have been included in the layout, giving architectural variety and good orientation for all living rooms. Stores are incorporated in the main body of the houses.

The density of the estate averages between thirty-five and forty persons per acre.

In the south-east corner of the site, old persons' dwellings have been planned to form an open square adjoining the garden of Goldington Hall, which should be used as a recreation centre.

0   100   200   300

end of Ampthill Road. The housing consists almost entirely of working-class dwellings, built since the turn of the century following the establishment of a number of large works along the railway lines south of the river. Most of Bedford's industry is in this neighbourhood, and about 6,000 people are employed in its factories.

The two main problems of cross-town communications and neighbourhood amenities are more serious in this neighbourhood than in any other part of the town. Three of its sub-divisions—Southend, Elstow Road and London Road—are rigidly divided from each other by the railways, while the fourth—Harrowden Road—is the most distant part of Bedford from the town centre. The proposed Western Relief Road would link sub-divisions 6(a) and 6(b), and would also give the whole neighbourhood a more direct route to Kempston and Queen's Park. The Eastern Cross-Town Road from Willmer's Corner to Newnham Avenue would connect it with Newnham and Goldington. The proposals also include two cycle bridges linking Ampthill, Elstow and London Roads in the heart of the industrial area. The four sub-divisions would still remain separate communities in certain respects—e.g. for the provision of shopping services—but the improved communications would make it easier for them to share other amenities, e.g. open spaces, as well as bringing about a considerable shortening of daily journeys to work.

The present standards of both parks and playing fields are low, but the extension of the London Road Recreation Ground to Harrowden Road, and the provision of seventeen acres of playing fields near Elstow Village and fourteen acres in Cardington Meadows would bring the future standards up to the recognized minimum. In calculating these standards, the main area of Cardington Meadows has been excluded, since it is best regarded as a whole town space, but it will be mainly used by people from this neighbourhood, and access would be improved by the proposed cycle tracks and bridges. There is a great need to raise the quality as well as the quantity of open space in the neighbourhood. The fine examples of Bedford Park and Russell Park should be copied in the layout and planting of the Recreation Ground and Cardington Meadows, so that the environment south of the river may begin to approach the high standard achieved on the north.

Sub-division 6(a) is the oldest part of the neighbourhood. About half of it was built during the nineteenth century, and some of the streets near the Britannia Works are nearing the end of their economic life, though none fall into the first and second categories of blight which it is proposed to clear during the next twenty years. Sub-division (b) (Elstow Road) contains the first Corporation housing estate—'The White City'—developed in the twenties, together with private development of the thirties, and post-war 'prefabs' and Corporation houses. It also includes the ramshackle Ministry of Supply huts off Mile Road, which have been the subject of much concern in the town, and should be pulled down and replaced as soon as possible. The London Road and Harrowden Road sub-divisions have been built almost entirely since 1930. The former has a residential density as high as forty-seven persons per acre, due to the large number of families with young children, and to the building of two-storey flats on part of the Council estate. The only large housing site in the neighbourhood is in Eastcotts Road. It forms part of sub-division 6(d), whose population will eventually be nearly 3,000.

Once again there are considerable differences in shopping provision and habits between the various sub-divisions. Southend, the oldest part of the neighbourhood, has the greatest variety of shops, but London Road is not far behind. Exactly the same proportion (seventy-seven per cent) of the population of each of these sub-divisions is registered in the local centre. It is interesting to note that the number of persons per shop in London Road is three times the number in Ampthill Road. This shows the trend towards larger shops in more recent developments, and also shows that fewer shops are necessary when they are grouped in a compact centre. At the same time, the London Road centre is too near the edge of the neighbourhood, and there are parts of the new estate on the Cardington Road side which are more than a quarter of a mile not only from the local centre but also from the nearest isolated shop. A small strictly local centre, possibly of only two shops but comparable in status to the centre at Wendover Drive, is needed in the Mareth Road area.

Elstow Road presents a complete contrast to sub-divisions (a) and (c). Its population is slightly greater than that of Southend, yet it has only one-third as many shops, none of which can be said to form a local centre. More than half the population shop outside the neighbourhood, presumably in the central area, since there is no direct access to either of the neighbouring sub-divisions. The need for local shops is as great in Elstow Road as in any other part of the town, for there are more children under five than in any other sub-division, and the present bus service is quite inadequate. It is proposed that when the blighted huts at the corner of Mile Road and Lancaster Avenue are demolished, a small shopping centre should be developed to serve the greater part of the neighbourhood. The site is within a quarter of a mile of almost every house in the sub-division, and is on the bus route.

At present seventy-five per cent of the people of the fourth sub-division—Harrowden Road—shop outside, although there are nine isolated shops. When the Eastcotts Road housing site has been developed, there will be nearly 3,000 people in the sub-division, and a small shopping centre should be built on Harrowden Road between Worcester and Hastings Roads (6D, Map 14, *p.* 110).

The same contrast is shown in the provision of public houses. There is one licence for every 700 people in Southend, one for every 2,250 people in Elstow Road, and one for every 3,500 in London Road. Like shops, public houses are tending to serve more people, and in the case of London Road it seems they are trying to serve altogether too many, for some parts of the sub-division are more than a third of a mile from the nearest public house. The Cardington Road estate would have been a better place to live in if its layout had included a few corner shops and a 'local'. Sub-division 6(d) will be served by 'The Anchor' at Fenlake, and by a proposed new house at the junction of Eastcotts and Harrowden Roads. Another new public house is proposed in Elstow Road at its junction with the Western Relief Road, where it would not only help to bring the provision of drinking space in sub-division 6(b) up to the recognized standard, but would also attract customers using the new main road.

There is only one public hall and one welfare centre in all of Bedford south of the river, and both are in the London Road district, in Faldo Road and Barford Avenue, respectively. Because the railway barriers will never be completely broken down—even after the proposed improvements in communications have been carried out—there is a need for two community centres, one to serve the 8,000 people of Southend and Elstow Road, and the other to serve the 9,000 people of London Road and Eastcotts. The first could be sited in Kent Avenue, opposite the 'Gloucester Arms', when the blighted huts are demolished; the second could be built in Cardington Road, between Mareth Road and 'The Anchor'. A second welfare centre is also needed to serve the Cauldwell end of the neighbourhood (i.e. sub-divisions (a) and (b)), and this should be associated with the community hall in Kent Avenue. Apart from the site in Faldo Road already earmarked for the new St Michael's Church, there are sites for a Roman Catholic Church in London Road by the re-designed junction with Harrowden Road and Mile Road, and for another church or chapel at the western end of Mile Road by its junction with the proposed Western Relief Road. This would serve the Elstow Road sub-division where the only place of worship at present is a Salvation Army Hut. Southend is well provided with churches, but the population of the Harrowden Road sub-division is unlikely to be great enough to support any.

KEMPSTON This urbanized village stands out on Map 5 (page 45) as a striking example of piecemeal development. While still preserving its original form as a long, straggling roadside village, several isolated groups of streets have been added at various times during the last seventy years until the population has now reached 8,000. Kempston has maintained its independence as an Urban District, even though its people look to Bedford for all major urban amenities, and even for much of their employment. The Kempston neighbourhood, as defined in this plan, is not the same as the Urban District, however. The latter's extension east of the main railway line about the southern end of

Map 14

SHOPS

Existing centres

Proposed centres

Main centre

Sub-centres

Quarter-mile circles

Neighbourhood boundaries

Isolated shops

New housing sites

There are big differences in shopping provision between the various Bedford neighbourhoods, and none of them has perfect facilities. If large compact groups of shops are encouraged, every house cannot be within a quarter of a mile of a local centre, and isolated general stores should be provided in the more remote parts of housing estates. The tendency for straggling sub-centres to grow up along the main approach roads will be arrested by the westward extension of the principal shopping centre.

Ampthill Road clearly belongs to Bedford's Southend sub-division, while, on the other hand, the three Bedford streets west of the railway near the Barracks must be considered part of the Kempston neighbourhood.

Although equally isolated from the rest of the town by the river and railways, Kempston does not at present form such a coherent community as does Queen's Park. The scattered nature of recent developments, which now extend further from the centre of Bedford than any other part of the town, and the large number of allotments and other open spaces remaining within the built-up area, have prevented the establishment of any single focus for the neighbourhood. These gaps provide a number of excellent housing sites, and their use would make it more necessary—and at the same time easier—to develop a neighbourhood centre for the whole district.

The best site for a neighbourhood centre is at the corner of Bunyan Road, Elstow Road and St John's Street, which is not quite central in relation to the existing built-up area, but is equidistant between the large new housing sites off Cemetery Road and Woburn Road to the west, and at either side of Elstow Road to the east. A large community centre to serve the whole neighbourhood is proposed on the very fine site between the orchard and the cross-roads, and there should be a small neighbourhood cinema. The extension of shopping facilities to serve the increased population should also take place in this vicinity, although, owing to the scattered nature of development, there is also a need for a number of isolated shops closer to the houses. At present about three-quarters of Kempston's population shop in Bedford Road, and the rest in High Street–St John's. Bedford Road will remain the shopping centre for the New Town district, but a number of shops may be transferred to the new centre, since the latter would tend to attract not only the people on the new estates but also some of those who now shop in Bedford Road.

Sub-division 7(c) (Austin Canons) has only 638 people, but has to be considered separately since it is isolated both from Bedford and from the main part of Kempston. These five short streets have their own public house and seven isolated shops, but four-fifths of the people are registered elsewhere. There will be no further housing in the sub-division, and ultimately, when these streets have reached the end of their economic life, they should not be replaced. The part south of Kempston Road should be devoted to industry, and the part adjoining Austin Canons to open space. So long as the houses remain, however, their isolation would be greatly reduced by the construction of the Western Relief Road, which would cross the middle of the sub-division along the line of the present Bedford–Kempston boundary.

The Western Relief Road, together with the cycle track from The Grange to Honey Hill, would effect a considerable reduction in the distance from Kempston to Queen's Park, for the benefit of Allens' workers in particular, and of contact between the two neighbourhoods in general (Map 8, *p.* 63).

Like Queen's Park, Kempston enjoys direct access to the river. The development of a strip of 116 acres as a permanent public open space would greatly enhance this amenity, but it has not been considered in calculating the open space standard for the neighbourhood, since it would be used by people from all over the town. Kempston is more fortunate than any of the other neighbourhoods south of the river in already having a very fine open space—Grange Park—the whole of which has recently become available for public enjoyment through the generosity of Mrs Howard. This, together with the Lodge grounds at the west end of High Street, gives a standard of four acres per thousand for the present population. This standard would be maintained for the future population by the proposed open spaces which are well distributed within the neighbourhood.

There are nearly fifty acres of sports fields in Kempston, but all of them belong to works' Sports Clubs. We propose the extension of sports facilities in the land between Grange Park and the river; in Cemetery Road; and south-east of the Sewage Works. These, together with the existing works' Sports Fields, and the new one suggested for the Britannia Works, would give 6·1 acres per thousand of the proposed population, or 1·8 acres per thousand if the works' fields are excluded.

The present standard of allotments provision in Kempston is even higher than in Bedford. There are 127 acres, more than fifteen per 1,000 people. At the same time, many of the old cottages have very large gardens, and most of the new houses are also built on bigger plots than similar houses in Bedford. It is suggested that ten acres of allotments near the Barracks should be taken for the Western Relief Road and its associated industrial sites, and thirty-four acres off Elstow Road for housing; but forty-two acres of new allotments could be provided along the Woburn Road, and the neighbourhood would also have access to the proposed fifty acres of allotments south of the Borough boundary in Ampthill Road.

There are eleven public houses in the Kempston neighbourhood—one to every 700 people. These would be enough to serve the proposed future population, but the more distant new developments would be more than a third of a mile from a pub, so three new sites are suggested—in Cemetery Road, south of Elstow Road and north of Woburn Road.

CONCLUSION These proposals for the improvement of neighbourhood amenities throughout the town do not mean that local centres in the outer districts would usurp the functions of the main town centre. The latter would become a greater attraction as a result of the developments suggested in Chapter 4. The effect of the proposals taken as a whole would be that people would no longer have to make journeys to the centre for services they have a right to expect closer at hand, but that occasional journeys to the centre would be made more worth while by the greater range of services eventually to be provided there.

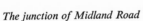

The junction of Midland Road   *with the central relief road*

7

66 There are considerable variations in the daily flow of the river and the Ouse is capable of increasing its volume by as much as one thousand times 99

The River

The River Great Ouse penetrates many sides of life in the town. Besides supplying Bedford and much of the surrounding district with water, it is also a source of pleasure and sport; it gives the town a characteristic that sets it apart from many places of similar size, and is the main feature that brings visitors to Bedford. But the river is not always an amenity—it can also be a menace; continuous measures have to be taken to guard against flooding. Even this has its positive side, however, for it ensures that much of the land bordering the river will not be built upon but preserved as open space. The effect of the river in hampering cross-town communications, and the proposed solution of this problem, have been dealt with in Chapter 3. Bedfordians appreciate their river, and have done much to enhance its beauty; few can fail to admire the view downstream from the Town Bridge. On a calm evening when the swans float among the reflections of the lights along the Embankment it challenges comparison with any other urban riverside scene. By arrangement with the Catchment Board, the Corporation is responsible for the cleanliness and maintenance of the river within the Borough boundary, and this work leaves little to be desired. Many other improvements could, however, be made, particularly to those parts of the river which flow through the outskirts of the town. There are no really satisfactory swimming facilities. Then there is the question of whether Bedford, the largest town on one of the chief rivers of England, will ever again be able to play the part of a 'river port' as she did for nearly two and a half centuries. If the Ouse could once more be made navigable as far as Bedford, yet another interest would be added to the town.

COURSE The Great Ouse rises between Banbury and Brackley in Northamptonshire, and flows 155 miles to enter the Wash, just below King's Lynn. Together with its tributaries it drains an area of nearly 3,200 square miles, but this catchment basin does not form a single natural region. Passing through districts with sharply contrasting physical features, the course of the Ouse can be divided into four sections (Map 15, *p.* 116):

1. From its source in the uplands of the Northamptonshire/Buckinghamshire border, through Newport Pagnell—where it is joined by the Tove and the Ouzel—and Olney, to Turvey.
2. From Turvey to Bedford there is a series of large meanders so that the distance by river is about thirty-four miles, though only seven miles as the crow flies.
3. From Bedford to St Ives the river flows through a valley about seventy feet above sea level, eastwards to Great Barford, then north through a constriction at St Neots to Huntingdon, picking up the Ivel on the way. From Huntingdon the river again follows an easterly course.
4. From St Ives to the Wash. In this Fenland section the Ouse is joined by its tributaries—the Cam, Lark, Wissey, and Little Ouse. For the last sixteen miles, below Denver Sluice, the river is tidal.

FLOODING AND DRAINAGE Much of the catchment area is affected by flooding, and nearly every year hundreds of acres are inundated; there were disastrous floods as recently as 1947, and their effect on Bedford is seen in the photograph on page 118. Ever since the Middle Ages schemes have been put forward to master the flow of the river. Today flood control is the responsibility of the Great Ouse Catchment Board, which is tackling the very different problems of the Fenland river and of the upper reaches.

Until the seventeenth century the drainage of the Fens remained a local concern. The Crown, when necessity arose, granted a commission to inquire into and remedy the flood damage, but no attempt was made to solve the problem on a large scale. During the first quarter of the seventeenth century conditions within the catchment area grew steadily worse. Until 1629 little effective work was done, but at that date Sir Cornelius Vermuyden was appointed to tackle the drainage problems. Under his direction works on what is now known as the Bedford Level were carried out. When he had finished, 40,000 acres had been reclaimed, although flooding still occurred; he was the pioneer who showed the way to further efforts in the following centuries.

In the eighteenth century windmills were used for drainage, and these were followed by steam pumps. Today, practically all drainage is done by electric pumps. A Flood Protection Scheme for the Fen area has recently been approved by Parliament, and is to be put into operation by the Catchment Board. It will, however, have no effect on conditions above St Ives.

In the upper reaches a programme has been embarked upon of dredging, repairing old structures such as weirs and mill sluices and, where necessary, of constructing new weirs and sluice gates. It is individual treatment of short stretches of the river rather than an over-all scheme that is being carried out. For instance, at Langford on the Ivel new sluice gates have been constructed. Work has been done at Cardington and Harrold. At Thornton the weir has been lowered, and at Thornborough, Buckinghamshire, there is a new weir and sluice. The river is being dredged from Turvey to Pavenham, and the part between Turvey and Lavendon is nearing completion.

As far as Bedford is concerned the works at Harrold and Cardington are of the greatest interest. At the former a new weir sixty feet long has been built, the old one has been reconstructed and there is a new sluice gate at the mill. At Cardington a modern sluice has been put in the old mill throttle in order to give greater discharge capacity. The benefits of this work were felt in Bedford early this year, when, after heavy rains and a rapid thaw, the river rose suddenly but returned to normal more quickly than before.

The flow of the river can be measured at Bromham Mill, at a cable gauging station by the electricity works, and at Duckmill Weir. There are considerable variations both in the daily flow and in the monthly averages. These are well illustrated by Diagram 7 (p. 120), which shows changes in the volume of the river during an exceptionally wet year (1939) and a particularly dry one (1949). The figures were obtained from the Catchment Board. In January 1939, the daily flow was never below 500 million gallons; in 1949 the flow was less than this for a large part of the month. Similarly, in the summer months of the two years only for a few days in July, 1939, was the volume between ten and twenty-five million gallons, while in 1949 the river was flowing at this rate from June to October. The lowest recorded flow was in 1921, when between 5–16 August the daily average was only 5·56 million gallons. The maximum flow was on 15 March, 1947—5,286 million gallons. The Ouse is thus capable of increasing its volume by as much as one thousand times.

WATER SUPPLY Most of the water used in the Borough comes from the Ouse. Some is taken out of wells which are flooded by river water, but the rest is directly extracted. Near Clapham from two to two and a half million gallons are taken every day, the amount depending upon the weather and the demand. It is purified at Waterworks Hill and piped into the town. About 30,000 gallons go to Kempston, which obtains the remainder of its water from Biggleswade, and some 450,000 gallons are used by the Bedford Rural District. The latter is under agreement not to take more than 700,000 gallons per day. The Borough at present uses 1·8 million gallons, but permission to abstract six million per day is being sought by the Corporation. This would be enough to serve a future population of 80,000, and to provide for the additional needs of the Bedford Rural District which is asking for 1·2 million gallons. The Corporation can only take six million gallons on days when the flow exceeds eight millions, for at least two million gallons per day must flow between Clapham and Cardington. When demand reaches the high level envisaged, it may be necessary to provide storage capacity to tide the district over the very dry periods shown in Diagram 7.

NAVIGATION ON THE OUSE Among the functions of many rivers is the position they hold as 'national highways'. Today the upper reaches of the Ouse are closed to navigation, but at one time the efforts made to open them up met with success, and the men who achieved this were some of the pioneers in a general movement for river improvement in the seventeenth century. Parts of the Great Ouse had been navigable during the Middle Ages, but in 1618 it was surveyed by Sir Clement Edmondes and found to be 'generally foul and overgrown with weeds', and 'stopped with weirs' between Huntingdon and Ely. Later in the seventeenth century, however, the Ouse became the backbone of an extensive system of Inland Navigation from Lincoln to Bedford, Cambridge and Bury St Edmunds. There was a passage from Bedford to the sea, which gave the town access to coal and provided an outlet for the agricultural produce of the district.

The work of the seventeenth century in making Bedford accessible by river prepared the way for the increased traffic of the following century. The Ivel was also opened up as far as Biggleswade. Revenue from tolls was almost doubled, and in these years before the coming of the railway river-borne trade grew in importance, since carriage by water was cheaper than by land.

There are indications that in 1812 trading on the Great Ouse was still prosperous; a scheme was put forward for a canal between Newport Pagnell and Bedford, the terminus of navigation. This proposed canal was to pass through Marston, Lidlington, Wavendon and Woughton, and to join the Grand Junction Canal about three miles north of Fenny Stratford. It would have enabled Birmingham and Manchester to receive agricultural products from the Bedford district, which would have been able to obtain coal, iron and manufactured goods in exchange. In the prospectus, dated July 1812, it was stated that the canal would carry, among other goods, coal, iron, corn, malt, lime, timber, bricks, pottery and salt—'now in constant traffic, but to a limited extent, owing to present expense and difficulty of carriage'. It was expected that 60,000 to 70,000 tons of goods would be carried annually. But the canal was never built.

By the middle of the nineteenth century, as is evident from the toll records, trade on the River Ouse had been affected by the rise of the railway—between 1847 and 1848 the total revenue at St Ives, St Neots, Eaton Socon and Great Barford fell from £6,737 14s. 3d. to £4,868. For the years before 1847, the takings had all been between £6,000 and £7,000, while from 1848 onwards they continued to be between £4,000 and £5,000.

During the next half-century the river gave up an increasing amount of traffic to the railways. Locks fell into disrepair, and by the end of the century navigation beyond St Ives became impossible. In 1893 the upper navigation between Holywell and Bedford, which was in a bad condition, was bought by Mr L. T. Simpson, of Sevenoaks. He spent a large sum repairing the locks, but in 1894 a flood occurred and the lock gates were opened by the Godmanchester Corporation. This happened a second time. There followed a series of legal disputes, and the case was finally taken to the House of Lords. Simpson lost the suit, it being held that the Corporation might protect their own land by opening the lock gates in time of flood. Simpson then gave up all further restoration work.

In 1908, a company called the 'Ouse Navigation Ltd' was formed with the aim of re-opening navigation as far as Bedford. The same year an inspection of the river between St Ives and Bedford was carried out by A. F. Fowler, M.I.C.E., for the St Ives Transport Company. He estimated that it would cost £1,150 to re-open this stretch of the river, followed by £150 a year maintenance. This would have entailed some dredging and cutting of weeds. The locks, apart from that at Heming-

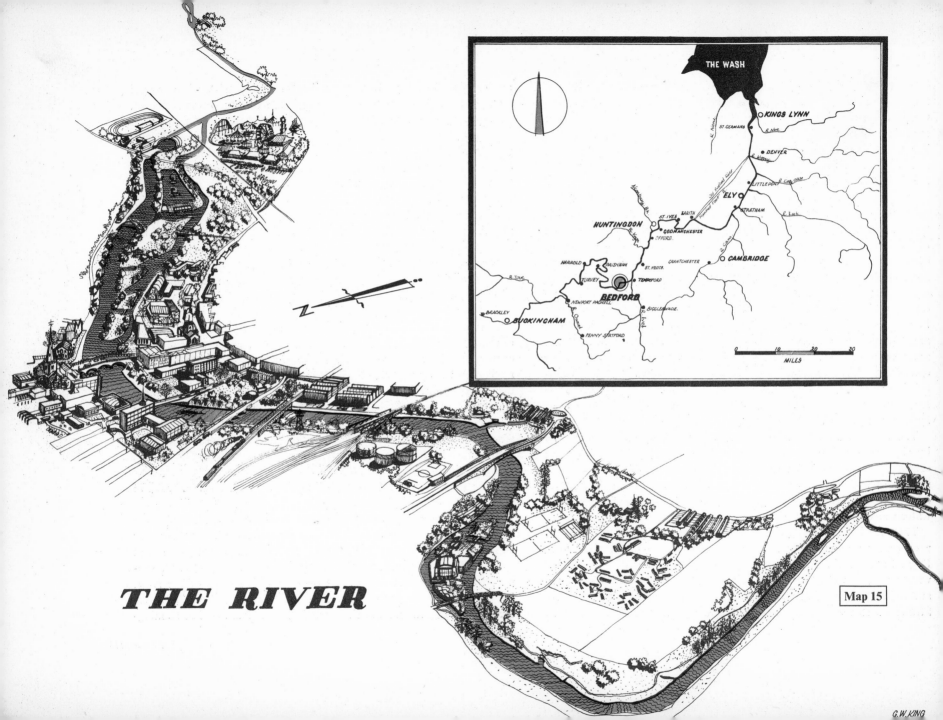

THE RIVER

Map 15

Inset map labels

THE WASH

KINGS LYNN

ST. GERMANS · R. Nene

DENVER · R. Wissey

LITTLEPORT · R. Little Ouse

ELY

STRETHAM · R. Lark

EARITH

ST. IVES

HUNTINGDON

GODMANCHESTER

OFFORD

CRANTCHESTER · CAMBRIDGE · R. Cam

HARROLD · PAVENHAM

ST. NEOTS

TURVEY · TEMPSFORD

BEDFORD

BRACKLEY · NEWPORT PAGNELL · BIGGLESWADE · R. Ivel

BUCKINGHAM

FENNY STATFORD

R. Tove

R. Ouse

0   10   20   30
MILES

G.W.KING

Overleaf is shown **The Town Bridge** from an unusual viewpoint. Few places can boast such a scene in the very heart of the town. Bedford should make even better use than it already has done of its one outstanding natural feature—the River Ouse. We propose the clearance of the blighted area nearby, and the building of a river-side recreational centre with a theatre, cinema and covered swimming pool.

The river is Bedford's showpiece and play-ground. In the Embankment Gardens the town possesses an urban riverside second to none in the country. But the need for less formal relaxa-tion is shown by the weekend scene at **Honey Hill**. Despite the effort that has been made the Lido still falls short of what is really wanted and what could be provided. There is an opportunity to develop first-class recreational facilities along this stretch of the river.

Although the Ouse gives Bedford so many opportunities for excelling other towns, it also raises many problems. Its hampering effect on cross-town communications is mentioned more than once in this book; there is also the menace of flooding. The **1947 floods** were exceptional, but every year a large area within the Borough is affected. Serious flooding may occur at any time, and it would be foolish to permit any further building on land liable to flood.

ford, were found to be in fair condition. Willington sluices would have required attention, and Bedford staunch would have had to be demolished. The work, however, was never carried out.

The Ouse is now navigable as far as Tempsford, eight miles east of Bedford. To open it as far as the town, eight lock structures would have to be reconditioned or rebuilt. Before the war, locks at Brampton, Offord, St Neots and Eaton Socon were repaired at a cost of £4,000 each. This suggests that the cost of renovating the locks between Tempsford and Bedford would be considerably greater, both because of the increase in prices and because of the additional decay which must have taken place since 1939. The actual amount necessary to re-open the river naturally depends on the extent of damage suffered by each structure. A figure of £50,000 has been quoted, but there are those who say the cost would be much less than this. One of the first jobs of the Committee recently established to campaign for the restoration of navigation on the Upper Ouse should be to have the river fully surveyed, and obtain an accurate estimate of the cost. At present there is no body with the authority to carry out the necessary measures. The Great Ouse Catchment Board owns the navigation, but being a land drainage authority, is unable to finance an effort which is not directly concerned with drainage and flood control, even though it might benefit the countryside and the river towns. There is no doubt that it would be welcomed by the increasing number of people who use pleasure craft, and would bring far more of them to the Ouse and to Bedford. Visitors who know other rivers with far less charm than the Ouse but better navigational facilities are shocked to find when they hire a boat in Bedford what a short distance of the river is open for their enjoyment. The view is widely held that commercial navigation on Britain's inland waterways can make a valuable contribution to the transport of bulky goods, but it must be said that its protagonists have not yet proved their point. If firm figures were to be quoted, the case for restoration could be fairly judged.

As regards the effect this would have on the flood problem, land drainage and navigation are to some extent conflicting interests, since the water level behind the locks must be kept artificially high to allow boats to pass. However, with careful regulation at the weirs the danger of increased flooding can be avoided. There is clearly a need for a single representative authority charged with the responsibility for every aspect of river control.

FISHING Many Bedfordians are keen fishermen, and the Ouse provides them with excellent opportunities for angling. The stretch of water between Kempston and Cardington is open to the public, because the Corporation owns most of the banks, and with them the fishing rights. By joining the Bedford Angling Club—which has a membership of over 500—command can be gained over much of the remaining water in Bedfordshire. Several types of water are represented in this section of the Ouse, both fast and shallow, deep and slow, and in addition there is the lake at Longholme. The maintenance of the high water level in the centre of the town is another asset to anglers. A large variety of fish is found in the Ouse, mainly roach, bream, chub, dace, rudd and perch. There are no trout or graylings, but some yearlings have been put into the water near Great Barford, though it is doubtful whether they will survive because of the large number of pike who prey upon them. The effluent discharged by the brewery has not reduced the numbers of fish; on the contrary, catches appear to increase! The best stretch of water for fishing is along the Embankment and Cardington Walk. An annual competition is held here by the Angling Club, and the proceeds are devoted to various charities in the town; last year there were more than 500 entries. A number of firms in the town also have angling clubs.

THE RIVER AT BEDFORD The section of the river between Kempston Mill and Cardington Mill can be divided into four parts:
1. Kempston Mill to Honey Hill.
2. Honey Hill to the Town Bridge.
3. Town Bridge to the eastern end of Longholme Island.
4. Longholme Island to Cardington Mill.
Between Kempston Mill and Honey Hill Lido, the river meanders, flowing first north for about half a mile and then turning due east. There

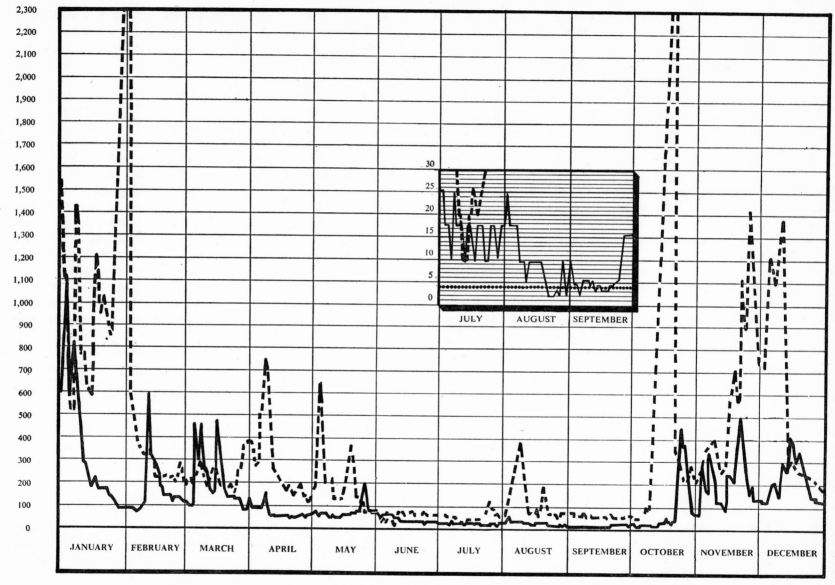

1939 ▬ ▬ ▬ ▬ 1949 ▬▬▬ Average daily amount to be taken for
water supply in addition to that already
taken, which is not included in the flow of
the river. •••••••••••••••

are stretches of woodland along the south bank, and a few hundred yards north of the Mill there is a small island. The Mill itself is a beautiful old building, and though equipped with modern roller machinery, still uses the river to supplement electric power. Just east of the Borough boundary the river widens, and at Honey Hill the main flow is again interrupted by two small wooded islands. The north bank in this part presents a slight slope, where the 100 feet contour line is just above the water's edge, and there is a footpath alongside the river. On the south bank the low plain is occupied by tree-less meadowland.

East of Honey Hill the north bank again widens out into a plain, and it is the south bank which has the chief attractions with the boat-house and gardens of Cauldwell House. From here the river passes under a series of railway bridges followed by Prebend Street Bridge, and reaches the centre of the town. The view from either bank is completely spoilt by the industrial development on both sides—Britannia Works, the gas-works and the power station—as well as the jumble of railway lines, goods yards and allotments. Beyond Prebend Street Bridge are the Commercial Road swimming baths and the Cattle Market on the north side, and after Batts' Ford, the brewery, followed by the backs of the Shire Hall buildings, which rise straight from the water. Opposite are the attractive St Mary's Gardens.

East of the Town Bridge the old river flows south of a series of large islands linked by footbridges. The islands and adjacent banks are well laid out in gardens, providing an excellent open space in the centre of the town. On the south bank there are boathouses and landing stages, and it is here that the King's Ditch joins the river. Between two of the islands are the Duckmill Weir and the Town Lock. The latter requires considerable repairs before it can be put into operation again. There is another weir a little further downstream by the club boathouses on Longholme Island. The islands are joined to the northern embankment by the 'rainbow' suspension bridge. In the centre of Longholme there is an artificial lake, well used by children for safe boating, and also by model boat enthusiasts and fishermen. The lake freezes quickly, and is therefore popular for skating.

At the end of the Embankment there are the Newnham Baths, and the remains of an old mill. The river then passes under another railway bridge and over a weir into further open country known as Cardington Meadows. Here the County Show is held whenever it visits Bedford, and travelling circuses also use the site. The improvement of this major open space by extensive tree planting would provide a better setting for such events. On the last stretch from Fenlake to Cardington Mill the south bank is bordered by trees, and there are several private houses with their own landing stages, while the north bank is open flat land crossed by a number of small streams. Any gravel workings that may be permitted in this vicinity should be carefully controlled in the interests of amenity.

THE FUTURE OF THE RIVER Few places can boast of so beautiful a river flowing right through the middle of the town. To the east of Wing's Bridge this asset has been used to the best advantage. Here the Embankment Gardens, the islands, and the Mill Meadows on the south side offer quiet and pleasant walks within easy reach of the shopping centre. The water itself is used extensively by rowing clubs, by the schools and by punts in the summer time, the annual Regatta providing the highlight of the year. This part of the river is marred by the blighted housing and cramped confusion of uses behind the Picturedrome. If cleared this would provide an ideal site for a cultural and recreational centre including a cinema, theatre, restaurant and covered swimming pool, grouped in an imposing ensemble against the background of the Rink Island trees, and making the south bank a worthy partner of the north. The Frontispiece shows what we have in mind.

West of the Town Bridge there is even more room for improvement, and the basis of this has been laid in the proposals for the town centre described in Chapter 4. The new Shire Hall and Assembly Hall on the north bank, the College of Further Education and the County Museum and Art Gallery on the south, would all have gardens running down to the water's edge. The new bridge carrying the Central Relief Road would span the river in the centre of these developments, and should be a sheer concrete structure contrasting with the formal Georgian stonework of Wing's Bridge and the ornamental Victorian ironwork of Prebend Street Bridge. The brewery must remain, but it would no longer dominate this stretch of the river, and when the new buildings had arisen, it might no longer be the eyesore that so many Bedfordians deprecate (Map facing *p. 74*).

Further upstream much needs to be done to enhance the natural beauty and hide the inevitable scars made by industrialization. Although there is a path along the north bank, the factories and railways with their uncared-for surroundings spoil the view. Attractive gardens, similar to those east of Wing's Bridge, should be laid out, and should include a large number of tall trees to screen them from industry. A feature of the triangle of land between the railway lines and the river should be an observation tower from which small boys could indulge in one of their favourite pastimes—'watching the trains'. During a large part of the year the paths along the banks become exceedingly muddy, and this should be remedied.

Besides the necessity of improving the appearance of the banks there is the question of using the water itself for the purposes of swimming and boating. There is a strong demand for better facilities. At the east end of the Embankment are the Newnham Baths, consisting of four pools for both swimmers and non-swimmers, with lawns and other amenities. Access from the south would be improved by the new road from Newnham Avenue to Willmer's Corner which would bridge the Ouse beside the baths. The Commercial Road Baths are in an unsatisfactory position because the water is polluted by the effluent from the gasworks and the power station, but would in any case be moved to make way for the developments described above. Further west there is the Queen's Park bathing area, and near that the popular Honey Hill Lido.

The photograph on page 118 shows that this stretch of the river still falls short of the need and the opportunity. Its natural attractions will draw many more people, and the proposed Western Relief Road and cycle tracks would give easy access from Kempston and south Bedford. There is a need for an amenity such as Newnham Baths at this end of the town, and a chance for the Corporation to provide additional outdoor and indoor recreational facilities at Honey Hill.

The aerial perspective, on page 116, gives a broad impression of the Ouse from Cardington Mill to Kempston Mill as it would appear after our proposals had been carried out. The river is Bedford's chief attraction, and could in the future be an even prouder boast.

The castle mound opened up to the river

bove The central portico, Bromham Road Terrace: a Regency detail

right top St Peter's Church and The Green

right bottom The Town Bridge

The Portico of the Swan Hotel: An essay in fine proportions

One of the few remaining half-timbered buildings in the area: The King William IV public house, Kempston

'The cream façade reveals the full beauty of its proportions': The County Architect's Department, St Paul's Square

Lea Cottage, Cardington Road, 1611

charming house which faces St Mary's Square is one
town's many fine Georgian residences
should be preserved

The Crofton Rooms, St Cuthbert's Street, shows
an interesting use of sliding window shutters
in the treatment of the façade

8

" It is the harmonious grouping of dissimilar elements . . . that makes this riverside town a place of restrained beauty "

Townscape

The planner's job does not include the design of individual buildings, but he must be constantly aware of the visual implications of his proposals. We have traced the relationship between the town's economic functions and the pattern of land use, and we have seen how the latter must be altered during the next twenty years to bring the two into full conformity. It is now necessary to consider the third dimension of the physical fabric, to examine the architectural character of the buildings in the town, and the way their combination has determined the townscape of Bedford. Our proposals aim at enriching the townscape by preserving and enhancing what is good, removing or disguising what is bad, and ensuring that future buildings are worthy of the town.

Bedford today shows little evidence of the ancient fortified town. Although the Castle has gone, the Mound, which was there long before the Normans built their keep upon it, is still there. It forms the central feature of the Castle Gardens, a quiet retreat close to the main shopping centre. Folk dances are performed on the ancient bowling green that crowns the Mound. The King's Ditch, a tenth-century defence work filled by the river, can be seen behind the old houses on either side of St John's. It is a great deal shallower than the original fortification, is uncared for and befouled, but could be made into a unique feature of the new developments south of the river.

Apart from the churches, few buildings remain from the medieval period, and there is very little standing evidence of the seventeenth century. Bedford's four old churches contain many interesting features which have been well described in a number of guides to the town and

county. St Paul's has almost the scale of a cathedral (which it once nearly became), rising majestically above the buildings near the river to mark the heart of the town. There are many unexpected views of its graceful spire, as from the streets in Black Tom running down from Cemetery Hill, from some of the hump-backed railway bridges and from parts of the riverside walks. These views should be carefully preserved, and new ones opened up.

The architecture of Bedford's central area is mainly a pleasant mixture of Regency and Victorian buildings, punctuated by a few examples of the Georgian period. This mixture of architectural styles, each with strong local characteristics, gives the town an air of quiet dignity and a marked personality of its own. Bedford is not rich in really old buildings, nor are there many of great architectural merit. It is the harmonious grouping of dissimilar elements (which can only be put down to a fortunate accident) that makes this riverside town a place of restrained beauty.

THE TOWN CENTRE *High Street*, which is one of the oldest thoroughfares in the town and the backbone of the present commercial centre, is typical of Bedford's assembly of architectural styles. With a few exceptions individual buildings are of no great architectural merit, but collectively they form a street of great character. Unfortunately, High Street has not completely escaped the pretentious architecture of the 'modern' multiple store, and the hand of the irresponsible shop-front designer.

The most interesting townscape in the High Street is that part facing St Paul's Square, beginning at the riverside Swan Hotel, one of Bedford's finest Georgian buildings, and extending past Lloyds Bank, with its dignified white classic façade, and on to the highly textured elevation of Messrs Wells' store. On the other side, and half-way from the Square to Mill Street, stands one of the town's oldest buildings—Sell and Wilshaw's shop, built in 1664. It is a charming survival of the late Stuart period, but is urgently in need of restoration. The rest of the High Street is a curious mixture, one of the more interesting features being Clare & Son's quaint little watchmaker's shop, with its traditional sign jutting out over the pavement.

St Paul's Square is now bounded on two sides by local government offices, and displays little of its former beauty. A drawing of 1830, a copy of which hangs in the Modern School Museum, shows the Square to have had many well-proportioned Georgian buildings. Some have since been removed to make way for buildings of such inferior architecture as the Shire Hall and the Corn Exchange, whose scale and decoration express the new pretensions of the closing years of the nineteenth century but lack the good taste of earlier periods. Of the remaining buildings the County Architect's Department, 1764, is a fine example of local style. The Town Hall, 1767, with its later addition, is a well-weathered stone building showing a strong Wren influence. Evidence of the Georgian tradition is also provided by the professional offices on the corner of the Square and Harpur Street, and by the present building of the Medical Officer of Health, once the Headmaster's House of Bedford School, which has a Mansard roof of rather special design.

St Mary's and St John's Streets form a typical 'approach' road, relieved only by St Mary's Church and the fine Georgian house opposite, which make a pleasant group. St Mary's Square is at present the main feature south of the river, and when freed of traffic congestion by the new circulation system at Willmer's Corner, it should be opened up by the demolition or setting back of the public houses on the south side. It is particularly unfortunate that there are, in this thoroughfare, a number of seventeenth-century houses and shops which have been allowed

to fall into disrepair. The restoration of these buildings would do much to enhance this potentially attractive area.

Cardington Road, originally called 'Potter Street' as far as the crossing of the King's Ditch, has an atmosphere of studied charm, due to a group of large villas set in generous gardens. The hotel on the north side is an interesting building of the early Renaissance, with a particularly fine dining room. On the south side stands St Mary's House, a residence of the Queen Anne period, now surprisingly used as a factory, and Lea Cottage, a small but charming example of early Stuart work.

Harpur Street is a street of contrasts. It has everything from the mean to the monumental. The Gothic Revival Modern School by Blore—the architect of Buckingham Palace—stands opposite the Regency Classic portico of the Borough Library, which in turn is adjacent to the heavy red-brick Victorian Sunday School of the adjoining Regency Methodist Chapel. This very interesting group of public buildings forms an extension of the civic centre in St Paul's Square. The rest of the street is a succession of façades ranging from the 'terra cotta' grandiose to the broken-down cottage type shop. At the corner of Harpur Street and St Loyes is an illustration of what *not* to do in a town like Bedford. Here is an example of a modern building out of scale and sympathy with its surroundings, and lacking interest in design. The cinema which is to be built on the adjoining car park, opposite the almshouses and commanding the Bromham Road entrance to the town, should be designed with careful attention to its relationship with other buildings in the vicinity and its effect on the general townscape. It will be left to another generation to demolish Telephone House and put a more worthy structure in its place.

Mill Street is the town's non-conformist street—a street of chapels. The present Bunyan Meeting was built in the same year (1849) as the Howard Chapel was reconstructed, and the Baptist Church was built twenty years later. It is said that on Sunday mornings in the closing years of the century Mill Street was full of jostling carriages waiting to pick up members of the three congregations. Now the street is congested every day—but the causes are different. John Howard's town house stands at the corner of Mill Street, by St Cuthbert's Church. Opposite is No. 38 Mill Street—a fine example of local Georgian architecture with a hipped mansard roof. Another beautiful house of the period is the Crofton Rooms in *St Cuthbert's Street*, which shows an interesting use of sliding window shutters in the treatment of the façade.

Dame Alice Street, leading to Bromham Road, provides evidence of the generosity of the Harpur Trust in the early nineteenth century. Most of the north side is taken up by two rows of Regency Gothic almshouses of pleasing design. These were built between 1802 and 1806, to house distressed families following the disastrous fire in the St Loyes district. The original terrace was divided centrally at a later date to make way for the northward extension of Harpur Street to Tavistock Street.

The aristocrats among Bedford's domestic buildings are found in *Bromham Road* and the *Crescent*, which show how architectural continuity and proportion may be achieved in two different ways. The gracious Priory Terrace, illustrated on page 72, is an example of the design of a number of houses as a single unit. It should never have been defaced by commercial additions, and the decay which has already set in should be arrested. In the Crescent a similar effect is gained by another method—the careful siting and treatment of individual houses and the use of tree planting to bind the various elements into a coherent whole.

Another example of visual continuity achieved by tree planting is *Kimbolton Road*, which also shows the staggered siting of individual buildings now used extensively in modern housing schemes. Some of the houses on the west side below Glebe Road are most elegant in design, especially No. 10/12, which was one of the first extensions in this direction in the early 1800's.

Tavistock Street was one of the last main roads to be incorporated in the town structure, and contains few buildings of interest except the ancient Flower Pot Inn. This was formerly a combined farm and inn, with extensive land at the rear. It is said that it was once called 'The Madonna Lily'; but that owing to the objections of the church the inn was eventually given its present name.

Only the more outstanding buildings have been mentioned in this review, but there are others of architectural or historic interest which are included in the list on page 133. They combine with their fellows of lesser merit or significance to form a townscape that is nearly always intimate and friendly, though rarely exciting or dramatic. The element of drama is difficult to achieve in a town built on an almost flat site, but every opportunity should be taken to use the river as a source of contrast and surprise.

Behind this façade the town centre contains many 'blighted' dwellings and other buildings in an advanced state of decay. Between Midland Road and Bromham Road is a particularly bad area. Greyfriars Walk, Greenhill Street, Allhallows Lane and their neighbours are streets of which Bedford has reason to be ashamed. Their demolition and replacement by modern buildings would raise the general quality of townscape throughout the central area, and at the same time give Bedford a chance to introduce innovations such as multi-storey flats that would give a new interest to the appearance of the town.

THE OUTSKIRTS On the fringes of the town centre, as in most other towns, are areas of high density housing of rather mean appearance. But in Bedford there is also the special feature of the high-class residential areas with spacious villas designed to house the families who settled here to take advantage of the unique educational facilities.

Further out are typical low density layouts of the inter-war period, with the sort of uninspired semi-detached and detached houses that can be seen in most towns. This type of development is devoid of character, and has no visual continuity. The people who live there know the effect on their daily life of this unimaginative approach to street architecture. In the effort to provide 'private' semi-detached or detached 'Englishmen's castles' the spirit of neighbourliness has been lost. As many houses must be built during the next twenty years as were built between the two wars. Besides having higher standards of internal planning and fittings, they should be a handsome addition to the town's architecture, and a suitable setting for the social life of the new neighbourhoods.

PRESERVATION OF BUILDINGS OF INTEREST AND BEAUTY The interesting buildings in Bedford, coloured red on Map 10 (*p.* 73), should as far as possible be preserved. We have done our best to respect them in making proposals for the reconstruction of the town centre, but we were unable to avoid suggesting the demolition of a few buildings of architectural interest, as for example, three Georgian houses in Cauldwell Street on the line of the Central Relief Road. The rest should remain, and wherever necessary they should be repaired and decorated. The position should never again be allowed to arise where the destruction of such historic treasures as the Friary, which once stood in Priory Street, and the old mills, could be justified on the grounds that they had fallen into a state of disrepair.

COLOUR IN THE TOWN It appears that many property owners in Bedford are not sufficiently aware of the part played by paint in determining the appearance of the town. There is seldom a positive use of colour; in most cases the paint applied to buildings is at best neutral in effect. Many delicate architectural details are hidden under heavy greens and browns. Bright colours can introduce an air of gaiety to a town, and reduce the effects of a dull day to a minimum. An example of well-chosen paintwork is the County Architect's Department on the south side of St Paul's Square; the cream façade reveals the full beauty of its proportions. These remarks do not only apply to large buildings; in Farrer Street, a tiny cul-de-sac off Cauldwell Street, is an example of a small terrace house which stands out from its neighbours of identical design by reason of an imaginative but discriminating use of paint. This street would be demolished during the next twenty years, but a similar use of colour could do much to enliven other areas of old and monotonous housing which must remain for a longer period.

TREE PLANTING Trees can do much to humanize an uncompromising group of buildings, and there should be a lot more planting in the outer parts of the town. The avenues of chestnuts flanking London Road help to relieve the monotony of the ribbon development; similar planting could revolutionize the appearance of such older areas as Queen's Park. Trees, however, should be carefully chosen and arranged to conform to the scale of their surroundings.

FUTURE ARCHITECTURAL DESIGN In the next twenty years many buildings of a wide range of type and function will be built in Bedford. Their architecture should be of the age in which they were designed rather than inferior copies of past styles. The personality of Bedford should be expressed in their design, but the buildings should honestly reflect their purpose. They should be good neighbours to the existing buildings, respecting their scale and alignment and having proportions as beautiful as those of Bedford's finest Georgian buildings.

Some of the buildings proposed are larger structures than exist today, but their siting and layout has been considered carefully so as not to dwarf existing buildings yet at the same time provide a stimulating contrast.

We conclude this study of Bedford with some words written by one of its first historians, Matthiason, in 1831. His final prediction is no doubt somewhat extravagant, but the proposals in this book will ensure that Matthiason's remarks are fulfilled in spirit, if not in letter.

'Not that as a town it has, as yet, attained to that marked superiority, either of general architecture, consequence, or enterprize, at which it is excellently calculated to arrive; but possessing, as it does, the elements of all, in a population, industrious, intelligent and wealthy; and in a great, popular, and munificent benefaction, the application of the continually increasing funds of which must necessarily call forth the noblest energies of the mind; the natural course of circumstances will tend rapidly to raise it, so as ere long probably to vie with some of the proudest cities in the world.'

Mill Street: John Howard's house can be seen in the left foreground

The oldest inhabitant of the High Street, a late Stuart survival (circa 1664)

Cardington Road: The dignified approach to the town from the south-east

What not to do in a town like Bedford. An example of a modern building out of scale and sympathy with its surroundings: Telephone House, Harpur Street

Model and Plans of a proposed block of flats which could bring a new element into the Bedford Townscape

This flatted factory was recently completed in Rotterdam. A similar building is proposed to meet some of the needs of business in Bedford

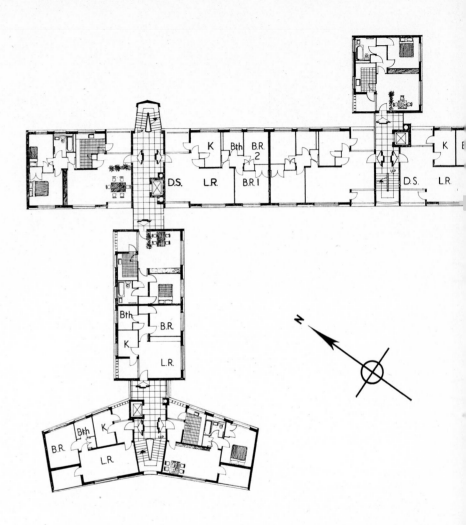

Proposed Flats at Ashburnham Road, by Max Lock and Associates: ground floor plan
The first part of the Plan to be put into effect will be the erection of this block of fifty-four flats. To be let at an economic rent, it replaces eight Victorian houses at present occupied by thirty-two families, and will help to restore a rapidly fading residential area near the town centre and railway station.

Table 8: LIST OF SITES, WORKS AND BUILDINGS OF ARCHITECTURAL and/or HISTORIC INTEREST

NAME, if any	ADDRESS	CLASS[1]	PERIOD	NAME, if any	ADDRESS	CLASS[1]	PERIOD
H.M. Prison	Bromham Road	A	1849	Terrace	32/38 Kimbolton Road	A	c. 1850
Priory Terrace[2]	18/48 Bromham Road	A	c. 1820	Houses	66/76 Kimbolton Road	A	c. 1850
The Den	122 Bromham Road	A	—	House of Industry (St Peter's			
Maple Cottage	126 Bromham Road	A	—	Hospital)	Kimbolton Road	A	1796
Ivy Cottage	128 Bromham Road	A	—	Howard Chapel	Mill Street	H	1772
St. Etheldreda (Orphanage)	9 Bromham Road	A	—	Bunyan Chapel	Mill Street	A	1849
Methodist Church	Bromham Road	A	c. 1830	House[2]	38 Mill Street	A	c. 1760
Houses	2/8 Cardington Road	A	c. 1650	Houses	43, 45, 47 Mill Street	A	c. 1800
House	11 Cardington Road	A	—	John Howard's House	55 Mill Street	H	1772
Lea Cottage	13 Cardington Road	A	1611	Town Bridge (Wing's)[2]	River	A	1813
St. Mary's House[2]	15 Cardington Road	A	1707	Crofton Rooms[2]	St Cuthbert's Street	A	18th cent.
House	19 Cardington Road	A	part 17th cent.	Ship Inn	St Cuthbert's Street	A	18th cent.
House	26 Cardington Road	A	19th cent.	Houses	9/11/15 St Cuthbert's Street	A	18th cent.
Abbey Hotel and Cottage[2]	32/34 Cardington Road	A	17th cent.	Bunyan Statue	St Peter's Green	H	1874
Houses	46/50 Cardington Road	A	19th cent.	House	24 St Peter's Street	A	18th cent.
House	26 Cauldwell Street	A	—	House	26 St Peter's Street	A	18th cent.
Houses[3]	31/35 Cauldwell Street	A	c. 1775	Willows Shop	27 St Peter's Street	A	17th cent.
Houses[2]	The Crescent—West side and			Houses and Shops	33/5/7, St John's Street	A	c. 1750
	19/19a	A	c. 1820		36/8, St John's Street	A	c. 1700
Almshouses	Dame Alice Street	A	1802		39, St John's Street	A	from 1650
Swan Hotel[2]	Embankment	A	Georgian	St. John's Hospital	St John's Street	H & A	from 13th cent.
Castle Mound	Embankment	H	—	House	26 St John's Street	A	17th cent.
Houses	2/4 Goldington Road	A	c. 1840	Shops	9/11/11a St Mary's Street	A	18th cent.
'The Towers'	6 Goldington Road	A	19th cent.	King's Arms Hotel	St Mary's Street	A	c. 1725
Terraced Houses	7/17 Goldington Road	A	c. 1830	House[2]	St Mary's Square	A	18th cent.
House	136 Goldington Road	A	19th cent.	Offices	8 St Paul's Square	A	c. 1730
Almshouses	41/47 Harpur Street	A	c. 1820	Offices	15a St Paul's Square	A	c. 1780
Bedford Modern School	Harpur Street	A	1832	County Architect's Dept.[2]	St Paul's Square	A	1764
Methodist Church	Harpur Street	A	1804	Mayes Corn Yard	St Paul's Square	A	c. 1820
Public Library	Harpur Street	A	1830	Public Health Dept.	St Paul's Square	A	c. 1750
Murkett Bros.	3 High Street	A	18th cent.	Town Hall[2]	St Paul's Square	H & A	1763
Mark Rutherford's Birthplace[3]	5 High Street	H	18th cent.	National Provincial Bank	St Paul's Square	A	c. 1820
Electricity House	9 High Street	A	18th cent.	John Howard Statue	St Paul's Square	H & A	—
Belfast Linen	11 High Street	A	18th cent.	Billiard Saloon	Castle Hill	A	18th cent.
Lloyds Bank to Henry Bacchus				King's Ditch	From Mill Meadows to New		
Ltd.	19/35 High Street	A	18th cent.		Wharf	H	10th cent.
Fisher—Butcher's Shop[2]	42 High Street	A	c. 1664	Flower Pot Inn	Tavistock Street	A	c. 1700
Sell and Willshaw—Shop[2]	44 High Street	A	c. 1664	Houses—Pleasant Place	Tavistock Street	A	c. 1825
Lion Hotel	55 High Street	A	18th cent.	Houses—Maqueen Terrace	Tavistock Street	A	c. 1833
Laxton Bros.	63 High Street	A	c. 1750	Medical Officer of Health Dept.[2]	Town Hall Yard	A	c. 1770
Margents Ltd.	77 High Street	A	18th cent.	Albert Terrace	Union Street	A	c. 1850
Dickins Bros.	79 High Street	A	18th cent.	Houses	Windsor Place	A	c. 1830
Clare & Son	82 High Street	A	18th cent.				and 1850
The Prioratus	(Yard) High Street—ANCIENT			Kempston Grange[2]	Bedford Road, Kempston	A	19th cent.
	MONUMENT	H	15th cent.	King William P.H.[2]	High Street, Kempston	A	16th cent.
Howard Statue	High Street	H	1894	Elstow School (Cosmic Works)	Ampthill Road, Kempston	A	1869
Houses	10/12 Kimbolton Road	A	c. 1820	Kempston Mill	Mill Lane, Kempston	A	from 13th cent.
Houses	14/22 Kimbolton Road	A	c. 1850	Goldington Hall[2]	Goldington Green	A	1650
Terrace	24/30 Kimbolton Road	A	c. 1850	Goldington Bury[2]	Goldington Green	A	c. 1800

[1] H =HISTORIC—Buildings having associations with famous persons or notable events.   A =ARCHITECTURAL—Buildings of architectural merit or significance.   [2] It is suggested that these buildings should be classified as 'buildings for preservation'.   [3] These buildings would have to be demolished in the course of implementing the road proposals.
Note: Buildings for preservation excluded from this list are the churches of St Paul, St Peter, St Mary, St John, St Cuthbert; St Mary, Goldington; All Saints, Kempston (Church End).

Table 9: PRESENT AND FUTURE NEIGHBOURHOOD POPULATIONS

NEIGHBOURHOOD	PRESENT POPULATION				PROPOSED HOUSING SITES			8—Numbers cleared not rehoused on present sites 9—Adjustment for Housing List[4]		FUTURE POPULATION
	Age composition			Total	5—Location and Number on Map 12 6—Acreage 7—Population[1]					
	0–4	5–18	19+							
	1	2	3	4	5	6	7	8	9	10
1—QUEEN'S PARK	6·6%	17·1%	76·3%	5,200	1—Honey Hill 2—Old Ford End	22 13	1,100 400 · 1,500+		450—	6,250
2—BROMHAM ROAD a—Poets' Corner b—Alexandra Road	 8·6% 9·1%	 15·7% 13·6%	 75·7% 77·3%	 3,925 2,175 · 6,100	3—Biddenham Turn 4—Day's Lane 5—Evans Field	25 23 25	500 300 500 · 1,300+	225— 50+[2] 175—	325— 175— 500—	4,675 2,050 · 6,725
3—BLACK TOM—DE PARYS a—Black Tom b—de Pary's	 6·9% 7·1%	 16·3% 16·5%	 76·8% 76·4%	 4,800 3,900 · 8,700	 6—Kimbolton Road 7—Putnoe 8—Cave's Lane[3]	 187 60 45	 5,600 1,800 1,400 · 8,800+	300+[2] 300+	400— 300— 700—	4,700 12,400 · 17,100
4—GOLDINGTON —	7·2%	19·0%	73·8%	1,750	9—Goldington	233	7,000+		150—	8,600
5—NEWNHAM a—Rothsay Road b—Castle Road c—Wendover Drive	 7·7% 6·5% 14·5%	 13·5% 16·2% 22·0%	 78·8% 77·3% 63·5%	 2,120 4,420 1,310 · 7,850					175— 360— 115— 650—	1,945 4,060 1,195 · 7,200
6—CAULDWELL—KINGSBROOK a—Southend b—Elstow Road c—London Road d—Harrowden Road	 6·6% 15·2% 11·7% 13·3%	 15·4% 22·8% 25·9% 23·4%	 78·0% 62·0% 62·4% 63·3%	 3,930 4,530 7,040 1,500 · 17,000	 17—Mile Road 18—Eastcotts	 12 35	 500+ 1,400+ 1,900+		325— 375— 575— 125— 1,400—	3,605 4,655 6,465 2,775 · 17,500
7—KEMPSTON a—Old Kempston b—New Town c—Austin Canons	 12·7% 7·1% 8·9%	 20·9% 17·2% 16·8%	 66·4% 75·7% 74·3%	 3,400 3,970 630 · 8,000	10—Cemetery Road 11—Woburn Road 12—Balliol Road 13—Manor 14—Foster Road 15—Elstow Road 16—Orchard Street	36 45 4 16 8 20 45	1,400 1,800 100 800 4,100 400 1,000 1,800 3,200 · 7,300+	115— 200— 315—	275— 325— 50— 650—	7,110 6,645 580 · 14,335
8—TOWN CENTRE a—North of River b—St. John's c—Pilcroft Street	 7·2% 7·3% 9·3%	 17·3% 18·4% 18·4%	 75·5% 74·3% 72·3%	 3,920 920 1,060 · 5,900				850— 200— 500— 1,550—	325— 100— 75— 500—	2,745 620 485 · 3,850
BEDFORD AND KEMPSTON	9·0%	18·5%	72·5%	60,500			27,800+	1,740—	5,000—	81,560

[1] Populations in accordance with suggested densities shown on Map 12. [2] In these cases more people will be accommodated in new dwellings than are displaced from cleared houses. [3] The Cave's Lane site is shown on the maps in Neighbourhood 4, but when developed will belong to Neighbourhood 3 (b). [4] An estimate of 5,000 for the number of people seeking homes has been distributed between the neighbourhoods in accordance with their present populations. *Sources: Population Count and Housing Survey*

Table 10: EXISTING AND PROPOSED PUBLIC OPEN SPACES (*shown on Map 3, page 29*)

NEIGHBOUR-HOODS	PARKS AND GARDENS							SPORTS FIELDS						
	EXISTING			PROPOSED		TOTAL		EXISTING			PROPOSED		TOTAL	
	Location	Acreage	Acres per 1,000[1]	Location	Acreage	Acreage	Acres per 1,000[2]	Location	Acreage	Acres per 1,000[1]	Location	Acreage	Acreage	Acres per 1,000[2]
	1	2	3	4	5	6	7	8	9	10	11	12	13	14
1—QUEEN'S PARK	Recreation Ground / River Walk	8·8 / 1·7 / 10·5	2·0	Cox's Pits / River Walk / N. of Allen Park	5·0 / 2·0 / 3·0 / 10·0	20·5	3·2	Allen Park	20·5 / 20·5	4·0	Cox's Pits / N. of Allen Park	6·0 / 6·0 / 12·0	32·5	5·1
2—BROMHAM ROAD	Priory Street Lodge Grounds	0·8 / 42·2 / 43·0	6·7					Clapham Road / Priory Street	9·5 / 1·1 / 10·6	1·6	Spenser Road / Beverley Grove	6·5 / 9·0 / 15·5	26·1	3·8
3—BLACK TOM/ DE PARY'S	Bedford Park	51·0	5·9	Brickhill Farm	6·0	57·0	3·3	Bedford Park	10·5	1·1	Kimbolton Road	60·0	70·5	4·0
4—GOLDINGTON	The Green	14·0 / 14·0	8·0	The Bury Neighbour-hood	8·0 / 8·0 / 16·0	30·0	3·5	Tennis Clubs	7·6 / 7·6	4·4	The Bury Neighbour-hood	7·2 / 25·0 / 32·2	39·8	4·0
5—NEWNHAM	Russell Park / Embankment / Wendover Drive	14·3 / 11·0 / 2·0 / 27·3	3·5			27·3	3·8	Russell Park / Newnham Avenue	5·7 / 9·6 / 15·3	2·0			15·3	2·1
6—CAULDWELL/ KINGSBROOK	Offa Road / Miller Road / Faraday Square / Elstow Brook / London Road	0·6 / 0·5 / 0·8 / 16·0 / 8·7 / 26·6	1·6	London Road (Jubilee Park extension) / Mile Road / Duchess Road	16·0 / 2·5 / 2·0 / 20·5	47·1	2·7	London Road / Britannia Tennis / Cardington Meadows / Meltis	4·9 / 1·0 / 6·0 / 8·1 / 20·0	1·2	London Road / Cardington Meadows / Elstow Village	19·0 / 14·0 / 17·0 / 50·0	70·0	4·0
7—KEMPSTON	Grange Park / Lodge Grounds	29·6 / 7·2 / 36·8	4·0	Ditmas Avenue / Balliol Road / N. of The Grange / S.E. of Sewage Works	2·5 / 3·5 / 3·0 / 16·0 / 25·0	61·8	4·2	Cryselco / Igranic / Robertsons / Ashdowns / Sanders	5·6 / 10·3 / 19·0 / 5·3 / 8·5 / 48·7	6·0	N. of Grange Park / S.E. of Sewage Works / Cemetery Road / Britannia / Orchard Street	8·3 / 7·1 / 6·0 / 12·0 / 5·0 / 38·4	87·1	6·1
8—TOWN CENTRE	Castle Close / Rink Island / St. Peter's Green / St. Mary's Gardens / Cauldwell Street	2·0 / 1·4 / 0·4 / 3·0 / 1·3 / 8·1	1·4	Youth Centre	2·2	10·3	2·8							
WHOLE TOWN OPEN SPACES	Longholme and Mill Meadows	124·0 / 124·0		Cardington Meadows / River Walk / Clapham Road	145·0 / 116·0 / 29·9 / 290·9	414·9								
BEDFORD AND KEMPSTON		341·3	5·6		370·6	711·9	8·7		133·2	2·2		208·1	341·3	4·2

[1] Based on present populations shown in Table 9   [2] Based on future populations shown in Table 9.
Source: Field Survey

LIST OF ORGANIZATIONS AND INDIVIDUALS CONSULTED DURING THE SURVEY OF BEDFORD

DEPARTMENTS OF CENTRAL AND LOCAL GOVERNMENT

The Ministry of Local Government and Planning, Eastern Region
The Inland Revenue Department, Bedford
The Board of Trade, Eastern Region
The Ministry of Food, Local Office
The Ministry of Transport, District Road Engineer
The Ministry of Labour, Local Office and Eastern Region
The District Factory Inspector, Luton

THE BEDFORDSHIRE COUNTY COUNCIL
The Clerk of the County Council
The County Planning Office
The County Architect's Department
The County Agricultural Office
The County Education Office
The County Surveyor's Department
The County Librarian
The Youth Employment Office
The Chief Constable
The Chief Fire Officer

THE BEDFORD CORPORATION
The Town Clerk
The Borough Treasurer
The Medical Officer of Health
The Borough Engineer and Surveyor
The Borough Librarian
The Chief Sanitary Inspector
The Allotments Manager
The Housing Manager

FIRMS WHOSE REPRESENTATIVES WERE INTERVIEWED IN THE COURSE OF THE INDUSTRIAL SURVEY

Factory Equipment Limited (Woodworkers)
Frank Gray (Joiner)
J. H. Boggas (Bedford) Limited (Wholesale Leather and Grindery, Boot repairers)
W. C. A. Brinklow (Baker)
Gossard Limited (Corset manufacturers)
F. H. Anstee (Machinery manufacturer)
Mark H. Crummie & Sons (Engineers, Machine Tool Makers, Millwrights)
Ibbett Engineering Co. Ltd
Eagle Electrical Engineering Co.
Mitchells & Butlers Ltd (Maltsters)
Astell Bros Ltd (Timber merchants)
Hallwin Limited (Underwear manufacturers)
Gabriel Wade & English Limited (Timber merchants)
F. Gamman & Sons Ltd (House furnishers)
Francis Coales & Son (Bedford) Ltd (Millers)
Walter Darlow (Gun maker)
J. M. Hughes (Lingerie manufacturers)
Marston Valley Brick Co. Ltd
George Mann (Wholesale and retail pastrycook and confectioner)
W. J. Gilbert & Son (Bakers)
W. P. Griffiths & Sons Ltd (Printers)
Laxton Bros Bedford Limited (Novelty raisers, Nurserymen, etc.)
Weaver Manufacturing & Engineering Co. Ltd
J. Gent & Son (Bedford) Ltd (Mineral Water manufacturers)
J. T. Hobson & Co. (Timber merchants and portable building manufacturers)

Bedford Refrigeration Co. Ltd
The Bedfordshire Times Publishing Co. Ltd
The Sidney Press Ltd
W. H. & J. Rogers Ltd (Millers, Corn Merchants, Agricultural Engineers)
Charles Wells Ltd (Brewers, etc.)
Kempston Electrical Co. Ltd
George Horn (Kempston) Ltd (Millers)
Alfred Nightingale & Sons Ltd (Artificial Manure manufacturers)
C.W.S. Canister Works
C.W.S. Boot Factory
C.W.S. Architect's Department
Ashdown Bros & Co. (Engineers) Ltd
British Mica Co. Ltd (Mica merchants, etc.)
J. & G. Turner Ltd (Waterproof cover manufacturers, sacks, bags, etc.)
Aero Controls Ltd
Low Loading Trailer Co. Ltd (Trailer manufacturers)
Muntona Ltd (Malt products and malt extract manufacturers)

FIRMS WHO ANSWERED THE COUNTY PLANNING OFFICER'S QUESTIONNAIRE

Cosmic Crayon Co. Ltd
Motor Rail Ltd (Mechanical engineers)
Charles Franklin Ltd (Coal and coke merchants)
W. H. A. Robertson & Co. Ltd (Engineers)
Bedford Steam Laundry Co. Ltd
Henry Bacchus Ltd (Builders' merchants, heating engineers, etc.)
Bedford Plough and Engineering Co. Ltd
Howard & Dennis Ltd (Engineers)
Meltis Ltd (Chocolate manufacturers)
Swan Model Laundry
E. F. Taylor & Co. Ltd (Paper Box manufacturers)
Interlock Metal Tubings Ltd (Flexible Metallic Tubing manufacturers)
Ellis & Everard (Coal Merchants, etc.)
John P. White & Sons Ltd (Manufacturing Joiners)
Wilson Bros & Humphreys Ltd (Automobile Engineers, packaging specialists)
Grafton Cranes Ltd
Warton & Goodship (Builders)
Sterling Foundry Specialities Ltd
Igranic Electric Co. Ltd
Marion & Foulger (1933) Ltd (Picture-frame manufacturers)
Britannia Iron and Steel Works Ltd (Ironfounders—malleable iron tube fittings)
W. H. Allen, Sons & Co. Ltd (Electrical and Marine engineers)
Samuel Foster Ltd (Building contractors)
M.C.C. Co. Ltd (Athletic Goods manufacturers)
J. Hobkirk, Sons & Co. Ltd (Engineers, pattern makers, etc.)
Cryselco Ltd (Electric lamp manufacturers)
H. H. Bennett & Co. (Bedford) Ltd (Clothing manufacturers)
R. B. Sanders & Co. (Kempston) Ltd (Leather manufacturers)

FIRMS WHO ANSWERED THE FLATTED FACTORY QUESTIONNAIRE

Automatic Electrical Refrigerators Ltd
North End Motors
Grimbly Hughes & Co. Ltd (Wholesale Grocers)
Dobbs Brothers Ltd (Wholesalers)
W. T. Henley's Telegraph Works Co. Ltd (Cables)

Schweppes Ltd (Warehouse)
Ellis & Everard Ltd (Coal and Builders' merchants)
Fisher & Sons (Printers)
J. White (Wholesale fruit warehouse)
George Frederick Ford (Upholsterers)
M.C.C. Co. Ltd (Athletic Goods manufacturers)
W. S. Richards (Carpenter)
Carter Bros (Bedford) Ltd (Wholesale Grocers)
Yorkshire Factoring Co. Ltd
Post Office Telephones (Engineering Depot and Stores)
T. Wall & Sons Ltd (Ice cream depot)
T. H. Smith & Son (Millers)
D. Moloney & Sons (Basketware manufacturers)
J. & B. Saunderson (Building contractors)
Bedford Property Services (Builders and decorators)
W. Salsbury (Wholesale Tobacconist, etc.)
Henry Burt & Sons Ltd (Printers)
Taylor Brawn & Flood Ltd (Soft Drink factory)
W. & H. Peacock (Auctioneers, etc.)
Ministry of Food Packing Station (Eggs)
T. C. Ginn Ltd. (Haulage contractors)
Mead & Rogers (Coach and motor body builders)
Northamptonshire Newspapers Ltd
F. J. Berrington (Builder and Decorator)
Rush & Warwick (Bedford) Ltd (Printers)
Cadena Bakery
United Yeast Co. Ltd (Bakers' wholesalers)
Nicholls & Sons Ltd (Garage)
James Perkins & Son Ltd (Woodworking)
J. A. King (Cabinet maker)
George Langley Ltd (Motor engineers)
Wilson Bros & Humphrey Ltd (Automobile engineers and packaging specialists)
W. Course & Carne (Engineers)
Longhurst & Skinner (Furniture store)
Randalls Ltd (Wholesale and retail ironmongers, etc.)
The Lightfoot Refrigeration Co. Ltd (Cold store)
Wallengers (Sewing machine dealer)
Charles Negus Ltd (Building contractors, etc.)
Reginald Hadden (Wholesale tobacconist)
The Bedford Sheet Metal Works
Midland Motor Co. (Bedford) Ltd (Motor engineers)
Jays Furnishing Stores (Warehouse)
Geere & Co. (Monumental masons)
Humphrey Chetham (Boat Yards, etc.)
South Eastern Wholesale Meat Supply Association (Distributors)
Diemer & Reynolds Ltd (Printers)

MEETINGS ADDRESSED BY MEMBERS OF THE GROUP

The Bedford Chamber of Trade (*Secretary:* S. Northwood, FACCA)
The Bedford Industrial Planning Committee (*Chairman:* R. K. Fleming, Esq.)
All Saints Church Youth Fellowship, Bedford
Workers' Educational Association, Bedford Branch
Toc H (Women's Section), Bromham Road
Bunyan Meeting Men's Fellowship, Bedford
St Paul's Youth Fellowship, Bedford
Bedford and District Trades Council
The Round Table of Bedford
Standing Conference of Women's Organizations, Bedford Branch

Bedford Central (Afternoon) Townswomen's Guild
Queen's Park (Evening) Townswomen's Guild
Fabian Society—Bedford Branch

ORGANIZATIONS WHO ANSWERED THE CLUBS AND SOCIETIES
QUESTIONNAIRE

All Saints Church Youth Fellowship
Anglo-French Circle
B.-P. Guild of Old Scouts
Baptist Church Young People's Fellowship
Bedford and County Athletic Club
Bedford and District Burns Club
Bedford and District Philatelic Society
Bedford and District Young Farmers' Club
Bedford Angling Club
Bedford Arts Club
1st Bedford Boys Brigade Company
Bedford Branch Comrades Association Bedfordshire and Hertford-
    shire Regiment
Bedford Branch of the National League of Young Liberals
Bedford Camera Club
Bedford Catholic Youth Club
Bedford Central (Afternoon) Townswomen's Guild
Bedford Central (Evening) Townswomen's Guild
Bedford Chess Club
Bedford Club
Bedford Conservative Club
Bedford Council of Social Service
Bedford Croquet Club
94th Bedford Group Sea Scouts
Bedford Divisional Labour Party
Bedford Divisional Labour Party League of Youth
Bedford Division Conservative and Unionist Association
Bedford Dramatic Club
Bedford Fabian Society
Bedford Lawn Tennis Club
Bedford Liberal Club
Bedford Morris Men
Bedford Music Club
Bedford Natural History and Archaeological Society
Bedford Rifle Club
Bedford Gas Works Social Club
1st Bedford Girls' Life Brigade
Bedford Film Society
Bedford Postels Sports Association
Bedford Preparative Meeting of the Society of Friends
Bedford Society of Model and Experimental Engineers
Bedford South (Evening) Townswomen's Guild
Bedford Swimming Club
Bedford Swifts R.U.F.C.
Bedford Town and County Club
Bedford Telephone Area Sports and Social Club
Bedford Town Cricket Club
Bedford Typographical Society
Bedford West End Bowling Club
Bedford Agricultural Executive Committee—Staff Canteen
Bedfordshire Agricultural Society
Bedfordshire Association of Boys' Clubs
Bedfordshire County Council Fire Service Club
Bedfordshire County Rifle Association
Bedfordshire Federation of Women's Institutes
Bedfordshire Rural Music School
Britannia Sports and Social Club
British Red Cross Society—Bedfordshire Branch
Bunyan Meeting Young People's Society

Cave's Lane and Polhill Smallholders and Allotments Association
Central Committee of the Devon Road Tennis Clubs
Beds. Constabulary Social and Athletic Club—Northern Area
Christian Brethren (Bedford)
Christian Brethren (Kempston)
Cryselco Social Club
Darby and Joan Clubs
East End Working Men's Club
Full Gospel Free Pentecostal Mission
Girl Guide Association—Bedford Division (thirty-one groups)
Goldington Church Youth Club
Goldington Townswomen's Guild
Grosvenor Club
Holy Trinity Boys' Club
Honey Hills Juvenile Temple
Igranic Social and Sports Club
Kempston British Red Cross Society Old People's Club
Kempston East Methodist Youth Club
Meltis Social and Sports Club
Newnham Avenue Methodist Youth Club
North Bedfordshire College of Further Education Students' Associa-
    tion.
Rotary Club of Bedford
Royal Naval Association, Bedford Branch
Russell Park Baptist Church
Russell Park Working Men's Social Club and Institute
St Andrew's, 14–21 Club
St John Ambulance Brigade—No. 3 District—County of Bedford
St Martin's Youth Club
St Michael Church House
St John's Church—Children's and Youth Associations
St Paul's Youth Fellowship
St Peter's Young People's Sports Club
Salvation Army Torchbearers Youth Movement
Scots Society of St Andrew, Bedford
'Seekers', St Cuthbert's Youth Group
Silver Jubilee Boys' Club
Silver Jubilee Girls' Youth Club
South End Working Men's Social Club
Standing Conference of Women's Organizations
Star of Bedford Lodge—International Order of Good Templars
Sterling Social Club
United Commercial Travellers' Association of Gt Britain and Ireland
    Incorporated—Bedford Branch
Workers' Educational Association—Bedford Branch
Youth Hostels Association—Bedford Branch

SCHOOLS COVERED BY THE EDUCATION SURVEY (other than
those wholly maintained by the Local Education
Authority)

The Harpur Trust Schools: Bedford School
                          Bedford Modern School
                          Bedford High School
                          Dame Alice Harpur School
Convent of the Holy Ghost
Bedford Physical Training College
Bedford Training College
Rushmoor Preparatory School
St Andrew's School (Bedford) Ltd
Belmont School
Polam Private Preparatory School

INSTITUTIONS COVERED BY THE HEALTH SURVEY
North West Metropolitan Regional Hospital Board
Bedford Group Hospital Management Committee (Secretary: E. H. L.
    Stonebanks, FHA; Deputy Secretary: F. G. Marks, Esq.)

Springfield House (Private Mental Hospital), Elstow Road, Kempston
De Pary's Nursing Home Ltd
Rena Nursing Home Ltd
Nursing Home, Kimbolton Road
Kimbolton House Nursing Home
Rothsay Nursing Home
Riverside Nursing Home
Nursing Home, Chaucer Road
The Elms Nursing Home, Kempston
Nursing Home, Kimbolton Avenue
Goldington Green Welfare Centre
Brereton Road Welfare Centre
Barford Avenue Welfare Centre
Co-Partners Hall Welfare Centre
Mental Deficiency Sanatorium, Bromham
Three Counties Hospital, Arlesey
Bedfordshire Sanatorium, Mogerhanger
Clapham Hospital
Steppingley Hospital

OTHER ORGANIZATIONS AND INDIVIDUALS CONSULTED

'Bedfordshire Times': Managing Director: C. Hamson, Esq.
                      Editor: A. W. Janes, Esq.
Eastern National Omnibus Co. Ltd—District Superintendent: R. W.
    Spray, Esq.
Birch Bros (Omnibus Co.)
British Railways: District Passenger Superintendent, Surveyor, Estate
    Manager and Engineer (Euston), District Operating Superintendent
    (St Pancras), District Goods Manager (Broad Street), Station Master
    (Bedford).
Eastern Gas Board—District Engineer, Bedford
The Harpur Trust: Clerk to the Trust: R. L. Elgie, MA,LLB;
                  Architect: Geoffrey M. Inskip, Esq.
Beds. and Herts. Joint Church Planning Committee—Secretary: Miss
    Busby
National Farmers Union (Bedford Branch)—Secretary: J. E. Tiffen,
    Esq.
River Great Ouse Catchment Board—The Chief Engineer: W. E.
    Doran, OBE, BAI, MICE; The District Engineer: C. W. Lacey,
    MICE
The Georgian Group
National Buildings Record
Department of Scientific and Industrial Research
Inspectorate of Ancient Monuments and Historic Buildings
The Brian Anstey Valuation Research Group
University of Durham, King's College—Department of Town and
    Country Planning—Prof. J. S. Allen, Percy Taylor, Esq.
City Architect's Department, Sheffield
St John's Hospital—Clerk to the Trustees: R. O. Watson, Esq.
The Estate Office, Southill Park
Messrs J. R. Eve & Son—J. D. Trustram Eve, FRICS, FLAS, FAI,
    W. Ewart Wootton, FRICS, FAI, MRSanI
Robert M. Peacock, FRICS, FAI
Humphrey Whitbread, Esq.
W. N. Henman, Esq.
Father John H. Thomson
C. M. Lolly, Esq.
David Wells, Esq.
J. E. Hammond, LRIBA—Brewers' Planning Consultant
R. J. Harper, Esq.
J. Sharp, Esq.
T. E. North, FRIBA, Borough Architect, West Ham
H. J. Manzoni, CBE, City Engineer and Surveyor, Birmingham
Architect Van Tijen, Rotterdam

Index